Godless
150 Years of Disbelief

Edited by Chaz Bufe

Introduction by Dan Arel

Godless: 150 Years of Disbelief
Edited by Chaz Bufe
This edition © 2019 PM Press.

ISBN: 978-1-62963-641-2
Library of Congress Control Number: 2018949082

Cover by John Yates / www.stealworks.com
Interior design by briandesign

10 9 8 7 6 5 4 3 2 1

PM Press
PO Box 23912
Oakland, CA 94623
www.pmpress.org

Printed in the USA.

Contents

Introduction   1
Dan Arel

CHAPTER I   The God Pestilence   5
Johann Most

CHAPTER II   Woman, Church, and State   19
Matilda Gage

CHAPTER III   The Devil's Dictionary *(excerpts)*   33
Ambrose Bierce
American Heretic's Dictionary *(excerpts)*   35
Chaz Bufe

CHAPTER IV   The Failure of Christianity   39
Emma Goldman

CHAPTER V   Twelve Proofs of the Nonexistence of God   47
Sébastien Faure

CHAPTER VI   The Meaning of Atheism   77
E. Haldeman-Julius

CHAPTER VII   How Christianity Grew Out of Paganism   95
Joseph McCabe
Christianity and Slavery   104
Joseph McCabe
Judeo-Christian Degradation of Woman   110
Joseph McCabe

CHAPTER VIII Why Science Leaves Religion in the Dust   137
              Chaz Bufe
              Twenty Reasons to Abandon Christianity   140
              Chaz Bufe

CHAPTER IX   May the Farce Be with You: A Lighthearted Look at
              Why God Does Not Exist   163
              Pamela Sutter

CHAPTER X   Disbelief 101: A Young Person's Guide to
              Atheism *(excerpt)*   179
              S.C. Hitchcock

CHAPTER XI   Dogspell   195
              Earl Lee

              Afterword   197
              Chaz Bufe

              ABOUT THE AUTHORS   209

Introduction

by Dan Arel

"No Gods, No Masters," a mantra that almost seems long forgotten in today's radical political landscape. We've lost some of our fervor to call religion what it is and to hold it accountable for the terrible things it has caused humanity to do. Some of this disconnect is understandable when some of the loudest voices claiming to speak out against religion are showing themselves to be in bed with white supremacists or are flat-out white supremacists themselves.

Today's new wave of atheist figureheads—better known as New Atheists—are writers and public figures such as Sam Harris, known these days for calling the Nazis marching in Charlottesville "peaceful" and advocating for the racial profiling of Muslims, or retired biologist Richard Dawkins, who has defended "light" pedophilia and referred to the phrase "Allah Akbar" as "violent sounding." This is not intellectually challenging religion, this is racism and bigotry.

Yet, while these people may mask their racism and bigotry behind the criticism of religion, we often allow religion to act unchecked. Christian extremists continue to terrorize and murder abortion doctors and staff. Christian politicians continue to use their religious beliefs to fight for laws that limit a women's abortion rights or fight to weaken protections for the LGBTQIA community.

Once upon a time, these critiques of religion were an everyday part of radical left politics and theory. In our modern life, we tend to ignore the impact religion has on climate denial. Ken Ham, the evangelical Christian owner of the Creation Museum, claims that while the climate is changing, there's nothing humans can do about it, God is in control. Others believe there is no climate change at all and attempt to root this ignorance in biblical claims, much like that of Ham, that God controls the heavens and earth and gave humans fossil fuels to burn and animals to slaughter.

Schools throughout the U.S. continue to debate whether or not evolution or sex education should be a part of a child's education. Tax dollars from the working class have been sunk into Noah's Ark theme parks, and so-called leaders in this country continue to push religion into our daily lives.

Maybe we have forgotten this, maybe we are too afraid to critique religion because of the New Atheist bigotry, or maybe we have simply forgotten how important this discussion can be. This is what makes *Godless* such an important anthology. It takes us back to a time before atheism was overrun with rampant bigotry and racism. This was a time when the discussion around the existence of God or the importance of Jesus was discussed and/or debated in a philosophical way that focused not on the believer but on the belief. This was when religion was properly challenged by those wanting to create a better world.

This does not mean the left doesn't believe in a person's right to religion or to believe in god. What it does mean is working to remove the shackles of control religious leaders have over people and removing a politician's ability to use their religious beliefs to dictate how we live our lives.

The authors within these pages spoke out before atheism was a profitable business that got you invited on cable news networks or took you on campus tours around the world. They spoke out not for fame or fortune, but because it was the right thing to do. They spoke out because someone had to.

The new atheist movement, though important to challenge, is also static. It's disrupting our message, and it has put us off course. This book rights that ship; let it be our compass.

We've forgotten the importance of what "No God, No Masters" means. For me, this collection of works serves as a reminder. It reinvigorated my atheism, for a lack of a better term. It's a return to the naturalist argument for the existence of everything, but it also serves as a reminder that just like our desire to abolish the state and return to a world of autonomy, as long as humans continue to believe that they must answer to a higher power and allow the self-proclaimed masters of that power to dictate so many aspects of their lives, we are still dealing with a force with the same kind of controlling power as that state.

Religion, at its most powerful, is used to control and subjugate women, turning them into property. It's used to excuse the abuse of children, by turning away from lifesaving medicine or from "sparing the rod," giving parents permission to physically abuse their children. It was and in many ways still is used to condone rape and slavery.

We know that the world can exist without the good that religion claims to provide, and oftentimes exists in spite of it. It is we, those fighting for self-determination, free association, and, above all, mutual aid, who understand best that we as humans must care for one another. We don't seek a higher power to grant us this authority. We don't want authority. We simply want to build a better world, and it's the gods and the masters who are standing in our way.

Today, we begin tearing them down.

CHAPTER I

The God Pestilence

by Johann Most

Among all mental diseases which man has systematically inoculated into his cranium, the religious pest is the most abominable.

Like all things else, this disease has a history; it only regrettable that in this case nothing will be found of the development from nonsense to reason, which is generally assumed to be the course of history.

Old Zeus and his double Jupiter were still quite decent, jolly, we might even say, somewhat enlightened fellows, if compared with the last triplet on the pedigree of gods who, on examination, can safely rival with Vitzliputzli as to brutality and cruelty.

We won't argue at all with the pensioned or dethroned gods, for they no longer do any harm. But the more modern, still officiating cloud lollers and terrorists of hell we shall criticize, expose, and vanquish the more disrespectfully.

The Christians have a threefold God; their ancestors, the Jews, were content with a single simpleton. Otherwise both species are quite a humorous crowd. "Old and New Testament" are to them the sources of all knowledge; therefore, willing or not, one must read the "holy writ" if one wants to fathom their shallowness and learn to deride them.

If we only take the "history" of these deities, we find an ample sufficiency for the characterization of the whole. In a short sketch the case stands thus: in the beginning God "created" heaven and earth—consequently he found himself next of all in a complete void, where it surely may have been dreary enough to bore even a deity. And it being but a trifle for a god to conjure worlds out of nothing by magic, like a juggler shaking eggs or silver dollars out of his coat sleeves, he (God) "created" heaven and earth. Somewhat later he molded the sun, moon, and stars to suit himself.

It is true, certain heretics, called astronomers, have established long since that the earth neither is nor could have been the center of the universe, nor could its existence have antedated that of the sun, around which it revolves. These people have proved it to be sheer lunacy to speak of sun, moon, and stars and with the same breath of the earth as being, compared with the former, something special and of great preponderance. It has been taught to every schoolboy that the sun is only a star, the earth one of its satellites, and the moon an under-satellite of the earth; and, furthermore, that the earth, compared with the universe, far from acting a conspicuous part, is only an atom, looking like a rain of dust.

But why should a God concern himself about astronomy? He does what he pleases and poohoos science and logic. For this reason, he made, after manufacturing the earth, first the light and afterwards the sun. Today even a Hottentot can understand there can be no light on earth without the stuff, but God—well, he is no Hottentot.

But let us continue to investigate. Thus far the "creation" was quite a success, but there was still something lacking—things were not lively enough. The creator wanted some pastime, therefore he finally made man. Curiously enough, he now deviated entirely from the method previously applied. Instead of accomplishing this creation by a simple and imperative "Let it be!" he made it exceedingly trouble-some. He took a prosaic lump of common clay in his hand, modelled it into the figure of a man "after his own image" and "breathed into his nostrils the breath of life." God being of infinite wisdom, benign, just, in short—amability itself—it occurred to him that this Adam, as he had named his last article, being alone, would find life exceedingly tedious (perhaps he remembered his own former lonely existence to "Nothing"), and so he made him quite a nice, enticing little Eve. But, in the meantime, experience had evidently taught him that the handling of a lump of clay was a rather unclean business, especially for a god, therefore he applied another new method of manufacture. He tore (dexterity is no witchcraft, least of all for a god) a rib out of Adam's body and changed it into a charming female. Whether this rib, extracted from Adam was restored at a later period or whether, after the performed operation, Adam had to run about in the world as a "one-sided" individual is a matter upon which the polite historian says nothing.

Modern natural science has established that animals and plants have, through the most manifold ramifications, developed during the course of millions of years from simple molluscous matter to their present forms. Man is nothing but the most perfect form of this development, and that he not only had, some thousands of years ago, a very brutish appearance, without language, but also that he—every other supposition excludes itself—must have developed from inferior animal species.

Consequently, natural science stamps God with his self-proclaimed creation of man as a preposterous braggart. But of what avail is all this?—God won't have any tomfoolery. Whether his tales have a scientific ring, or whether they sound like foolish babble, he commands belief in them, otherwise he will let it come to pass that his competitor, the "devil," will get you into his clutches, which is supposed to be quite uncomfortable. For in hell there is not only moaning and the gnashing of teeth but an eternal fire burns, an indefatigable worm is gnawing your soul, and a dreadful stench of burning pitch and sulfur fills the air. To all these discomforts the bodiless man is supposed to be exposed. His flesh, of which he is void, is stewed; his decayed and fallen-out teeth clatter; he howls without a throat or lungs; he smells without a nose—and all this eternally. A devil of a god! Taking all in all, God is, as he candidly informs us in his autobiographical chronicle—the Bible—extremely whimsical and revengeful; actually, an ideal model of a despot.

Hardly were Adam and Eve in existence, before God took it as a matter of course that this rabble must be governed. He decreed a penal code, which said categorically, "Thou shalt not eat of the fruit of the tree of knowledge!" Since that time no tyrant has existed anywhere who did not lay down the same decree for the people.

Adam and Eve did not respect this prohibition, therefore, they were exiled and sentenced to hard labor for life—they and their descendants for all time to come. Beyond this, "civil rights" were taken away from Eve, she being declared to be a bond servant to Adam, whom she was to obey. Besides, both of them were to be under eternal divine police surveillance. Verily, not even William (the German Emperor) has got ahead of him as a haberdasher of human affairs.

But in spite of God's useless severity to mankind, they angered him more and more in proportion as they multiplied. How rapidly this multiplication took place is demonstrated by the history of Cain and Abel. After the former had slain his brother, he went into "a strange land, and took unto himself a wife." Where the location of this strange land and whence the women that were to be found there, God has forgotten to mention, a matter of no surprise, considering the burden of overwork he had to perform at that time.

At last the cup was overflowing. God resolved to destroy all mankind by means of water. Only a few specimens of the race were excepted, with which to make another trial. Unfortunately, notwithstanding all his wisdom, he had made a misgrab, for Noah, the chief of the saved, was soon unmasked as a drunken sot who disported with his own daughters. What good could ever come of so degraded a family?

Again mankind spread; again they developed to such simpletons and rapscallions in sin—about whom the renowned Mecklenburger psalmbook states so much viciousness—that God felt like bursting with heavenly wrath, the more so, as all his exemplary local punishments, such as the destruction of whole cities with fire and brimstone, were entirely disregarded and "thrown to the dogs." He resolved to destroy the whole mob, root and branch, when a really remarkable event occurred which toned him down considerably. Otherwise mankind would have been done for long ago.

One fine day, a certain "Holy Ghost" suddenly appeared upon the stage. He came hither like a wart overnight, nobody knew whence. The Bible scribe (God) merely says he himself was the Holy Ghost. All at once we have to deal with a dual deity. Said Holy Ghost took a notion to descend in the shape of a dove, or rather of a cock pigeon, and to enter into an intimacy with an obscure woman named Mary. In a sweet hour he "overshadowed" the selected of his heart, and lo! she gave birth to a baby boy, which occurrence, as God positively avers in the Bible, never encroached the least bit upon her virginity. Now, this boy was not only human, he was also God, being the Son of God (of the Holy Ghost). The first mentioned God now called himself God the Father, at the same time assuring us of his identity not only with the Holy Ghost but also with God the Son. The father to be his own son, the son his own father, and either or both the Holy Ghost. Thus the "Holy Trinity" was shaped.—Neat!

And now, poor human brain, stand firm, for what now follows is enough to stagger a horse. We know that God the Father had resolved to friccasee the whole human rabble. This intention filled the Son with unbearable sorrow. He (being his own father), shouldered all the guilt of man, and allowed himself, to appease the fury of the Father (being his own son), to be cruelly put to death by the "to be redeemed" rabble—of course, not without subsequently ascending hale and hearty to heaven. This sacrifice of the Son (who is one with the father) tickled the Father (who is one with the Son) to such an extent that he immediately proclaimed a general amnesty—under conditions—which partly remain in force today.

That is the "historical" part in the "Holy Scriptures." Here we see that absurdity and nonsense are put on so thick that those who are already idiotic enough to digest such stuff are susceptible to the most crazy hallucinations. Among these must be classed first and foremost the doctrine of reward and punishment of mankind in the "great hereafter." It has long ago been scientifically proved that there is no existence of a soul independent of the body. That which the religious humbuggers call soul is nothing more or less than the seat of thought, the brain, which receives impressions by means of the living senses, and by such impressions becomes active; and, consequently, at the moment of physical dissolution this action necessarily must cease. But what care the deadly enemies to human reason for the results of scientific research? Just as much as is necessary to prevent their promulgation among the people.

And so they preach the immortality of the soul. Woe to it in the "hereafter" if the body which here held it has not punctiliously respected God's penal code during life. As these folks assure us, their "all bountiful," "all righteous," "all benevolent," "all merciful" God is a super highly developed pokenose, sniffling into the minutest affairs and trifles of each and every individual and making entries of all their shortcomings in his blacklist. He is quite a queer coon anyway. Under danger of giving newborn babes a bad cold, he desires that, to his glory, they be drenched with water (otherwise, baptized).

He takes a heathenish delight in hearing an innumerable herd of his faithful sheep bleat their litanies to hire from their church stalls consecrated to such practices, or when the most devoted of his adherents send aloft without cessation their pious "caterwaulings" and pray, or rather beg, for all things possible and impossible, while he

participates in bloody wars and receives the thanksgivings and frank-
incense of the victors as the "God of battles."

He gets rip-roaring mad if anybody doubts his existence, or when
a Catholic eats meat on Friday or does not by repeated application to
the confessional chair scrub off his sins; or when a Protestant does not
hold in contempt the bones of saints and the paraphernalia and images
prescribed for Catholics, or when he does not, as a rule, toddle through
the world with a face long enough to stop a clock, turned up eyes, bent
back, and folded hands.

If such a person dies impenitent, then his "all merciful" God
decrees a punishment to him, in comparison to which all the scourges
of the knout or cat-o'-nine-tails, all pangs and sufferings of prison life,
all privations of deportation and exile, all emotions of those sentenced
to the scaffold, all pains of the rack and other instruments of torture
that human tyrants ever invented are only pleasant, agreeable, tick-
ling sensations. This God exceeds in bestial cruelty everything malignant that we know of on earth. His prison is hell, his handman the
devil, and his punishments last forever. He employs worms that never
cease gnawing, fires which are never quenched, and other deviltries a
thousandfold as chastisements and only shows mercy for minor trans-
gressions after long periods of time, provided the transgressor died
a Catholic; for these he has under certain circumstances provided a
"purgatory," which differs from hell about as much as a jail from prison.
It is fitted up only for comparatively transient inmates, with somewhat
more lenient regulations—but, at any rate, even in purgatory you will
be singed mercilessly.

The so-called "cardinal sins" are never punished with purgatory,
always with hell. These include, among others, "blasphemy" perpe-
trated by word, by writing, or by thought. Consequently, in this direction God permits neither freedom of the press nor speech, not even
of the unspoken thought. This in itself is enough to stamp him from
the outset as a successful competitor in churlishness with the basest
despots and tyrants of any country or time, but the means and the
duration of his punishments augment the baseness of his nature to
the utmost. Consequently, this God is the most atrocious monster
conceivable.

His attitude is the more infamous in that he allows it to be said of
him that the entire world, and especially mankind in their behavior,

are regulated by his omnipotent divine providence. He maltreats man for actions of which he himself is the originator or prime cause. How amiable, compared with this monster, are the tyrants of earth of the past and present time. Should it please God, however, to permit a person to live and die happy in accordance with his (God's) conceptions, he maltreats him still worse, because the promised "heaven," examined by gaslight, is a good deal worse institution than hell itself; for there you have no desires, you are always satisfied, without ever having a longing for anything. (But as without desire and attainment thereof no gratification is possible, so existence in heaven is without enjoyment.) Eternally employed in "beholding the Lord," eternally listening to the same strains from the same harps, eternally singing that same new and entrancing song in the same melody, if not the one of "Gabriel blowing the trumpet in the morning," surely not anything more exhilarating.

This is the highest degree of "getting tired after a whilishness." The occupancy of an isolated prison cell would be decidedly preferable. It is not surprising, then, that those who are rich and mighty enough to enjoy paradise on earth, should laughingly proclaim with Heine:

The angels and the birds may own
The heavens for themselves alone!

And yet the rich and mighty foster and nourish divine idiocy and religious stupidity. It is, in fact, part of their business; it is really a question of life or death to the domineering and exploiting classes whether the people at large are dumbfounded religiously or not. With religious lunacy stands and falls their power. The more man clings to religion, the more he believes—the more he believes, the less he knows—the less he knows, the more stupid he is—the more stupid, the easier he is governed—the easier to govern, the better he may be exploited—the more exploited, the poorer he gets—the poorer he, the richer and mightier the domineering classes get—the more riches and power they amass, the heavier their yoke upon the neck of the people.

The tyrants of all time and of all countries were always well acquainted with this train of thought, and for that reason always were on good terms with the priesthood of all creeds. Casual quarrels between these two kinds of enemies to mankind were at all times only of a domestic character, merely a struggle for supremacy. The priests or preachers know that they are done for, unless they have the support of the circle of cronies at the governmental top. It is no secret to the rich and powerful that mankind can only be enslaved and exploited when the necromancers of the churches ingraft sufficient servility into the hearts of the masses of the people to make them look upon the earth as a vale of tears, to imbue their minds with the justness of the godly decree; "Serve ye your master" (those in authority), and to buy them off with an alleged "sparerib," of which the people will get the soup in that home beyond the skies, the "Nobodyknows."

Mr. Windthorst, member of the German Parliament, arch-Jesuit, and champion of the clerical faction, once in the heat of debate gave us plainly to understand what the frauds and charlatans of society think in regard to this matter. "When the people lose their faith"—said he—"they will no longer bear their intolerable misery, but rebel!"—That was to the point, and should have aroused the minds of all working people to earnest reflection, if—yes—if the great majority of them had not become religious imbeciles to such an extent that it were an utter impossibility to comprehend the simplest ideas, though heard with normal ears.

It is not in vain that the priesthood of all sorts—i.e., the "black gendarmerie" despotism—have always so strenuously exerted themselves to prevent the retrogression of religious sentiment, although, as is well-known, when among themselves they could burst with laughter over the nonsense they preach for ready cash.

During thousands of years these brain defilers have instituted a reign of terror, without which the religious craze would long since have been abolished. Scaffold and sword, dungeon and chains, poison and poignards, assassination and judicial murder, these were the means by which the religious insanity was upheld, forever a blot of shame in the history of the human race. Hundreds of thousands have been slowly roasted to death at the stake "in the name of God," because they dared to find a stink in the biblical mire. Millions have in tedious wars been compelled to break each other's heads, to burn and sack entire countries, and, after wholesale murder and incendiarism, to spread disease and pestilence, all to maintain religion. The most excruciating tortures were invented by the priests and their accomplices to scare those who had ceased to fear God into religion by the application of mundane devilishness.

When a man maims the hands or feet of another, we say he is a criminal. What shall we call those who maim the intellect of man and, failing in that attempt, with refined cruelty destroy the body inch by inch?

It is certainly true that today they cannot carry on their nefarious "godly" brigandage in the manner formerly in vogue, but in lieu thereof have taken to worming into domestic affairs of families, influencing women, kidnapping children, and misusing the schools for the furtherance of their ends. Their hypocrisy has rather increased than diminished. After their attempts to abolish the newly discovered art of printing had signally failed, they, with their usual cunning and craftiness, utilized it and have gradually to a great extent made the press of today servile to their cause.

An old adage says, "Where a priest has trod, no grass will grow!" That means, in other words, if a person is once in the clutches of the priests, his intellect becomes barren—his intellectual functions cease to operate in a normal way, and instead religious maggots and divine worms wriggle through his brain. He resembles a sheep that has the staggers.

These misguided, unhappy wretches have been defrauded of the real object of life; and, what is worse, they form the great crowd in the train of the opponents to science and the march of reason, to evolution and liberty. Whenever new chains are to be forged for mankind, they are willing to work at the anvil as if possessed by demons. Whenever the road of progressive development is to be blockaded by obstacles, these Kaffirs oppose in their broadest front to the spirit of the times. The attempt to cure such imbeciles is not only a piece of good work to them, it is really an attempt to cauterize a cancer which brings suffering to the whole people and which must ultimately be unconditionally extirpated if this earth is to become a fit habitation for mankind instead of being a playground for gods and devils to torment us.

Out then with religion from the heads of the people, and down with priesthood! The latter are in the habit of saying, "The aim sanctifies the means." Very well, let us apply this precept against them. Our aim is to make mankind independent of every condition of slavery, of the yoke of social servitude, as well as of the shackles of political tyranny, and, not least because last, of all bane of religious darkness. All means to attain this object and made use of at all opportunities offering will be acknowledged just and right by every true philanthropist.

Every person possessing common sense in place of religious insanity, neglecting to do the utmost in his power daily, hourly, to overthrow religion, shirks a duty. Every person, released from deistic superstition, forbearing to oppose priesthood where, when, and however an opportunity presents itself, is a traitor of his cause. Therefore, war to the black hounds! Implacable war to the knife! Incite against the seducers of man, enlighten the seduced! Let us make every means of strife subservient: the scourge of derision and scorn, the torch of science and knowledge, and where these are insufficient—weightier arguments—those that will be felt.

For the ignorant, or rather those craftily made and kept so, if they appear to have a little sense left, the following questions will be proper: "If God desires that we know, love, and fear him, why does he not show himself?—If he is as good as the clergy tell us, what reason is there to fear him?—If he is omniscient, why bother him with private affairs and prayers?—If he is omnipresent, why build him churches?—If he is just, why the supposition that man, whom he created full of faults, shall be punished?—If man does good only by the grace of God, why should he be rewarded?—If he is omnipotent, how can he permit that we blaspheme?—If he is inconceivable, why shall we occupy ourselves with him?—If the knowledge of God is necessary, why does he remain obscure?" Such questions are puzzles to them.

Every thinking person must admit that not one single proof of the existence of a God has ever been found; and, besides this, there is not the least necessity for the existence of God. As we know the inherent properties and laws of nature, the presence of God, either within or beyond this nature, is really to no purpose, quite superfluous, and evidently untenable. Morally the necessity for his existence is still more insignificant.

There is a large empire ruled by a potentate whose demeanor creates differences of opinion in the minds of his subjects. He wants to be known, loved, and honored, and that all shall obey him, but he never shows himself. Everyone endeavors to confound the conception of him by individual nations. The people, subjected to his power, have only such ideas about the character and laws of their invisible sovereign as his ministers see fit to make known, although the latter admit, at the same time, that they are unable themselves to form a conception of their master, that his will is inscrutable, his views of things and his properties unfathomable, and that even his servants disagree about the decrees sent forth by him; for in every province of his empire, the laws differ, and they accuse each other of having altered and forged them. These edicts and commandments, which they claim to have authority to promulgate, are obscure; they are conundrums which the subjects for whose special benefit and enlightenment they are issued can neither understand nor solve. The laws of this hidden monarch require explanation, but those who explain are ever at variance themselves.

Everything that they relate about their concealed sovereign is a chaotic mass of contradictions. They do not say one word that could not at once be proved as a lie. They speak of him as exceedingly good, but still there is no individual existing who does not complain of his mandates. They speak of him as infinitely wise, but yet in his administration everything opposes common sense and reason. They praise his justice, and still the best of his subjects are, as a rule, the least favored. They assure us that he sees everything, still his omnipresence alleviates no distress. He is, they say, a friend of order, yet in his domain everything is confusion and disorder. All his actions are self-determined, yet occurrences seldom, if ever, bear out his plans. He can penetrate the future but does not know the things that will come to pass. He permits no insult to himself to go unpunished but still submits to them from everyone. They are amazed at his knowledge and the perfection of his works, yet his works are imperfect and of short duration, for he creates, destroys, and constantly improves upon that which he has made, without ever being satisfied with his productions. All his enterprises are for the sake of glory, yet his purpose, to be universally glorified, is never attained. He labors incessantly for the welfare of his subjects, but the most of them are in dire distress for the necessities of life. Those whom he apparently seems to favor most are the least satisfied with their lot. We see them nearly all refractory to a master whose grandeur they admire, whose wisdom they praise, whose benevolence they honor, whose justice they fear, and whose commandments they revere but never keep. The empire is the earth; this sovereign is God; his vassals are the priests; his subjects are mankind—a fine conglomeration.

The God of the Christians, as we have seen, is the God who makes promises only to break them; who sends them pestilence and disease in order to heal them; a God who demoralizes mankind in order to improve them. A God who created man "after his own image," and still the origin of evil in man is not accredited to him. A God who saw that all his works were good and soon after discovered that they were bad; who knew that man would eat of the forbidden fruit and still eternally damned him therefore. A God who is so dull as to allow himself to be outwitted by the devil; so cruel that no tyrant on earth can be compared with him—that is the God of the Jewish-Christian theology. He is an all wise bungler who created mankind perfectly, yet could not keep them in that state; who created the devil, yet could not keep him under control; a God who is omnipresent, yet descended from heaven to see what mankind was doing; who is merciful, and yet has, at times, permitted the slaughter of millions. An Almighty who damned millions of innocent for the faults of a few, who caused the deluge to destroy mankind excepting a very few with whom to start a new generation no better than the preceding—who created a heaven for the fools who believe in the "Gospel" and a hell for the enlightened who repudiate it. A divine charlatan who created himself through the Holy Ghost, and then sent himself as mediator between himself and others, and who, held in contempt and derided by his enemies, was nailed to a cross like a bat on a barndoor; who was buried—arose from the dead—descended to hell—ascended to heaven, and since then for eighteen hundred years has been sitting at his own right hand to judge the living—and the dead when the living cease to exist. A terrible despot! whose history should be written in letters of blood, because it is a religion of terror.

Away then with the Christian theology! Away with a God invented by preachers of the bloody faith, who, without their important nothing, by means of which they explain everything, could no longer revel in superfluity; no longer glorify poverty and live in luxury themselves; no longer preach submission and practice arrogance; but who would, through the march of reason, be hurled into the deepest depths of oblivion.

Away then with the malignant Trinity—the murderous Father—the unnatural Son—the lascivious Ghost! Away with all the debasing phantasies in whose name man is degraded to miserable slavery, and through the almighty power of falsehood has been deluded into hoping for the joys of heaven as an indemnification for the miseries of earth.

Away then with those who with their sanctified hallucinations are the curses of liberty and happiness—the priesthood of all sorts!

God is merely a specter fabricated by designing scoundrels through which mankind is tyrannized and kept in constant dread. But the phantom instantly dissolves when examined under the glass of sober reflection. The defrauded masses become impatient . . . and no longer fear the bugbear, but will rather hold out to the priesthood the word of the poet:

> A curse to the idols to whom we pray'd,
> That in winter our hunger and cold be stay'd,
> In vain did we hope, in vain did we wait,
> To be humbugg'd and fool'd was ever our fate.

It is to be hoped that they will not stand humbugging and fooling much longer but will, one of these fine days, throw their crucifixes and saints into the fire, "transform their crucifixes and chalices into useful utensils, and make of their church" theatres, concert and assembly halls or, should they not be serviceable for that purpose, use them as corn bins or stables—find useful work for the priests and nuns, and then be surprised at themselves for not having done it long before.

This short and terse method will, of course, only be consummated in the storm of the coming social revolution; in fact, at that moment, when the conspirators of priesthood, the princes, the nobility, the bureaucrats, the capitalists, and the exploiters of all kinds are swept away as by a whirlwind, thereby cleaning state and church with an iron broom of the accumulated mire of centuries.

CHAPTER II

Woman, Church, and State

by Matilda Gage

The most important struggle in the history of the church is that of woman for liberty of thought and the right to give that thought to the world. As a spiritual force the church appealed to barbaric conception when it declared woman to have been made for man, first in sin, and commanded to be under obedience. Holding as its chief tenet a belief in the inherent wickedness of woman, the originator of sin, as its sequence the sacrifice of a God becoming necessary, the church has treated her as alone under a "curse" for whose enforcement it declared itself the divine instrument. Woman's degradation under it dating back to its earliest history, while the nineteenth century still shows religious despotism to have its stronghold in the theory of woman's inferiority to man. The church has ever invoked the "old covenant" as authority, while it also asserts this covenant was done away with at the advent of the new dispensation. Paul, whose character as persecutor was not changed when he veered from Judaism to Christianity, gave to the church a lever long enough to reach down through eighteen centuries in opposition to woman's equality with man. Through this lengthy period, his teaching has united the Christian world in opposition to her right of private judgment and personal freedom.

Each great division of Christianity alike proclaims the supreme sinfulness of woman in working for the elevation of her sex. In this work she has been left outside of religious sympathy, outside of political protection, yet in the interest of justice she claims the right to tear down the barriers of advancing civilization and to rend asunder all beliefs that men hold most sacred. Freedom for woman underlies all the great questions of the age. She must no longer be the scapegoat of humanity upon whose devoted head the sins of all people are made to rest. Woman's increasing freedom within the last hundred years is not due to the church but to the printing press, to education, to free thought and other forms of advancing civilization. The fashions of the Christian world have changed but not its innermost belief. The power of the pulpit, built up by a claim of divine authority, with the priest as an immediate representative of God, has been reacting upon the priesthood itself, and now while vainly struggling for light this order finds itself bound by chains of its own creating. Today the priesthood is hampered by creeds and dogmas centuries old, yet so fully outside of practical life that the church has become the great materialistic force of the century; its ideas of a God, its teachings of a future life, all falling within the realm of the physical senses; the incorporeal and spiritual are lost in the grossest forms of matter. Although a body professing to inculcate pure spiritual truths, the church teaches the grossest form of materialism. It asserts principles contradictory to natural laws; it presents chaos as the normal condition of the infinite; it bids people live under faith outside of evidence, and in thus doing is guilty of immeasurable evils to mankind. A bark without compass, it steers upon a sea of night, no star illumining the darkness; the control and guidance by humanity of the psychic part of being, generally spoken of as "supernatural," although the truest to nature, has become nearly lost through the materialization of spiritual truth by the church, the worst form of idolatry. Christianity was a stern reality to the men of the Early and Middle Ages, who believing themselves to have been created nearer to God than woman also believed themselves to have lost earthly immortality through her. Permeated with this idea, it is not strange that men through many hundred years taught that woman was especially under control of the Evil One. The devil was an objective form to the clergy and people alike. Nor, under such belief, is it strange that priests should warn their flocks from the pulpit against the wiles of woman, thus degrading her self-respect and teaching men to hold her in that contempt whose influence is felt today. The result of this teaching has been deplorable to humanity; men equally with women having sunk under this degradation of one half of the race.

The most stupendous system of organized robbery known has been that of the church towards woman, a robbery that has not only taken her self-respect but all rights of person; the fruits of her own industry; her opportunities of education; the exercise of her own judgment, her own conscience, her own will. The unfortunate peculiarity of the history of man, according to Buckle, is that although its separate parts have been examined with considerable ability, hardly anyone has attempted to outline them into a whole and ascertain the way they are connected with each other. While this statement is virtually true as regards the general history of mankind, it is most particularly so in reference to the position of woman in its bearings upon race development. A thorough investigation of her connection with our present form of civilization, or even with that of the past, as compared with each other, or as influencing the whole, has never yet been authoritatively undertaken. This failure has not been so largely due to willful neglect as to incapacity upon the part of man to judge truly of this relation. Woman herself must judge of woman. The most remote feminine personality is not less incomprehensible to man than the woman of today; he now as little understands the finer qualities of her soul or her high intuitive reasoning faculties as in the past. Reason is divided into two parts, theoretical and practical; the former appertains to man; the latter, composed of those intuitive faculties which do not need a long process of ratiocination for their work, inhere in woman. Although the course of history has given many glimpses of her superiority, and the past few decades have shown in every land a new awakening of woman to a recognition of her own powers, man as man is still as obtuse as of yore. He is yet under the darkness of the patriarchate, failing to recognize woman as a component part of humanity, whose power of development and influence upon civilization are at least the equal of his own. He yet fails to see in her a factor of life whose influence for good or for evil has ever been in direct ratio with her freedom. He does not yet discern her equal right with himself to impress her own opinions upon the world. He still interprets governments and religions as requiring from her an unquestioning obedience to laws she has no share in making and that place her as an inferior in every relation of life. Ralph Waldo Emerson, with keen insight into the fallibility of lawmakers, declared that "good men must not obey the laws too well." Woman is showing her innate wisdom in daring to question the infallibility of man, his laws, and his interpretation of her place in creation. She is not obeying "too well," and yet man fails to analyze her motives in this defection. The church and the state have long done man's thinking for him, the ideas of the few, whose aim is power, have been impressed upon the many; individualism is still characterized as the essence of evil; self-thought, self-control as heretical. The state condemns both as a crime against itself, the church as a sin against heaven. Both church and state claiming to be of divine origin have assumed divine right of man over woman; while church and state have thought for man, man has assumed the right to think for woman.

As man under fear of eternal damnation surrendered to the irresponsible power of church and state, so woman yielded to that power which closed every external avenue of knowledge to her under pretext of her sinfulness. One-tenth of the human race, within the period covered by modern civilization, has compelled the other nine-tenths to think their thoughts and live lives according to their commands. This has been the chief effort of governments and religion. The most formidable general evil under which woman has suffered during the Christian ages has been that of protection; a non-recognition of her ability to care for herself, rendering watchful guardianship over her a recognized part of man's law; not alone to prevent her sinking into depths of vice but to also prevent her entire subversion of government and religion. Buckle and other writers have recognized the protective spirit as the greatest enemy to civilization, its influence causing the few to establish themselves as guardians of the many in all affairs of life. The American Revolution in proclaiming the rights of humanity struck a blow at the protective system. This system has ever based itself upon a declaration of the supreme rights of a God and certain rights as pertaining to certain classes of men by virtue of authority from that God. The defense of such authority has ever been the chief business of church and state, and thus religions and governments have neither found time nor inclination to uphold the rights of humanity. Under the Christian system, woman as the most rebellious against God, in having eaten a forbidden fruit, has found herself condemned through the centuries to untold oppression in order that the rights of God might be maintained. Yet while constantly teaching that woman brought sin into the world, the church ever forgets its own corollary; that if she brought sin she also brought God into the world, thus throwing ineffable splendor over mankind. The whole theory regarding woman, under Christianity, has been based upon the conception that she had no right to live for herself alone. Her duty to others has continuously been placed before her, and her training has ever been that of self-sacrifice. Taught from the pulpit and legislative halls that she was created for another that her position must always be secondary even to her children, her right to life has been admitted only in so far as its reacting effect upon another could be predicated. That she was first created for herself, as an independent being to whom all the opportunities of the world should be open because of herself, has not entered the thought of the church; has not yet become one of the conceptions of law; is not yet the foundation of the family.

But woman is learning for herself that not self-sacrifice but self-development is her first duty in life; and this, not primarily for the sake of others but that she may become fully herself; a perfectly rounded being from every point of view; her duty to others being a secondary consideration arising from those relations in life where she finds herself placed at birth or those which later she voluntarily assumes. But these duties are not different in point of obligation, no more imperative upon her than are similar duties upon man. The political doctrine of the sovereignty of the individual, although but partially recognized even in the United States, has been most efficacious in destroying that protective spirit which has so greatly interfered with the progress of humanity. This spirit yet retains its greatest influence in the family, where it places a boundary between husband and wife. Of all circumstances biasing the judgment and restricting the sympathies, none have shown themselves more powerful than physical differences, whether of race, color, or sex. When those differences are not alone believed to be a mark of inferiority but to have been especially created for the pleasure and peculiar service of another, the elements of irresponsible tyranny upon one side and irremediable slavery upon the other are already organized. If, in addition, that inferior is regarded as under an especial curse for extraordinary sin, as the church has ever inculcated in reference to women; and when, as in the case of woman and man, an entire separation of interests, hopes, feelings, and passions is impossible, we have reached the extreme of injustice and misery under the protective system. Consequently, no other form of "protection" has possessed so many elements of absolute injustice as that of man over woman. Swedenborg taught, and experience declares, that morality cannot exist except under conditions of freedom. Hence, we find much that has been called morality is the effect of dependence and lessened self-respect and has really been immorality and degradation. While in every age the virtues of self-sacrifice have been pointed to as evidence of the highest morality, we find those women in whom it has been most apparent have been those doing least justice where justice first belongs—to themselves. Justice as the foundation of the highest law is a primal requirement of the individual to the self. It is nonetheless a serious impeachment of the religious-moral idea that the doctrine of protection and the duty of woman's self-sacrifice were taught under the theory of divine authority. No faith was more profound, none could be more logical if resting on a true foundation, than the church theory regarding woman. Life assumed a sterner reality to men who believed themselves in point of purity and priority nearer their Creator than woman. Thereafter, she was to be protected from herself, the church and man cheerfully assuming this duty. Under the protective spirit it is not so very long since men sold themselves and their families to some other man in power, either lay or religious, under promise of protection, binding themselves to obey the mandates of such lord evermore. The church protected and directed the thought of the world. To think for one's self is not even now the tendency of mankind; the few who dare, do so at great peril. It will require another hundred years of personal and political freedom for men to appreciate what liberty really is—for them to possess confidence in their own judgment upon religious questions—for the man of humble station to fully believe in himself and in his own opinions when opposed to the authority of church or state.

Women of the present century whose struggle for equal opportunity of education with men for a chance to enter the liberal professions, for a fair share of the world of work, for equal pay in that work, for all demands of equality which make the present a noted age in the world's history, have met their greatest opposition from this protective spirit. No less than during the darkest period of its history does the church still maintain the theory that education and public life are not fitting for woman—indelicate for herself and injurious to the community. During the Christian ages, the church has not alone shown cruelty and contempt for woman but has exhibited an impious and insolent disregard of her most common rights of humanity. It has robbed her of responsibility, putting man in place of God. It has forbidden her the offices of the church, and at times an entrance within its doors. It has denied her independent thought, declaring her a secondary creation for man's use to whom alone it has made her responsible. It has anathematized her sex, teaching her to feel shame for the very fact of her being. It has not been content with proclaiming a curse upon her creative attributes but has thrust the sorrows and expiations of man's "curse" upon her, and in doing these things the church has wrought her own ruin. A religious revolution of the most radical kind has even now assumed such proportions as to nearly destroy the basic creeds of various sects and undermine the whole fabric of Christendom. It everywhere exists, although neither the world nor the church seem to realize the magnitude of its proportions. As a legitimate result of two opposing forces, a crisis in the life of the church is at hand; nay, even upon it. While we see it making organized effort for extension of power and entire control of the state, we also find great increase of radical thought and development of individual conscience and individual judgment. With thought no longer bound by fear of everlasting punishment, mankind will cease to believe unproved assertions, simply because made by a class of men under assumed authority from god. Reason will be used, mankind will seek for truth come whence it may, lead where it will, and, with our own Lucretia Mott, will accept "truth for authority and not authority for truth."

In knocking at the door of political rights, woman is severing the last link between church and state; the church must lose that power it has wielded with changing force since the days of Constantine, ever to the injury of freedom and the world. The immeasurable injustice of woman and her sufferings under Christianity, her intellectual, moral, and spiritual servitude, will never be understood until life with its sorrows shall be opened to our vision in a sphere more defined than the present one. The superstitions of the church, the miseries of woman, her woes, tortures, burnings, rackings, and all the brutalities she has endured in the church, the state, the family, under the sanction of Christianity, would be incredible had we not the most undeniable evidence of their existence, not alone in the past but as shown by the teachings, laws, and customs of the present time. "She has suffered under a theology which extended its rule not only to her civil and political relations but to her most significant domestic and personal concerns, regulating the commerce of husband and wife, of

25

parent and child, of master and servant, even prescribing her diet and dress, her education and her industries." Edmund Noble speaks in like manner of the ancient Russians under the tyrannical provisions of the Greek church, saying, "clearly, such a system of theocratic supervision and direction as this is compatible only with the lowest possible spiritual condition of the subject, or the lowest possible conception of God." Possessing no proof of its existence, the church has ever fostered unintelligent belief. To doubt her "unverified" assertion has even been declared an unpardonable sin. The supreme effort of the church being maintenance of power, it is but recently that woman has been allowed to read history for herself or, having read it, dared to draw her own conclusion from its premises. Ignorance and falsehood created a sentiment in accord with themselves, crushing all her aspirations. In the family, man still decides the rights and duties of the wife, as of old. As legislator and judge, he still makes and executes class laws. In the church, he yet arrogates to himself the interpretation of the Bible; still claims to be an exponent of the Divine will, that grandest lesson of the reformation, the right of private interpretation of the scriptures not yet having been conceded to woman. The premises upon which the church is based being radically false, and this, most especially in everything related to woman. Trained from infancy by the church to a belief in woman's inferiority and incapacity for self-government, men of the highest station have not hesitated to organize societies in opposition to her just demands. As early as 1875, an anti-woman's franchise association was formed in London under the name of "Association for Protecting the Franchise from the Encroachment of Women"; Hon. Mr. Bouverie, a leading opponent of woman suffrage in the House of Commons, being its chairman. Among the promoters of the movement were Sir Henry James, formerly attorney general (for the Crown), Hon. Mr. Claflin, and Mr. Leathers, correspondent of the *New York Tribune*.

Since this period, a number of women distinguished as "the wives of" have petitioned legislative bodies for protection against freedom for themselves and all others of their sex, in asking that legislatures shall not recognize woman's self-governing right. The deepest depth of degradation is reached when the slave not only declares against his own freedom but strives to tighten the bonds of fellow slaves; and the most cruel wrong resulting from such slavery is the destruction of self-respect in the enslaved, as shown by the course of these women petitioners. The protective theory reached its lowest depth for woman by an attack upon her already vested rights of the ballot in the former territory, now State, of Washington, on the Pacific coast, in the case of Nevada M. Bloomer (a woman) against John Wood and others, to have the women of that territory deprived of their already existing right of suffrage. In line with the general opposition to the enfranchisement of woman, men of even the most liberal tendencies declare that her political freedom will be used to sustain the church, apparently forgetting that man alone has placed the church in power, and that man alone holds it in power. And proof of man's complicity is even greater than this. Despite what is said of the larger church membership of women, the most noted modern evangelist, Moody, recently declared that he "found men tenfold, aye, an hundredfold" more receptive of his preaching than women. While speaking in Farwell Hall, Chicago, 1886, he said, "For fifteen years I have preached to women in the afternoon and very often as near as I could, have preached the same sermon to men at night, and in ninety-nine cases out of a hundred have had five times more result in preaching to men than to women." This pseudo-argument, as to woman's susceptibility to church teaching, brought up by the enemies of her freedom, possesses no more real value than the pseudo-political argument sometimes presented in opposition to woman's admission into active politics; that is, her emotional temperament. To one who has been present at four great presidential nominating conventions and several large state conventions, knowledge upon this point is practical. When one has seen a cordon of police, enforced by the mayor upon the platform, protecting the officers of such a convention, while its members, standing upon seats, stamped, shouted, gesticulated, threatened with revolvers, acting more like uncaged wild beasts than like men, when one has witnessed the wildest enthusiasm at the mention of a name, the waving of flags, of hats, of handkerchiefs, the shaking of umbrellas, chairs, canes, with violent stamping, amid a hubbub of indistinguishable voices, all shouting, screaming so loud that people for blocks away are roused from slumber in affright of a fire or the approach of an ungovernable mob, such objections to woman's freedom as her "emotions" fall to their lowest value.

In church and in state, man has exhibited the wildest passions, the most ungovernable frenzy—has shown himself less controlled by reason than possible for woman under the most adverse circumstances.

Judaism, and its offspring, Christianity, show the results of the patriarchate in some of its most degenerate forms; industrial servitude, educational restrictions, legal thralldom, political slavery, false religious teachings are but a portion of the evils existing under its most enlightened forms, and equally with the more pronounced polygamy and infanticide they show a total perversion of moral ideas. Woman dearly pays for the rights she has secured. Labor opposes, in less pay for the same work; literature, at first welcoming her only through the cookbook, next compelled her to conceal her sex under a male pseudonym, in order that her writings might be received with the same respect as those of man; art has given her similar experiences, and while today admitting her to the same advantage of study with man, yet compels her to pay twice the price for the same instructions.

The careful student of history will discover that Christianity has been of very little value in advancing civilization but has done a great deal toward retarding it. "Civilization, a recognition of the rights of others at every point of contact," has been carried forward by means of rebellion against church teaching and church authority. The experience of science is familiar to all, even school children quoting Galileo and Dr. Faust. What are called reformations in religion, the work of Huss, of Luther, of the Waldenses, the Huguenots, are equally familiar instances to the youngest student of rebellion against the church. These and a myriad of others known to the historian have all been brought about by refusal to accept the authority of the church as final. The Peasant War in France, the struggles of Wat Tyler and of Hampden in England, the French and the American Revolutions looking toward equality of rights, and a thousand minor forms of political progress have all been opposed by the church as rebellions against its teachings, yet all have been marked steps in civilization. The church and civilization are antipodal; one means authority, the other freedom; one means conservatism, the other progress; one means the rights of God as interpreted by the priesthood, the other the rights of humanity as interpreted by humanity. Civilization advances by free thought, free speech, free men. The uprising of the women of all peoples in assertion of their common humanity with man is exemplification of that fact recognized in the Declaration of Independence, that while patient endurance of wrongs to which persons are accustomed, always long borne, rather than by change, perhaps to meet evils they know not of, shows its absolutely certain ultimate effect, no matter how long delayed, in rebellion. A time comes in the history of souls, as of nations, when forbearance ceases to be a virtue, and self-respecting life is only to be retained through defiance of and rebellion against existing customs. The soul must assert its own supremacy or die. It is not one woman or the women of one nation that have thus suddenly shown desire to rule themselves—to act for themselves alone. A strange identity of thought pervades all parts of the world—India, China, Japan, Russia and all of Europe, North and South America, the vast continents of the southern seas and the isles thereof, and even barbaric Africa, all evince proof of the wide psychic undercurrent which, seething through women's souls, is overthrowing the civilizations built upon the force principles of the patriarchate and will soon reinstate the reign of truth and justice. During those long ages of priestly intolerance, of domestic and governmental tyranny, in which woman seemed to accept the authority of the priest as that of God, there still existed a consciousness hardly perceptible to herself that she was an independent being to whom by virtue of her humanity all opportunities in life belonged. From century to century mothers transmitted this scarcely developed perception to daughters, until suddenly within the past fifty years these dominant ideas woke to thought, and the women of all nations began to proclaim their same right to self-control as that claimed by man.

It is impossible to write of the church without noticing its connection with the great systems of the world during its course of life. The history of Christendom is the history of the myriad institutions which have arisen through its teachings or that have been sustained by its approval. The world has not grown wise under it, except with a wisdom that is leading the purest humanitarian thought in a direction contrary to its footsteps. Slavery and prostitution, persecutions for heresy, the inquisition with its six hundred modes of torture, the destruction of learning, the oppression of science, the systematized betrayal of confiding innocence, the recognized and unrecognized polygamy of man, the denial to woman of a right to herself, her thought, her wages, her children, to a share in the government which rules her, to an equal part in religious institutions, all these and a myriad more are parts of what is known as Christian civilization. Nor has the church ever been the leader in great reforms. During the anti-slavery conflict, the American church was known as "the bulwark of American slavery." Its course continues the same in every great contest with wrong. A memorial history of the American Episcopal Church, an extensive work in two volumes of seven hundred pages each published within the past few years devotes but seven pages to the "Attitude of the Church during the Civil War," and the general refusal of the church to take part in the great struggle for national life is referred to with complacent satisfaction. Penitentiaries and prisons, asylums and reformatories, all institutions of a repressive character which the church prides herself as having built up are no less evil than the convents, monasteries, and religious orders belonging to it. They have all risen through perversion of nature. Crimes and criminals are built up and born because of the great wrong first done to mothers; they are the offspring of church and state. Science now declares crime to be a disease, but it has not yet discovered the primal cause of this disease. It is an inheritance from centuries of legalized crime against woman, of which the church in its teachings is prime factor.

Woman will gain nothing by a compromising attitude toward the church, by attempt to excuse its great wrong toward her sex, or by palliation of its motives. On the contrary, a stern reference to facts, keeping the face of the world turned toward its past teachings, its present attitude, is her duty. Wrongs of omission equal in magnitude those of commission.

Advance for woman is too well-established, woman has had too much experience, has borne too much ridicule, misrepresentation, and abuse to now hesitate in an attack upon the stronghold of her oppression—the church. She possesses too full knowledge of its subtle touch upon civil law to dare leave it alone; it has become one of woman's first duties, one of her greatest responsibilities, to call public attention to its false doctrines and false teachings in regard to the origin, condition, and subjection of woman. She has engaged in too many battles, weathered too many storms, to longer hesitate in exposure of its stupendous crimes toward one half of humanity. Let those who fear hide themselves, if they will, until the storm is past. Let those who dare, defiantly rejoice that they are called upon to bear still more, in order that woman may be free. A brighter day is to come for the world, a day when the intuitions of woman's soul shall be accepted as part of humanity's spiritual wealth; when force shall step backward and love, in reality, rule the teachings of religion; and may woman be strong in the ability and courage necessary to bring about this millennial time. The world is full of signs of the near approach of this period; as never before is there an arousing sense of something deeper, holier in religion than the Christian church has given. The world has seemingly awaited the advent of heroic souls who once again should dare all things for the truth. The woman who possesses love for her sex, for the world, for truth, justice, and right, will not hesitate to place herself upon record as opposed to falsehood, no matter under what guise of age or holiness it appears. A generation has passed since the great struggle began, but not until within ten years has woman dared attack upon the veriest stronghold of her oppression, the church. The state, agent and slave of the church, has so long united with it in suppression of woman's intelligence, has so long preached of power to man alone, that it has created an inherited tendency, an inborn line of thought toward repression. Bent in this line before his birth, man still unwittingly thinks of woman as not quite his equal, and it requires a new creation of mind to change his thought. A second generation has arisen, in whom some slight inherited tendencies toward recognition of a woman's right to herself are seen. In the next generation this line of inherited thought will have become stronger, both church and state more fully recognizing woman's inherent right to share in all the opportunities of life; but at what cost to all who have taken part in the great struggle.

Has woman no wrongs to avenge upon the church? As I look backward through history I see the church everywhere stepping upon advancing civilization, hurling woman from the plane of "natural rights" where the fact of her humanity had placed her, and through itself and its control over the state, in the doctrine of "revealed rights," everywhere teaching an inferiority of sex; a created subordination of woman to man; making her very existence a sin; holding her accountable to a diverse code of morals from man; declaring her possessed of fewer rights in church and in state; her very entrance into heaven made dependent upon some man to come as mediator between her and the Savior it has preached, thus crushing her personal, intellectual, and spiritual freedom. Looking forward, I see evidence of a conflict more severe than any yet fought by reformation or science; a conflict that will shake the foundations of religious belief, tear into fragments and scatter to the winds the old dogmas upon which all forms of Christianity are based. It will not be the conflict of man with man upon rites and systems; it will not be the conflict of science upon church theories regarding creation and eternity; it will not be the light of biology illuminating the hypothesis of the resurrection of the body; but it will be the rebellion of one half of the church against those theological dogmas upon which the very existence of the church is based. In no other country has the conflict between natural and revealed rights been as pronounced as in the United States; and in this country where the conflict first began, we shall see its full and final development. During the ages, no rebellion has been of like importance with that of woman against the tyranny of church and state; none has had its far-reaching effects. We note its beginning; its progress will overthrow every existing form of these institutions; its end will be a regenerated world.

CHAPTER III

The Devil's Dictionary (excerpts)

by Ambrose Bierce

and

American Heretic's Dictionary (excerpts)

by Chaz Bufe

The Devil's Dictionary

Adore, v.t. To venerate expectantly.

Altar, n. The place whereon the priest formerly raveled out the small intestine of the sacrificial victim for purposes of divination and cooked its flesh for the gods. The word is now seldom used, except with reference to the sacrifice of their liberty and peace by a male and a female fool.

Christian, n. One who believes that the New Testament is a divinely inspired book admirably suited to the spiritual needs of his neighbor. One who follows the teachings of Christ in so far as they are not inconsistent with a life of sin.

Divination, n. The art of nosing out the occult. Divination is of as many kinds as there are fruit-bearing varieties of the flowering dunce and the early fool.

Evangelist, n. A bearer of good tidings, particularly (in a religious sense) such as assure us of our own salvation and the damnation of our neighbors.

Faith, n. Belief without evidence in what is told by one who speaks without knowledge of things without parallel.

Heathen, n. A benighted creature who has the folly to worship something that he can see and feel.

Immoral, adj. Inexpedient.

Indigestion, n. A disease which the patient and his friends frequently mistake for deep religious conviction and concern for the salvation of mankind. As the simple Red Man of the western wild put it, with, it must be confessed, a certain force: "Plenty well, no pray; big bellyache, heap God."

Infidel, n. In New York, one who does not believe in the Christian religion; in Constantinople, one who does.

Koran, n. A book which the Mohammedans foolishly believe to have been written by divine inspiration, but which Christians know to be a wicked imposture, contradictory to Holy Scriptures.

Magic, n. The art of converting superstition into coin. There are other arts serving the same high purpose, but the discreet lexicographer does not name them.

Orthodox, n. An ox wearing the popular religious yoke.

Pantheism, n. The doctrine that everything is God, in contradistinction to the doctrine that God is everything.

Pray, v. To ask that the laws of the universe be annulled in behalf of a single petitioner confessedly unworthy.

Rack, n. An argumentative implement formerly much used in persuading devotees of a false faith to embrace the living truth.

Religion, n. A daughter of Hope and Fear, explaining to Ignorance the nature of the Unknowable.

Reprobation, n. In theology, the state of a luckless mortal prenatally damned. The doctrine of reprobation was taught by Calvin, whose joy in it was somewhat marred by the sad sincerity of his conviction that although some are foredoomed to perdition, others are predestined to salvation.

Revelation, n. A famous book in which St. John the Divine concealed all that he knew.

Reverence, n. The spiritual attitude of a man to a god and a dog to a man.

Satan, n. One of the Creator's lamentable mistakes, repented in sashcloth and axes. Being instated as an archangel, Satan made himself multifariously objectionable and was finally expelled from heaven. Halfway in his descent he paused, bent his head in thought a moment, and at last went back. "There is one favor that I should like to ask," said he.

"Name it."

"Man, I understand, is about to be created. He will need laws."

"What, wretch! You his appointed adversary, charged from the dawn of eternity with hatred of his soul—you ask for the right to make his laws?"

"Pardon; what I have to ask is that he be permitted to make them himself."

It was so ordered.

Scriptures, n. The sacred books of our holy religion, as distinguished from the false and profane writings on which all other faiths are based.

Universalist, n. One who foregoes the advantage of hell for persons of another faith.

Virtues, n. pl. Certain abstentions.

Worship, n. Homo Creator's testimony to the sound construction and finish of Deus Creatus. A popular form of abjection having an element of pride.

Zeal, n. A certain nervous disorder afflicting the young and inexperienced. A passion that goeth before a sprawl.

American Heretic's Dictionary

Atheist, n. A person to be pitied in that he is unable to believe in things for which there is no evidence, and who has thus deprived himself of a convenient means of feeling superior to others.

Believer, n. One who wisely chooses to avoid unnecessary work, especially that of thinking for himself.

Catholicism, n. A popular form of self-degradation involving ritual cannibalism.

Christian, n. One who generously seeks to transfer his expertise in morality into provisions in the penal code.

Compassion, n. Mercy. A virtue so rare in Christian lands that when discovered by chance it is always deemed newsworthy.

Cruelty, n. The most important and highly valued element in entertainment in Christian and Muslim countries, especially in entertainment provided by the legal and penal systems.

Death, n. For Christians, a blessing—the gateway to heaven, the portal to paradise. It speaks volumes of the generosity of Christians that they so freely bestow this blessing upon their enemies, yet routinely do all in their power, even in extreme old age, to deny this same blessing to themselves.

Faith, n. An attribute of desperation. An attempt to make the intolerable tolerable. When achieved, it gives its holders a satisfying feeling of superiority over those so unfortunate as to see things as they are.

Fundamentalist, n. One in whom something is fundamentally wrong.

God, n. 1) An unsavory character found in many popular works of fiction; 2) A three-letter justification for murder.

Hell, n. A place of everlasting torment, much like the United States during an election year.

Islamophobia, n. 1) The unspeakable act of pointing out that acts committed by Islamists in the name of Islam just might have something to do with Islam; 2) The ever popular American mass participation sport of scapegoating and further victimizing an already victimized minority. While both definitions are accurate, those who accept one will never accept the other. This provides an example of yet another popular American mass participation sport: rejection of reality.

Jesus Christ, int. A common exclamation indicating surprise, anger, disgust, or bewilderment.

Life, n. 1) A series of minor annoyances and missed opportunities punctuated by blinding pain; 2) According to pro-lifers, the most beautiful, precious thing in the world, from the moment of conception to the moment of execution.

Moral, adj. 1) In the conventional religious sense, anything tending to increase human misery, as in "moral conduct" and "moral standards"; 2) A term of self-approbation used by those who enjoy locking other human beings in cages.

Mystic, n. A man or woman who wishes to understand the mysteries of the universe but is too lazy to study physics.

Pascal's Wager, n. A cunning stratagem based on the premise that God's last name is "Ed," his first name is "Special," and that he can't tell the difference between lip service and belief.

Piety, n. An uncommonly strong fear of death.

Prayer, n. 1) A form of begging, unusual in that it's often practiced as a solitary activity. When practiced in groups, it is normally referred to as "worship"; 2) A humble supplication, the premise of which is that the omnipotent, omniscient creator of the universe will benefit from the guidance of the humble supplicator.

Priest, n. A holy individual who follows—often to excess—the divine injunction to "love the little children."

Rapture, n. An eagerly awaited religious event in which the world will be rid of much unwanted rubbish.

Religious Extremist, n. A term used by religious liberals to condemn anyone who shows the poor judgment to follow to the letter the inerrant word of God.

Spirituality, n. 1) A meaningless but uplifting term of self-congratulation often found in dating site profiles.

Televangelist, n. Ideally suited to his profession, the televangelist makes a career of denouncing greed, gluttony, dishonesty, drunkenness, drug abuse, prostitution, adultery, fornication, and homosexuality—and thus speaks from a wealth of personal experience.

Ten Commandments, n. pl. The fundamental moral precepts of the Christian and Jewish faiths and a fine set of guiding lights for us all. Some low-minded skeptics have suggested that God could have improved upon these inspired moral principles if it had dropped the commandments concerning swearing, idol worship, sexual exclusivity, and resting on the sabbath, and had instead instituted bans on slavery, torture, and cruelty, but these suggestions are obviously sacrilegious. If slavery, torture, and cruelty were true moral evils, organized Christianity would not have condoned, instigated, and practiced all three for the better part of two millennia. Fortunately, most Christians realize this and do not bother themselves about such trifles. Instead, they rightly concentrate their moral outrage on the true evils of "obscene" books and pictures, "filthy" language, and the sexual practices of their neighbors.

Witch, n. To fundamentalist Christians, a burning curiosity—and a curiosity which many of them, even at this late date, hope to reignite.

CHAPTER IV

The Failure of Christianity

by Emma Goldman

The counterfeiters and poisoners of ideas, in their attempt to obscure the line between truth and falsehood, find a valuable ally in the conservatism of language.

Conceptions and words that have long ago lost their original meaning continue through centuries to dominate mankind. Especially is this true if these conceptions have become a commonplace, if they have been instilled in our beings from our infancy as great and irrefutable verities. The average mind is easily content with inherited and acquired things or with the dicta of parents and teachers, because it is much easier to imitate than to create.

Our age has given birth to two intellectual giants who have undertaken to transvalue the dead social and moral values of the past, especially those contained in Christianity. Friedrich Nietzsche and Max Stirner have hurled blow upon blow against the portals of Christianity, because they saw in it a pernicious slave morality, the denial of life, the destroyer of all the elements that make for strength and character. True, Nietzsche has opposed the slave morality idea inherent in Christianity in behalf of a master morality for the privileged few. But I venture to suggest that his master idea had nothing to do with the vulgarity of station, caste, or wealth. Rather did it mean the masterful in human possibilities, the masterful in man that would help him to overcome old traditions and worn-out values, so that he may learn to become the creator of new and beautiful things.

Both Nietzsche and Stirner saw in Christianity the leveler of the human race, the breaker of man's will to dare and to do. They saw in every movement built on Christian morality and ethics attempts not at the emancipation from slavery but for the perpetuation thereof. Hence, they opposed these movements with might and main.

Whether I do or do not entirely agree with these iconoclasts, I believe, with them, that Christianity is most admirably adapted to the training of slaves, to the perpetuation of a slave society; in short, to the very conditions confronting us today. Indeed, never could society have degenerated to its present appalling stage, if not for the assistance of Christianity. The rulers of the earth have realized long ago what potent poison inheres in the Christian religion. That is the reason they foster it; that is why they leave nothing undone to instill it into the blood of the people. They know only too well that the subtleness of the Christian teachings is a more powerful protection against rebellion and discontent than the club or the gun.

No doubt I will be told that, though religion is a poison and institutionalized Christianity the greatest enemy of progress and freedom, there is some good in Christianity "itself." What about the teachings of Christ and early Christianity, I may be asked, do they not stand for the spirit of humanity, for right and justice?

It is precisely this oft-repeated contention that induced me to choose this subject, to enable me to demonstrate that the abuses of Christianity, like the abuses of government, are conditioned in the thing itself and are not to be charged to the representatives of the creed. Christ and his teachings are the embodiment of submission, of inertia, of the denial of life; hence, responsible for the things done in their name.

I am not interested in the theological Christ. Brilliant minds like Bauer, Strauss, Renan, Thomas Paine, and others refuted that myth long ago. I am even ready to admit that the theological Christ is not half so dangerous as the ethical and social Christ. In proportion as science takes the place of blind faith, theology loses its hold. But the ethical and poetical Christ myth has so thoroughly saturated our lives that even some of the most advanced minds find it difficult to emancipate themselves from its yoke. They have rid themselves of the letter but have retained the spirit; yet it is the spirit which is back of all the crimes and horrors committed by orthodox Christianity. The Fathers of the Church can well afford to preach the gospel of Christ. It contains nothing dangerous to the regime of authority and wealth; it stands for self-denial and self-abnegation, for penance and regret, and is absolutely inert in the face of every [in]dignity, every outrage imposed upon mankind.

Here I must revert to the counterfeiters of ideas and words. So many otherwise earnest haters of slavery and injustice confuse, in a most distressing manner, the teachings of Christ with the great struggles for social and economic emancipation. The two are irrevocably and forever opposed to each other. The one necessitates courage, daring, defiance, and strength. The other preaches the gospel of non-resistance, of slavish acquiescence in the will of others; it is the complete disregard of character and self-reliance and, therefore, destructive of liberty and well-being.

Whoever sincerely aims at a radical change in society, whoever strives to free humanity from the scourge of dependence and misery, must turn his back on Christianity, on the old as well as the present form of the same.

Everywhere and always, since its very inception, Christianity has turned the earth into a vale of tears; always it has made of life a weak, diseased thing, always it has instilled fear in man, turning him into a dual being, whose life energies are spent in the struggle between body and soul. In decrying the body as something evil, the flesh as the tempter to everything that is sinful, man has mutilated his being in the vain attempt to keep his soul pure, while his body rotted away from the injuries and tortures inflicted upon it.

The Christian religion and morality extols the glory of the hereafter, and therefore remains indifferent to the horrors of the earth. Indeed, the idea of self-denial and of all that makes for pain and sorrow is its test of human worth, its passport to the entry into heaven.

The poor are to own heaven, and the rich will go to hell. That may account for the desperate efforts of the rich to make hay while the sun shines, to get as much out of the earth as they can: to wallow in wealth and superfluity, to tighten their iron hold on the blessed slaves, to rob them of their birthright, to degrade and outrage them every minute of the day. Who can blame the rich if they revenge themselves on the poor, for now is their time, and the merciful Christian God alone knows how ably and completely the rich are doing it.

And the poor? They cling to the promise of the Christian heaven as the home for old age, the sanitarium for crippled bodies and weak minds. They endure and submit, they suffer and wait, until every bit of self-respect has been knocked out of them, until their bodies become emaciated and withered, and their spirit broken from the wait, the weary endless wait for the Christian heaven.

Christ made his appearance as the leader of the people, the redeemer of the Jews from Roman dominion; but the moment he began his work, he proved that he had no interest in the earth, in the pressing immediate needs of the poor and the disinherited of his time. what he preached was a sentimental mysticism, obscure and confused ideas lacking originality and vigor.

When the Jews, according to the gospels, withdrew from Jesus, when they turned him over to the cross, they may have been bitterly disappointed in him who promised them so much and gave them so little. He promised joy and bliss in another world, while the people were starving, suffering, and enduring before his very eyes.

It may also be that the sympathy of the Romans, especially of Pilate, was given Christ because they regarded him as perfectly harmless to their power and sway. The philosopher Pilate may have considered Christ's "eternal truths" as pretty anemic and lifeless, compared with the array of strength and force they attempted to combat. The Romans, strong and unflinching as they were, must have laughed in their sleeves over the man who talked repentance and patience, instead of calling to arms against the despoilers and oppressors of his people.

The public career of Christ begins with the edict, "Repent, for the Kingdom of Heaven is at hand."

Why repent, why regret, in the face of something that was supposed to bring deliverance? Had not the people suffered and endured enough; had they not earned their right to deliverance by their suffering? Take the Sermon on the Mount, for instance. What is it but a eulogy on submission to fate, to the inevitability of things?

"Blessed are the poor in spirit, for theirs is the Kingdom of Heaven."

Heaven must be an awfully dull place if the poor in spirit live there. How can anything creative, anything vital, useful, and beautiful come from the poor in spirit? The idea conveyed in the Sermon on the Mount is the greatest indictment against the teachings of Christ, because it sees in the poverty of mind and body a virtue, and because it seeks to maintain this virtue by reward and punishment. Every intelligent being realizes that our worst curse is the poverty of the spirit; that it is productive of all evil and misery, of all the injustice and crimes in the world. Everyone knows that nothing good ever came or can come of the poor in spirit; surely never liberty, justice, or equality.

"Blessed are the meek, for they shall inherit the earth."

What a preposterous notion! What incentive to slavery, inactivity, and parasitism! Besides, it is not true that the meek can inherit anything. Just because humanity has been meek, the earth has been stolen from it.

Meekness has been the whip which capitalism and governments have used to force man into dependency, into his slave position. The most faithful servants of the state, of wealth, of special privilege, could not preach a more convenient gospel than did Christ, the "redeemer" of the people.

"Blessed are they that hunger and thirst for righteousness, for they shall be filled."

But did not Christ exclude the possibility of righteousness when he said, "The poor ye have always with you"? But, then, Christ was great on dicta, no matter if they were utterly opposed to each other. This is nowhere demonstrated so strikingly as in his command, "Render to Caesar the things that are Caesar's, and to God the things that are God's."

The interpreters claim that Christ had to make these concessions to the powers of his time. If that be true, this single compromise was sufficient to prove, down to this very day, a most ruthless weapon in the hands of the oppressor, a fearful lash and relentless tax gatherer, to the impoverishment, the enslavement, and degradation of the very people for whom Christ is supposed to have died. And when we are assured that "Blessed are they that hunger and thirst for righteousness, for they shall be filled," are we told the how? How? Christ never takes the trouble to explain that. Righteousness does not come from the stars nor because Christ willed it so. Righteousness grows out of liberty, of social and economic opportunity and equality. But how can the meek, the poor in spirit, ever establish such a state of affairs?

"Blessed are ye when men shall revile you and persecute you, and say all manner of evil against you falsely, for my sake. Rejoice, and be exceeding glad: for great is your reward in heaven."

The reward in heaven is the perpetual bait, a bait that has caught man in an iron net, a straitjacket which does not let him expand or grow. All pioneers of truth have been and still are reviled; they have been and still are persecuted. But did they ask humanity to pay the price? Did they seek to bribe mankind to accept their ideas? They knew too well that he who accepts a truth because of the bribe will soon barter it away to a higher bidder.

Good and bad, punishment and reward, sin and penance, heaven and hell, as the moving spirit of the Christ gospel, have been the stumbling block in the world's work. It contains everything in the way of orders and commands but entirely lacks the very things we need most.

The worker who knows the cause of his misery, who understands the makeup of our iniquitous social and industrial system, can do more for himself and his kind than Christ and the followers of Christ have ever done for humanity; certainly more than meek patience, ignorance, and submission have done.

How much more ennobling, how much more beneficial is the extreme individualism of Stirner and Nietzsche than the sickroom atmosphere of the Christian faith. If they repudiate altruism as an evil, it is because of the example contained in Christianity, which set a premium on parasitism and inertia, gave birth to all manner of social disorders that are to be cured with the preachment of love and sympathy.

Proud and self-reliant characters prefer hatred to such sickening artificial love. Not because of any reward does a free spirit take his stand for a great truth nor has such a one ever been deterred because of fear of punishment.

"Think not that I come to destroy the law or the prophets. I am not come to destroy, but to fulfill."

Precisely. Christ was a reformer, ever ready to patch up, to fulfill, to carry on the old order of things; never to destroy and rebuild. That may account for the fellow feeling all reformers have for him.

Indeed, the whole history of the state, capitalism, and the Church proves that they have perpetuated themselves because of the idea "I come not to destroy the law." This is the key to authority and oppression. Naturally so, for did not Christ praise poverty as a virtue; did he not propagate non-resistance to evil? Why should not poverty and evil continue to rule the world?

Much as I am opposed to every religion, much as I think them an imposition upon and crime against reason and progress, I yet feel that no other religion has done so much harm or has helped so much in the enslavement of man as the religion of Christ.

Witness Christ before his accusers. What lack of dignity, what lack of faith in himself and in his own ideas! So weak and helpless was this "Savior of Men" that he must needs the whole human family to pay for him unto all eternity, because he "hath died for them." Redemption through the Cross is worse than damnation, because of the terrible burden it imposes upon humanity, because of the effect it has on the human soul, fettering and paralyzing it with the weight of the burden exacted through the death of Christ.

Thousands of martyrs have perished, yet few, if any, of them have proved so helpless as the great Christian God. Thousands have gone to their death with greater fortitude, with more courage, with deeper faith in their ideas than the Nazarene. Nor did they expect eternal gratitude from their fellow men because of what they endured for them.

Compared with Socrates and Bruno, with the great martyrs of Russia, with the Chicago anarchists, Francisco Ferrer, and unnumbered others, Christ cuts a poor figure indeed. Compared with the delicate, frail Spiridonova, who underwent the most terrible tortures, the most horrible indignities, without losing faith in herself or her cause, Jesus is a veritable nonentity. They stood their ground and faced their executioners with unflinching determination, and though they too died for the people, they asked nothing in return for their great sacrifice.

Verily, we need redemption from the slavery, the deadening weakness, and humiliating dependency of Christian morality.

The teachings of Christ and of his followers have failed because they lacked the vitality to lift the burdens from the shoulders of the race; they have failed because the very essence of that doctrine is contrary to the spirit of life, exposed to the manifestations of nature, to the strength and beauty of passion.

Never can Christianity, under whatever mask it may appear—be it New Liberalism, Spiritualism, Christian Science, New Thought, or a thousand and one other forms of hysteria and neurasthenia—bring us relief from the terrible pressure of conditions, the weight of poverty, the horrors of our iniquitous system. Christianity is the conspiracy of ignorance against reason, of darkness against light, of submission and slavery against independence and freedom; of the denial of strength and beauty against the affirmation of the joy and glory of life.

CHAPTER V

Twelve Proofs of the Nonexistence of God

by Sébastien Faure

Comrades,

There are two ways to examine and resolve the problem of the non-existence of God.

The first involves eliminating the hypothesis of God from the field of plausible or necessary conjectures, through a clear and precise analysis, through the presentation of a positive system of the universe, of its origins, successive developments, and ends.

This account would make the idea of God useless and would destroy in advance all the metaphysical scaffolding with which the spiritualist philosophers and the theological scholars have propped it up.

Now, *in the present state of human knowledge*—limiting ourselves, as is proper, to what is demonstrated or demonstrable, verified or verifiable—that analysis is missing and the positive system of the universe is lacking. Of course, there are some ingenious hypotheses, which in no way shock the reason. There exist some more or less plausible systems which rest on a mass of observations and draw from those abundant observations an impressive degree of probability. We can boldly assert that these systems and suppositions compare favorably with the assertions of the deists, but, in truth, they are only theories, still not possessing scientific certainty. Each individual remaining free, in the end, to give preference to any given system—or to any other that is opposed to it—the solution of the problem would appear, *at least* from this point of view *and at present*, necessarily elusive.

The followers of all the religions so clearly grasp the advantage conferred upon them by the study of the problem when posed in this way that they all constantly attempt to bring it back to that position; and if, even on that terrain—the only terrain on which they can still maintain their composure—they do not leave the encounter with the honors of battle—not by a long shot—it is still possible for them to perpetuate doubt in the minds of their coreligionists. And, for them, that is the essential point.

In this combat, where the two opposing theses grapple and strive to lay each other low, the deists receive some hard blows, but they also give them. For better or worse, they defend themselves and, the outcome of this duel remaining uncertain in the eyes of the crowd, the believers, even when they seem to have been defeated, can cry victory.

They do not hesitate to do so with that impudence that is the public sign of their piety; and that comedy manages to keep the vast majority of the flock under the crook of the pastor.

That is all these "bad shepherds" desire.

The Problem Posed in Precise Terms

However, comrades, there is a second way of examining and attempting to resolve the problem of the non-existence of God.

That involves examining the existence of the God whom religions offer for our adoration.

Can any sensible and thoughtful man be found who could accept the existence of this God—of whom we speak as if he was not shrouded in any mystery, as if we were ignorant of nothing about him, as if we had penetrated all his thought, and as if we had received all his confidences: "He has done this and done that, and then this, and then that. He has said this and that, and then again that. He has acted and spoken with this aim and for that reason. He desires this thing, but he forbids this other thing. He will reward these actions and punish those others. And he has done this and wants that because he is infinitely wise, infinitely just, infinitely powerful, infinitely good"?

Just think of it! Here is a God who makes himself known! He abandons the realm of the inaccessible, clears away the clouds that surround him, descends from the heights, converses with mortals, confides his thought to them, reveals his will to them, and charges some privileged few to spread his doctrine, to communicate his law, and—let's be clear—to represent him here below, with full powers to bind and release, in heaven and on the earth!

This God is not a God of force, intelligence, will, and energy, which, like everything that is composed of energy, will, intelligence, and force, can be in turn, according to the circumstance and consequently indifferently, good or bad, useful or harmful, just or unjust, merciful or cruel. This god is the God in whom everything is perfection and whose existence is and can only be compatible—since he is perfectly just, wise, powerful, good, and merciful—with a state of things of which he would be the author and through which he would affirm his infinite justice, his infinite wisdom, his infinite power, his infinite goodness, and his infinite mercy.

You will recognize this God. He is the one who is taught through the catechism to the children. He is the living and personal God, the one to whom we raise temples, towards whom prayer mounts, in honor of whom we make sacrifices, and the one whom all the clergy, all the priestly castes, claim to represent on the earth.

He is not an "unknown," an enigmatic force, impenetrable power, incomprehensible intelligence, unknowable energy, or mysterious principle. He is not a hypothesis that the mind of man, in its continuing powerlessness to explain the how and why of things, is happy to employ. He is not the speculative God of the metaphysicians but a God abundantly described to us in luminous detail by his representatives.

He is, I repeat, the God of religion, and, since we are in France, the God of the religion that has dominated our history for fifteen centuries: the Christian religion.

This is that God that I deny, and it is only this God that I wish to discuss and this God that you must study, if you wish to draw from this lecture a positive profit and a practical result.

What is this God?

Since those who manage his business here below have been good enough to describe him to us in lavish detail, let us profit from the graciousness of his duly authorized representatives; let us examine him up close; let us go over him with a magnifying glass. In order to discuss him well, we must know him well.

This God is the one who, with a powerful and life giving gesture, has made all things from nothing, the one who has called the void to being, who has, by his will alone, substituted movement for inertia, universal life for universal death: *he is the Creator!*

This God is the one who, having accomplished this act of creation, far from returning to his age-old inaction and remaining indifferent to the thing created, concerns himself with his work, takes an interest in it, intervenes when he judges it appropriate, manages, administers, and governs it: *he is the Governor, or Providence.*

This God is the one who, as Supreme Tribunal, summons each of us after our deaths, judges us according to the acts of our lives, determines the balance of our good and bad actions, and pronounces, in the last resort and without appeal, the judgment that will make us, for all the centuries to come, the most fortunate or unfortunate of beings: *he is the Justice Bringer, or Magistrate.*

It goes without saying that this God possesses all attributes and that he does not just possess them to an exceptional degree; he possesses them all to an infinite degree.

Thus, he is not only just: he is infinite justice; he is not only good: he is infinite goodness; he is not only merciful: he is infinite mercy; he is not only powerful: he is infinite power; he is not only learned: he is infinite science.

This, I repeat, is the God whom I deny and whose impossibility I will demonstrate by twelve different proofs (although, strictly speaking, just one would suffice).

Division of the Subject

Here is the order in which I will present my arguments. They form three groups: the first of these groups will most specifically apply to the Creator God and will include six arguments; the second will most specifically concern the Governor God, or Providence, and will encompass four arguments; finally, the third and last of these groups will focus on the Justice Bringer God, or Magistrate, and will be composed of two arguments. Thus: six arguments against the Creator God; four arguments against the Governor God; two arguments against the Justice Bringer God. That will make twelve proofs of the nonexistence of God. The plan of my demonstration being known to you, you can better and more easily follow its development.

First Series of Arguments
Against the Creator God

First Argument
The Creative Act Is Inadmissible
What does it mean to create?

What is creation?

Is it to take scattered, separate, but existing materials, and then, making use of certain tested principles, applying certain known rules, to bring together, group, classify, combine, and modify these materials, in order to make something of them?

No! That is not creation. Examples: Can we say of a house that it has been created?—No! It has been constructed. Can we say that a piece of furniture has been created?—No! It has been manufactured. Can we say that a book has been created?—No! It has been composed, printed.

Thus, to take existing materials and make something of them is not to create.

What, then, is creation?

To create... My word! I am embarrassed attempting to explain the inexplicable, to define the indefinable. I will, nonetheless, attempt to make myself understood.

To create is to draw something out of nothing; it is to make something with nothing at all; it is to call the void to be something.

Now, I imagine that not a single reasonable person will be found who could imagine or accept that something could be drawn from nothing, that it would be possible to make something with nothing.

Imagine a mathematician; choose the most experienced calculator and place before them a gigantic blackboard; ask them to draw on that blackboard zeros and more zeros; they will add and multiply in vain; they may engage in all the operations of mathematics, but they will never succeed in extracting a single unity from the accumulation of these zeros.

With nothing, we make nothing; with nothing, we can make nothing, and the famous aphorism of Lucretius, ex nihilo nihil, remains the expression of a self-evident certainty.

The act of creation is an act that is impossible to accept, an absurdity.

To create is thus a mystical, religious expression, which may possess some value in the eyes of persons happy to believe what they do not understand and for whom faith is that much more necessary the less they understand; but to create is an expression void of sense for every astute, attentive man, in the eyes of those for whom words only have value to the extent that they represent a reality or possibility.

Consequently, the hypothesis of a truly creative Being is a hypothesis that reason rejects.

The Creator Being does not exist and cannot exist.

Second Argument
The "Pure Spirit" Could Not Have Determined the Universe

To the believers who, in defiance of all reason, persist in accepting the possibility of creation, I would say that it is, in any case, impossible to attribute that creation to their God.

Their God is *pure spirit*. And I say that the pure spirit, the immaterial, cannot have determined the universe, the material. Here is why: pure spirit is not separated from the universe by a difference in degree, in quantity, but by a difference in nature, in quality. So that the pure spirit is not and cannot be an amplification of the universe, any more than the universe is or can be a reduction of pure spirit. The difference here is not only a distinction but an opposition—and an opposition of an essential, fundamental, irreducible, and absolute nature.

Between pure spirit and the universe, there is not just a gap, more or less wide and deep, which it would be, in a pinch, possible to fill or cross; there is a veritable abyss of such depth and expanse that whatever they might try, no one could fill or bridge it.

And I challenge the most astute philosopher or the most consummate mathematician to build a bridge, to establish a relation of any kind (and particularly a relation as direct and close as that which links the cause to the effect) between pure spirit and the universe.

Pure spirit accepts no material alloy; it assumes no form, body, line, material, proportion, extent, duration, depth, surface, volume, color, tone, or density.

Now, in the universe, everything is, on the contrary, form, body, line, material, proportion, extent, duration, depth, surface, volume, color, tone, and density.

How could we accept that the latter was determined by the former?

It is impossible.

Having reached this point in my demonstration, I firmly plant the following conclusion atop the two arguments that have preceded it: we have seen, first, that the hypothesis of a truly creative power is inadmissible; we have seen, secondly, that even if one persists in believing in that power, one could not accept that the essentially material universe had been produced by an essentially immaterial pure spirit; if, despite it all, you persist, believers, in maintaining that it is your God that has created the universe, the moment has come to ask you where, given your theory of God, we are to find matter at the origin, at the commencement.

Well! One of two things must be true: either the matter was outside of God or else it was within God. (You could not assign it a third place.) In the first case, if it was outside of God, God had no need to create it, since it already existed; it coexisted with God, was concomitant with him, and, therefore, your God is not a creator; in the second case, if it was not outside of God, it was *within* God; and, in this case, I conclude:

1) That God is not pure spirit, since he bears within him a bit of matter—and what a bit: the totality of the material worlds!
2) That God, bearing matter within him, has not had to create it, since it existed; he had only to bring it forth; and, thus, the creation ceases to be an act of true creation and is reduced to an act of externalization.

In both cases, there is no creation.

Third argument
The Perfect Cannot Produce the Imperfect
I am certain that if I asked a believer this question: "*Can the imperfect produce the perfect?*" that believer would respond to me without the least hesitation and without fear of being mistaken: the imperfect cannot produce the perfect.

Now I say: the perfect cannot produce the imperfect, and I maintain that my proposition possesses the same force and the same exactitude as the previous one, and for the same reasons.

Here again, between the perfect and the imperfect there is not only a difference of degree, of quantity, but a difference of quality, of nature, an essential, fundamental, irreducible, absolute opposition.

Here again, between the perfect and the imperfect, there is not only a ditch, more or less deep and wide, but an abyss so immense and so deep that nothing could cross over or fill it.

The perfect is the absolute; the imperfect is the relative. Compared to the perfect, which is everything, the relative, the contingent, is nothing. Compared with the perfect, the relative is without value; it does not exist, and it is not within the power of any mathematician or philosopher to establish a relation—of any sort whatever—between the relative and the absolute; a fortiori, this relation is impossible when it is a question of a relation as rigorous and precise as the one that must necessarily unite cause and effect.

So it is impossible the perfect could have produced the imperfect.

There exists, however, a direct, inevitable, and, in some sense, mathematical relation between the work and the one who is its author. The work is only as good as the worker, and the worker is only as good as the work. It is by the work that we recognize the worker, as it is by the fruit that we recognize the tree.

If I examine an essay that has been written badly—where errors in French abound, where the sentences are constructed badly, where the style is poor and careless, where the ideas are scarce and banal, where the knowledge is inexact—I could not think of attributing this page of bad French to a sculptor of phrases, to one of the masters of literature.

If I look at a poorly executed picture, where the lines are badly drawn, the rules of perspective and proportion violated, I would never think to attribute that rudimentary sketch to a teacher, to a master, to an artist. Without the least hesitation, I would say: it is the work of a student, of an apprentice, of a child. And I am certain of not having committed an error, so true is it that the work bears the mark of the worker, and that through the work we can appraise its author.

Now, nature is beautiful; the universe is magnificent, and I passionately admire, as much as anyone, the incessant spectacle of splendor and magnificence that it offers us. However, as enthusiastic as I am about the beauties of nature and whatever homage I may render them, I cannot say that the universe is a work without defects, irreproachable and perfect. And no one would dare to maintain such an opinion.

So the universe is an imperfect work.

Consequently, I say: between the work and its author there is always a strict, close, mathematical relation; now, the universe is an imperfect work; thus, the author of that work can only be imperfect.

As a result of this syllogism, the God of the believers is stamped with imperfection and, consequently, denied.

I can then reason as follows: either it is not God who is the author of the universe (I express thus my conviction).

Or else, if you persist in claiming that he is its author, the universe being an imperfect work, your God is himself imperfect.

Syllogism or dilemma, the conclusion of the reasoning remains the same: *the perfect cannot produce the imperfect.*

Fourth Argument

The Eternal, Active, Necessary Being Cannot, at Any Moment, Have Been Inactive or Useless

If God exists, he is eternal, active, and necessary.

Eternal? He is eternal by definition. It is his reason for being. We cannot conceive of him confined within the limits of time; we cannot imagine him beginning or ending; he can neither appear nor disappear. He exists at all times.

Active? He is and cannot not be active, since it is his activity that has produced everything, since his activity is affirmed, say the believers, by the most colossal, the most majestic, of acts: the creation of worlds.

Necessary? He is and cannot not be necessary, since without him nothing would be; since he is the author of all things; since he is the original source from which everything has flowed; since, alone, sufficient unto himself, it is his will alone that has determined whether there is something or nothing. He is thus eternal, active, and necessary.

I maintain and I will demonstrate that if he is eternal, active, and necessary, he must be eternally active and eternally necessary; that, as a consequence, he cannot, at any moment, be inactive or useless; that, as a further consequence, he has never created.

To say that God is not eternally active is to admit that he has not always been active, that he has become active, that he has commenced to be active, that before being active, he was not; and since it is through creation that his activity is manifested, it is to admit at the same time that during the billions and billions of centuries that perhaps preceded the creative action, God was inactive.

To say that God is not eternally necessary is to admit that he has not always been necessary, that he has become necessary, that he has commenced to be necessary, that before being necessary, he was not, and since it is the creation that proclaims and attests to the necessity of God, it is to admit at the same time that during the billions and billions of centuries that perhaps preceded the creative action, God was useless.

God idle and lazy!

God useless and superfluous!

What a position for the essentially active and essentially necessary Being!

So it is necessary to confess that God is at all times active and necessary.

But then he cannot be responsible for the creation; for the idea of creation implies, absolutely, the idea of commencement, of origin. A thing that commences cannot have existed at all times. There was necessarily a time when, before being, it did not yet exist. As short or as long as that time may have been preceding the thing created, nothing can eliminate it; in any case, it exists.

It follows that God is not eternally active and eternally necessary; and, in this case, he has become active and necessary through creation. If this is the case, then before the creation, God lacked the two attributes of activity and necessity. This God was incomplete; he was a portion of God and no more; and he needed to create in order to become active and necessary, in order to complete himself.

Or else God is eternally active and necessary; and, in this case, he has created eternally; the creation is eternal; the universe has never commenced; it has existed at all time; it is eternal, like God; it is God himself and becomes mixed up with him.

In this case, the universe has had no commencement; it has not been created.

Thus: in the first case, God, before the creation, was neither active nor necessary, was incomplete, which is to say imperfect; and, thus, he did not exist; in the second case, God being eternally active and eternally necessary, he cannot have become active and necessary; and, thus, he has not created.

There is no escape from that.

Fifth Argument
The Immutable Being Cannot Have Created

If God exists, he is immutable. He does not change; he cannot change. While, in nature, everything changes, is metamorphosed and trans- formed; while nothing is once and for all, and everything becomes, God, a fixed point, immobile in time and space, is subject to no modification, does not know and could not know any change.

He is today as he was yesterday; he will be tomorrow as he was today. If we envisage God in the distance of the centuries passed or in that of the centuries to come, he is constantly identical to himself.

God is immutable.

I maintain that if he has created he is not immutable, because, in this case, he has changed twice.

To make up one's mind to want is to change. Quite obviously there is a change between the being who does not yet desire and the being who wants.

If I desire today what I did not want, what I had not even dreamed of forty-eight hours ago, it is because there have been produced in me or around me one or more circumstances that have determined my desire. This new desire constitutes a modification: there is no room to doubt it: it is indisputable.

Similarly: to decide to act or to act is to be change.

It is, furthermore, certain that this double modification—to want and to act—is that much more considerable and marked, as it is a ques- tion of a more serious resolution and a more important action.

God has created, you say?—So be it. Then he has changed twice: the first time, when he resolved to create; the second time, when, exe- cuting that determination, he accomplished the act of creation.

If he has changed twice, he is not immutable.

And if he is not immutable, he is not God; he does not exist.

The immutable Being cannot have created.

Sixth Argument
God Cannot Have Created without Motive; Now, It Is Impossible to Discern a Single One

However we consider it, the creation remains inexplicable, enigmatic, void of sense.

It is blindingly obvious that if God has created, it is impossible to accept that he has accomplished this grandiose act, the consequences of which must inevitably be proportionate to the act itself and, consequently, incalculable, without being set on that course by a motive of the highest importance.

Well! What can that motive be? For what reason has God been able to resolve to create? What cause has impelled him? What desire has gripped him? What plan has he formed? What aim has he pursued? What end has he proposed?

Multiply, in that order of ideas, questions upon questions: turn the problem over and over; consider it from all sides; examine it in every way—and I challenge you to resolve it, other than by quips or quibbles.

Look: here is a child raised in the Christian religion. His catechism tells him, his teachers teach him, that it is God who has created him and put him in the world. Suppose that he asks himself this question: Why has God created me and put me in the world? And suppose that he wishes to find a serious, reasonable response. He will not succeed. Now suppose that, confident in the experience and knowledge of his educators, persuaded that, through the sacred character with which they, priests or pastors, are clothed, they possess special insights and particular graces, convinced that, through their sanctity, they are closer to God than him and more fully initiated into revealed truths, suppose that this child was curious enough to ask his masters why God had created him and put him in the world—I maintain that they could make no plausible, sensible response to that simple question.

In truth, there is none.

Let us examine the question up close, look deeply into the problem.

Through thought, let us examine God before the creation. Let us take him in his absolute sense. He is all alone; he is self-sufficient. He is perfectly wise, perfectly happy, perfectly powerful. Nothing can increase his wisdom; nothing can augment his happiness; nothing can bolster his power.

This God can feel no desire, since his happiness is infinite; he can pursue no goal, since his perfection lacks nothing; he can form no plan, since nothing can extend his power; he cannot resolve to want anything, since he feels no needs.

Come now! Profound philosophers, subtle thinkers, prestigious theologians respond to this child who questions you, asking why God has created him and placed him in the world.

I am confident that you cannot respond, unless you say, "The plans of God are impenetrable." And you cannot consider that response sufficient.

And you would be wise to abstain from answering, for every response—I warn you charitably—would be the ruin of your system, the collapse of your God.

The conclusion, logical and pitiless, imposes itself: God, if he has created, has created without a motive, without knowing why, without an aim.

Do you know, comrades, where we would inevitably be led by the consequences of such a conclusion?

You will see.

What differentiates the acts of a man endowed with reason from the acts of a man afflicted with madness, what makes the one responsible and the other not, is that a reasonable man always knows, or in any event can know, the motives that have motivated him when he has acted, the reasons that have caused him to act. When it is a question of an important action, the consequences of which can seriously engage his sense of responsibility, it is enough for the man in possession of his reason to withdraw within himself, to give himself up to a serious, persistent, and impartial examination of conscience; it suffices for him to reconstruct, in memory, the framework within which events have enclosed him; in short, he need only relive the hour that has passed in order for him to discern the mechanism of the movements that have led him to act.

He is not always very proud of the reasons that have motivated him; he often blushes at the motive that have caused him to act; but whether these motives are noble or vile, generous or cheap, he always manages to uncover them.

A lunatic, on the contrary, acts without knowing why. Question him when his act accomplished; interrogate him; press him with questions; insist; badger him. Even when the act is one most laden with consequences, the poor madman will stammer out some extravagance, and you will not draw him out of his delirium.

Thus, what differentiates the acts of a sensible man from one who is insane is that the acts of the first are explicable. They exist for a reason, and we can distinguish their cause and their aim, their origin and their end. The acts of a man deprived of reason are inexplicable, and he is himself incapable of discerning their cause and aim; they have no reason to exist.

Well! If God has created without an aim, without motive, he has acted in the manner of a lunatic and *the creation would appear to be an act of insanity.*

Two Crucial Objections

In order to finish with the God of creation, it appears indispensable to examine two objections.

You can be certain that, here, objections abound, so when I speak of two objections to study, I talking about two crucial, conventional objections.

These two objections are that much more important since we can, with the tools of debate, reduce all the others to these.

First Objection
God Eludes You
Someone says to me:

"You have no right to speak of God as you have. You present to us a caricature of God, systematically shrunken to the proportions that your understanding deigns to grant him. That is not our God. Our God could not be conceived by you, for he surpasses you; he slips from your grasp. Know that what would be fabulous for the most powerful of men, the men most endowed with strength, wisdom, and knowledge, is for God only child's play. Do not forget that humanity cannot move on the same plane as divinity. Do not lose sight of the fact that it is as impossible for man to understand the ways in which God operates as it is for minerals to imagine the modes of action of animals and for animals to understand the actions of men.

"God soars in heights that you can never attain; he occupies summits that remain inaccessible to you.

"Know that however magnificent a human intelligence may be, no matter the effort achieved by that intelligence, whatever the persistence of that effort, human intelligence can never raise itself up to God.

Consider, finally, that, as vast as it might be, the brain of man is still finite and, consequently, cannot conceive of the infinite.

"So be faithful and modest enough to confess that it is not possible for you to understand or explain God. And what you can neither understand nor explain, you have no right to deny."

And I respond to the deists:

Gentlemen, with your recommendations of faithfulness I am entirely disposed to comply. You remind me of the legitimate modesty that befits the humble mortal that I am. I have no desire to stray from it.

You say that God surpasses me, that he eludes me. So be it. I agree to recognize this fact and affirm that the finite can neither understand nor explain the infinite. This is a truth so certain, and even obvious, that I haven't the slightest urge to oppose it. We are, thus far, very much in agreement, and I hope you are quite happy.

But, gentlemen, allow me, in my turn, to urge the same faithfulness; permit me, in my turn, to recall you to the same modesty. Are not you men, as I am? Does not God surpass you, as he surpasses me? Does he not elude you, just as he eludes me? Would you pretend to move on the same plane as the divinity? Would you have the impudence to think and the foolishness to declare that with a stroke of your wings you have climbed to the summits that God occupies? Would you be presumptuous enough to say that your finite brain has embraced the infinite?

I will not insult you, gentlemen, and believe you stricken with such extravagant vanity.

So, like me, be faithful and modest enough to confess that if it is impossible for me to understand and explain God, you meet with the same impossibility. Have the integrity to recognize that if I am not allowed to deny God, because I can neither understand nor explain him, you, who likewise are unable to understand or explain him, are not allowed to affirm his existence.

And do not imagine, gentlemen, that we are, from now on, in the same boat. It is you who first affirmed the existence of God, so it is you who must first put an end to your affirmations. Would I have ever thought to deny God, if, when I was very small, belief in him had not been imposed on me? If, as an adult, I had not heard his existence declared all around me? If, having become a man, I had not constantly observed churches and temples raised to God?

It is your affirmations that provoke and justify my negations. Stop affirming, and I will stop denying.

Second Objection
There Is No Effect without a Cause

The second objection would appear as formidable. Many still consider it as without reply. It comes to us from the spiritualist philosophers.

These gentlemen say to us, sententiously: "There is no effect without a cause; now, the universe is an effect; thus, that effect has a cause, which we call God."

The argument is well presented; it appears well constructed and seems solidly framed.

The whole question is to know if this is truly the case.

This form of reasoning is what is called, in logic, a syllogism. A syllogism is an argument composed of three propositions: the major, the minor, and the consequence; and including two parts: the premises, made up of the first two propositions, and the conclusion represented by the third.

In order for a syllogism to be unassailable, it is necessary: 1) that the major and minor propositions be exact; 2) that the third flow logically from the first two.

If the syllogism of the spiritualist philosophers meets these two conditions, it is irrefutable and I can only bow; but if one of these two conditions is lacking, it is null and void, without value, and the argument falls apart completely.

In order to know its value, let us examine the three propositions of which it is composed.

First, the major proposition: "*there is no effect without a cause.*"

Philosophers, you are correct. There is no effect without a cause; nothing is more precise. There is not and cannot be an effect without a cause. The effect is only the consequence, the extension, the outcome, of the cause. Whoever says effect says cause; the idea of effect *necessarily* and *immediately* calls for the idea of cause. If it was otherwise, the without cause would be an effect of nothing, which would be absurd.

Thus, on this first proposition, we are in agreement.

Second, the minor proposition: "*now, the universe is an effect.*"

Ah! Here I demand reflection and call for explanations. What is the basis of such a flat, peremptory affirmation? What is the phenomenon or

collection of phenomena, what is the observation or collection of observations, that allows you to express yourself in such an unequivocal tone?

First of all, do we have sufficient knowledge of the universe? Have
we studied, examined, searched, and understood it well enough that
we can be so positive? Have we penetrated its inner workings? Have
we explored its immeasurable spaces? Have we descended into the
depths of the oceans? Have we scaled all the heights? Do we know
everything to be found in the domain of the universe? Has it delivered
up all its secrets? Have we stripped away all the veils, penetrated all
the mysteries, and solved all the riddles? Have we seen everything,
heard everything, touched everything, smelled everything, observed
everything, and noted everything? Do we no longer have anything to
learn? Does there remain nothing for us to discover? In short, are we
in a position to make a positive appraisal, a definitive judgment, or an
incontrovertible decision regarding the universe?

No one could answer in the affirmative to all these questions
and we would feel deeply sorry for the reckless fool, we could say the
madman, who would pretend that they know the universe.

The universe!—we mean by that not only this tiny planet that we
inhabit and over which we drag around our miserable carcasses, not
only the millions of stars and planets that we know, which are part of
our solar system or which we will discover in the fullness of time, but
also those worlds upon worlds of whose existence we know or suspect
but whose number, expanse, and distance remain incalculable!

If I say that the universe is a cause, I am certain that I would spon-
taneously unleash the hoots and protests of the believers; and yet my
assertion would be no more ridiculous than their own.

My temerity would be equal to their own; that is all.

If I study the universe, if I observe the known facts to the extent
allowed to the man of today, I note an incredibly complex and involved
ensemble, an inextricable and colossal tangle of causes and effects,
which determine, enchain, succeed, repeat, and penetrate one another.
I perceive that the whole is formed like an endless chain, the links of
which are unbreakably connected, and I note that each of these links
is at once cause and effect: the effect of the cause that has determined
it, the cause of the effect that follows.

Who can say: "Here is the first link, the link called cause"? Who
can say: "Here is the last link, the link called effect"? And who can say:

"There is necessarily a cause we can number the first, there is necessarily an effect we can number the last"?

Thus, the second proposition—"now, the universe is an effect"—lacks the indispensable condition of precision.

Consequently, the famous syllogism is worth nothing.

I add that even in a case where the second proposition was exact, in order for the conclusion to be accepted, it would still have to be established that the universe is the effect of a unique cause, of a first cause, of the cause of causes, of a causeless cause, of the eternal cause.

I await that demonstration without distress, without worry. It is one of those that has been attempted many times but has never been made. It is one of those of which we can say, without being too rash, that it will never be seriously, positively, scientifically established.

I add, finally, that even in a case where the entire syllogism was flawless, it would be easy to turn against it, and in favor of my demonstration, the thesis of the Creator God.

Let us try. There are no effects without a cause?—So be it. Now, the universe is an effect?—Okay. So that effect is a cause and it is the cause that we call God?—Again, okay.

Do not be in a hurry to triumph, deists, and hear me well.

If it is obvious that there is no effect without a cause, it is as completely obvious that there is no cause without an effect. There is not, and there cannot be, a cause without an effect. Whoever says cause says effect; the idea of cause *necessarily* implies and *immediately* calls to mind the idea of effect; if it were otherwise, the cause without an effect would be a cause of nothing, which would be as absurd as an effect of nothing.

So it is well understood that there is no cause without an effect.

Now, you say that the universe has God as a cause. So it would be appropriate to say that the God Cause has the universe as an effect.

It is impossible to separate the effect from the cause; but it is equally impossible to separate the cause from the effect.

You maintain, finally, that the God Cause is eternal. I conclude from this that the universe effect is equally eternal, since to an eternal cause there must inescapably correspond an eternal effect.

If it were otherwise, if the universe had commenced during the billions and billions of centuries that have perhaps preceded the creation of the universe, God would have been a cause without effect, which is impossible, a cause of nothing, which would be absurd.

Consequently, God being eternal, the universe is also eternal, and if the universe is eternal, it is because it has never commenced, because it has not been created.

Is this clear?

Second Series of Arguments
Against the Governor God, or Providence

First Argument
The Governor Denies the Creator

There are those—and they are legion—who, despite everything, persist in believing. I understand that, strictly speaking, one can believe in the existence of a perfect creator; I understand that, strictly speaking, one can believe in the existence of a necessary governor; but it seems impossible to me that one can reasonably believe in both at the same time. These two perfect beings categorically exclude one another: to affirm one is to deny the other; to proclaim the perfection of the first is to admit the uselessness of the second; to proclaim the necessity of the second is to deny the perfection of the first.

In other words, we can believe in the perfection of one and the necessity of the other; but it is unreasonable to believe in the perfection of both: we must choose.

If the universe created by God had been a perfect work; if in the ensemble and in the least details this work had been without defect; if the mechanism of this gigantic creation had been flawless; if, in addition, its arrangement had been so perfect that there was no fear that it would produce a single derangement or a single bit of damage; if, in short, the work had been worthy of that brilliant worker, that incomparable artist and wonderful builder whom we call God, the need of a governor would never have been felt.

The initial helping hand once given, the formidable machine once set in motion, there would be nothing to do but to leave it to itself, without fear of any possible accident.

What need for this engineer, this mechanic, whose role is to monitor the machine, direct it, intervene when it is necessary, and provide the necessary modifications and successive repairs to the machine in motion? This engineer would be useless and this mechanic without purpose.

In this case, there is no place for a governor.

If the governor exists, it is because his presence, supervision, and intervention are indispensable. The necessity of the governor is like an insult, a challenge hurled at the creator; his intervention attests to the clumsiness, incompetence, and powerlessness of the creator. The governor denies the perfection of the creator.

Second Argument
The Multiplicity of the Gods Demonstrates That No Gods Exist

The Governor God is and must be powerful and just, infinitely powerful and infinitely just.

I claim that the multiplicity of religions testifies to his lack of power and justice.

Let us ignore the dead gods, the abolished cults and extinct religions. Those will number in the thousands. We speak only of the current religions.

According to the best estimates, there are presently eight hundred religions that fight for control of the sixteen hundred million consciences that occupy our planet. There is no doubt that each imagines and proclaims that it alone is in possession of the true, authentic, indisputable, and unique God, and that all the other Gods are laughable false Gods, cheap contraband Gods, whom it is a pious work to battle and crush.

I add that if there were only a hundred religions instead of eight hundred, if there were only ten, if there were only two, my argument would retain the same force.

Well! I claim that the multiplicity of these Gods demonstrates that none exist, because it certifies that God lacks power or justice.

Powerful, he could have spoken to all as easily as to some. Powerful, he could have shown himself, revealed himself to all, with no more effort than would have been required to reveal himself to a few.

A man—whoever he may be—can only show himself, can only speak to a limited number of men; his vocal cords have a power that cannot exceed certain limits; but God...!

God can speak to all—however great the multitude—as easily as to a small number. When it is raised, the voice of God can and must resound to the four cardinal points. The divine word knows neither distance nor obstacles. It crosses the oceans, scales the summits, and traverses spaces without the least difficulty.

Since he has seen fit—as religion affirms—to speak to men, to reveal himself to them, to confide his plans to them, to indicate his will and make known his law, he could have spoken to all without any more effort than to a handful of the privileged.

He has not done this, since some deny him, since others are unaware of him, and since others, finally, oppose this God to one of his competitors.

In these conditions, isn't it wise to think that he has not spoken to any and that the multiple revelations are only multiple impostures; or else that, if he has spoken to some, it is because he could not speak to all?

If this is the case, I accuse him of powerlessness.

And, if I do not accuse him of powerlessness, I accuse him of injustice.

What, indeed, are we to think of this God who shows himself to some and hides himself from others? What are we to think of this God who speaks to some and to others maintains his silence?

Do not forget that the representatives of this God maintain that he is the Father, and that we are all, by the same title and to the same degree, the well-loved children of the Father who reigns in the heavens.

Well! What do you think of this Father who, full of sympathy for a privileged few, snatches them, by revealing himself to them, from the anguish of doubt and the tortures of hesitation, while he intentionally condemns the immense majority of his children to the torments of uncertainty? What do you think of this Father who shows himself to some of his children in the dazzling radiance of his majesty, while for the others he remains shrouded in darkness? What do you think of this Father who, demanding a cult, respect, and worship from his children, calls a few elect to hear the word of truth, while he deliberately refuses that singular favor to the others?

If you reckon that this father is just and good, you will not be surprised that my judgment is different.

So the multiplicity of religions proclaims that God lacks power or justice. Now, God must be infinitely powerful and infinitely just; the believers affirm it; if he lacks one of these two attributes, power or justice, he is not perfect; if he is not perfect, he does not exist.

The multiplicity of gods demonstrates that no gods exist.

Third Argument
God Is Not Infinitely Good: Hell Demonstrates It
The Governor God, Providence, is and must be infinitely good, infinitely merciful. The existence of hell proves that he is not.

Follow my reasoning closely: God could—since he is free—refrain from creating us; he has created us.

God could—since he is all-powerful—make us entirely good; he has created the good and the wicked.

God could—since he is good—allow us all into his paradise after our deaths, contenting himself with the times of trials and tribulations through which we have passed on the earth.

God could, finally—since he is just—allow into his paradise only the good and refuse access to the wicked, but destroy the latter at their time of death, rather than condemn them to hell.

For he who can create can also destroy; he who has the power to give life also has the power to destroy it.

Let us see: you are not gods. You are not infinitely good nor infinitely merciful. I am, however, certain, without attributing qualities to you that you perhaps do not possess, that if it was in your power, without costing you a painful effort, without the chance of it causing you material harm or moral injury, if, I say, it was in your power, under the conditions that I have just indicated, to prevent one tear, one pain, one hardship for your brothers in humanity, I am certain that you would do it. And yet you are neither infinitely good nor infinitely merciful!

Would you be better and more merciful than the God of the Christians?

For, in the end, hell exists. The Church teaches it; it is the horrific vision with the aid of which they terrify the children, old folks, and timid spirits; it is the specter installed at the bedsides of the dying, in the hour when death's approach robs them of all energy and lucidity.

Well! The God of the Christians, a God known as a being of pity, pardon, indulgence, goodness, and mercy, casts some of his children—forever—into this place occupied by the cruelest tortures, the most unspeakable ordeals.

How good he is! How merciful!

You know that line from the scriptures: "Many are called but few are chosen." That phrase means, if I am not mistaken, that the number of elect will be tiny and the number of damned considerable. This affirmation is so monstrously cruel that some have attempted to give it another meaning.

It matters little: hell exists and it is obvious that the damned—in large or small number—will endure the most agonizing torments there.

Let us ask ourselves who can profit from the torments of the damned.

Would it be the elect?—Obviously not! By definition, the elect will be the most just, the virtuous, the fraternal, and the compassionate, and we could not imagine that their bliss, already inexpressible, would be increased by the spectacle of their tortured brethren.

Would it be the damned themselves?—Again, no, since the Church maintains that the torture of these wretches will never end, and that in billions and billions of centuries their torments will be as intolerable as on the first day.

So...?

So, apart from the elect and the damned, there is only God; there can only be God.

Is it then God who would profit from the sufferings of the damned? Is it this infinitely good, infinitely merciful Father who would revel sadistically in the sorrows to which he has deliberately condemned his children?

Ah! If that is the case, then God appears to me as the most savage executioner, the most implacable torturer that one could imagine.

Hell proves that God is neither good nor merciful. The existence of a good God is incompatible with that of hell.

Either there is no hell, or God is not infinitely good.

Fourth Argument
The Problem of Evil

It is the problem of evil that presents me with my fourth and final argument against the Governor God, as well as my first argument against the Magistrate God. I do not claim that the existence of evil, physical or moral evil, is incompatible with the existence of God; but I do claim that it is incompatible with the existence of a God who is *infinitely powerful and infinitely good.*

The reasoning is known, if only by the multiple refutations—always powerless, however—that have been opposed to it.

It can be traced back to Epicurus. So it has already been in exist-ence for more than twenty centuries; but no matter its age, it still main-tains all of its vigor.

Here it is: evil exists. All beings capable of feeling know suffering. God, who knows all, cannot be unaware of this. Well! One of two things must be true: either God would like to eliminate evil, but he cannot; or else God could eliminate evil, but he does not wish to.

In the first case, God would like to eliminate evil; he is good and sympathizes with the suffering that oppresses us, with the evil we endure. Ah! If it only depended on him! Evil would be wiped out, and good would flourish on the earth. Once more, he is good; but he cannot eliminate evil, and, thus, he is not all-powerful.

In the second case, God could eliminate evil. He need only wish it for evil to be abolished, as he is all-powerful, but he does not wish to eliminate it; and, therefore, he is not infinitely good.

Here, God is powerful, but he is not good; there, God is good, but he is not powerful.

Now, in order for God to exist, it is not enough that he possesses one of these perfections: power or goodness. It is indispensable that he possesses both.

This reasoning has never been refuted.

Now, listen: I do not claim that no one has ever attempted to refute it; I say that no one has every succeeded.

The best-known attempt at refutation is this: "You pose the problem of evil in an entirely erroneous manner. You are quite wrong to hold God responsible. Yes, certainly, evil exists and it is undeniable; but it is man who should be held responsible for it. God did not want man to be an automaton, a machine, whose actions are inevitable. In creating man, he gave him his liberty; he made him an entirely free being. In every cir-cumstance, God has left him the ability to make whatever use he wishes of the liberty that he has generously granted him; and if it should please man, instead of making a judicious and noble use of that inestimable good, to make an odious and criminal use, it is not God that we must accuse. That would be unjust; it would be equitable to accuse man."

That is the objection; it is classic.

What is it worth? Nothing.

I will explain: let us first distinguish physical from moral evil.

Physical evil is sickness, suffering, accident, and old age, with its process of flaws and infirmities; it is death, the cruel loss of those we love, of children born who die some few days afterward, without having known anything but suffering; it is a host of human beings for whom existence is only a long series of sorrows and afflictions, so that it would be better if they had never been born; it is, in the domain of nature, the plagues, cataclysms, fires, droughts, famines, floods, tempests, and the whole sum of tragic inevitabilities that are measured in sadness and death.

Who would dare say, regarding this physical evil, that man must be held responsible for it?

Who does not understand that if God has created the universe, if it is he who has endowed it with the formidable laws that rule it, and if physical evil is the ensemble of these inevitabilities that result from the normal play of the forces of nature, who does not understand that the author responsible for these calamities is, in all certainty, the one who has created this universe, the one who governs it?

I suppose that on this point no dispute is possible.

The God who governs the universe is thus responsible for physical evil.

That alone would be sufficient, and my response could stop there.

But I maintain that moral evil is imputable to God by the same title as physical evil, since, if he exists, he has presided over the organization of the moral world, just like that of the physical world, and, consequently, man, victim of moral and physical evil alike, is no more responsible for one than for the other.

But I must connect what I have to say regarding moral evil to the third and last series of my arguments.

Third Series of Arguments
Against the God of Justice

First Argument
Being Irresponsible, Man Can Be Neither Punished nor Rewarded
What are we?

Have we presided over the conditions of our birth? Have we been consulted on the simple question of whether we would like to be born?

Have we been called to settle our own destinies? Have we, on a single point, had a say in the matter?

If we had had a say, each of us would have been, from the cradle, furnished with all the advantages: health, strength, beauty, intelligence, courage, generosity, etc., etc. Each of us would have been a living summary of all the perfections, a sort of God in miniature.

What are we?

Are we what we wish to be?

Unquestionably not!

Supposing there is a God, we are, since he has created us, what he wanted us to be.

God, since he is free, could have chosen to not create us.

He could have made us less wicked, since he is good.

He could have made us virtuous, healthy, and splendid. He could have lavished upon us all sorts of physical, intellectual, and moral gifts, since he is all-powerful.

For the third time, what are we?

We are what God has wanted us to be. He has created us as he pleased, according to his whim.

There is no other response to that question—what are we?—if we accept that God exists and that we are his creatures.

It is God who has given us our senses, our capacity for understanding, our sensibility, our means of perceiving, feeling, reasoning, and acting. He has anticipated, willed, and determined our conditions of life: he has conditioned our needs, our desires, our passions, our fears, our hopes, our hatreds, our tender feelings, and our aspirations. The whole human machine corresponds to his wishes. He has designed and arranged all aspects of the environment in which we live; he has prepared all the circumstances that, in each moment, will mount an attack on our will and determine our actions.

Before this formidably armed God, man is irresponsible.

The individual who is dependent on no one is entirely free; the one who is *slightly* dependent on another is *slightly* enslaved and is free in other respects; the one who is *largely* dependent on another is *largely* enslaved and is only free in a few respects; finally, the one who is *entirely* dependent on another is *entirely* enslaved and enjoys no liberty.

If God exists it is in this last position, that of slavery, that the individual finds himself in relation to God, and his slavery is that much more complete as there is a greater distance between him and the Master.

If God exists, he alone knows and wills; he alone is capable and free. Man knows nothing, wants nothing, has no power; his dependence is complete.

If God exists, then he is everything, and man is nothing.

The man thus held in slavery, placed in full and complete dependence on God, can bear no responsibility.

And if he is irresponsible, he cannot be judged.

Every judgment entails a punishment or a reward; and the acts of an irresponsible being, having no moral value, are subject to no judgment.

The acts of the irresponsible can be useful or harmful; morally, they are neither good nor bad, neither meritorious not reprehensible; they could not be equitably rewarded or punished.

In setting himself up as a judge, by punishing or rewarding the irresponsible man, God is only a usurper; he has assumed an arbitrary right and has used it in ways contrary to all justice.

From what I have just said, I conclude:

a) that the responsibility for moral evil is imputable to God, like the responsibility for physical evil;
b) that *God is an unworthy magistrate, because, being irresponsible, man can neither be rewarded nor punished.*

Second Argument
God Violates the Fundamental Rules of Equity

Let us concede, for a moment, that man is responsible, and we will see that, even in this case, divine justice violates the most elementary rules of equity.

If we admit that the practice of justice could not be exercised without involving a sanction and that it is the mandate of the magistrate to establish that sanction, there is a rule regarding which our sentiments are and must be unanimous: just as there is a scale of merit and culpability, there must be a scale of rewards and punishments.

According to this principle, the magistrate who best practices justice will be the one who most exactly makes reward proportionate to merit and punishment proportionate to guilt; and the ideal, impeccable, perfect magistrate will be the one who establishes with a mathematical rigor the relation between the act and the sanction.

I think that this elementary rule of justice is accepted by all.

Well! God, through heaven and through hell, misjudges that rule and violates it.

Whatever the merit of man, it is limited (like man himself) and yet the sanction of reward—heaven is without bounds—is such only through its character of perpetuity.

Whatever the culpability of man, it is limited (like man himself) and yet the sanction of punishment—hell is without limits—is such only through its character of perpetuity.

There is thus a disproportion between the virtue and the recompense, a disproportion between the fault and the punishment. There is disproportion everywhere. Thus, *God violates the fundamental rules of equity.*

My thesis is completed; nothing remains for me but to sum up and conclude.

Summary

Comrades, I had promised you a tightly argued, substantial, decisive demonstration of the nonexistence of God. I believe I can say that I have kept that promise.

Keep in mind that I have not proposed to provide you a system of the universe that renders useless any recourse to the hypothesis of a supernatural force, of an otherworldly energy or power, of a principle superior or prior to the universe. I have had the fidelity, as I should, to tell you that, considered in this way, the problem does not entail, *in the present state of human knowledge*, any definitive solution, and that the only attitude appropriate for cautious and reasonable minds is uncertainty.

The God whose impossibility I wished to establish, whose impossibility I can now say that I have established, is the God of the religions, God as Creator, Governor, and Magistrate, God infinitely wise, powerful, just, and good, the God whom the clergy claim to represent on earth, and whom they attempt to set up for our veneration.

There is not, there can be no ambiguity. It is this God whom I deny; and if one wants to debate usefully, it is this God who must be defended against my attacks.

Every debate on another terrain will be—I warn you of it, for you must be on guard against the ruses of the enemy—every debate on another terrain will be a diversion and will be, moreover, a proof that the God of the religions cannot be defended or justified.

I have proven that, as Creator, he would be inadmissible, imperfect, inexplicable; I have established that, as Governor, he would be useless, powerless, cruel, horrible, despotic; I have shown that, as a Justice Bringer, he would be an unworthy Magistrate, violating the essential rules of the most elementary equity.

Conclusion

Such is, however, the God who, since time immemorial, has been taught and in our days is still taught to a multitude of children in so many families and schools. What crimes have been committed in his name!

What hatreds, wars, and calamites have been furiously unleashed by his representatives! Of what sufferings has this God been the source! What evils he still engenders!

For centuries, religion has held humanity bowed in fear, wallowing in superstition, prostrate in resignation.

Will the day never come when, ceasing to believe in eternal justice, in its imaginary judgments and questionable reparations, humans will work with tireless ardor for the advent on earth of an immediate, positive, and fraternal justice?

Will the hour never strike when, disillusioned with the consolations and fallacious hopes suggested by the belief in a compensatory paradise, humans will make our planet an Eden of abundance, peace, and liberty, whose doors will be fraternally open to all?

For too long, the social contract has been inspired by a God without justice; it is time that it is inspired by a justice without God. For too long, the relations between nations and individuals have stemmed from a God without philosophy; it is time that they proceeded from a philosophy without God. For centuries, monarchs, rulers, castes and clergy, conductors of people and directors of consciences have treated humanity like the vile flock, good only to be shorn, devoured, cast into abattoirs.

For centuries, the disinherited passively endured poverty and servitude, thanks to the deceptive mirage of heaven and the horrific vision of hell. We must put an end to this horrible enchantment, to this abominable trickery.

Oh, you who hear me, open your eyes and look, observe, understand. The heaven of which you speak endlessly, the heaven with the aid of which they try to numb your misery, anesthetize your suffering, and stifle the groan that, despite it all, rises from your chest, that heaven is unreal and deserted. Only your hell is peopled and positive.

Enough lamentations: the lamentations are in vain.

Enough prostrations: the prostrations are pointless.

Enough prayers: the prayers are powerless.

Stand up, oh man! And, upright, trembling, rebellious, declare an implacable war on the God whose mind-numbing veneration has for so long been imposed on you and your brethren.

Rid yourself of this imaginary tyrant and shake off the yoke of those who claim to be his deputies here below.

But remember that, this first act of liberation accomplished, you have completed only a part of the task that falls to you.

Do not forget that it will do you no good to break the chains that the imaginary, celestial, and eternal gods have forged for you, if you do not also break those forged for you by the passing, positive gods of the earth.

These gods prowl around you, seeking to starve and enslave you. These gods are only men like you.

Rich men and rulers, these earthly gods have peopled the earth with countless victims, with unspeakable torments.

May the damned of the earth finally rebel against these villains and found a city where these monsters will be forever rendered impossible!

When you have chased the gods from heaven and earth, when you have rid yourselves of the masters from above and the masters from below, when you have accomplished this double act of deliverance, then, but only then, oh, my brother, you will escape from your hell and you will achieve your heaven!

CHAPTER VI

The Meaning of Atheism
by E. Haldeman-Julius

Atheism is accurately defined as the denial of the assumptions of theism. The theist affirms that there is a God running the universe; he declares that the idea of such a God is necessary to an understanding of life; he offers various arguments or, as he rather presumptuously calls them, evidences for his God idea.

What is the position, logically, of the atheist? He will not say in a mild, uncertain fashion that he doesn't know whether the idea is true or that it is an open question. He has studied carefully the case for and against theism. He finds that case utterly insupportable, lacking any real or positive evidence, defended by arguments which are easily discovered to be casuistic and fallacious, and linking itself with other supplementary ideas which are incredible.

The atheist perceives that history, in every branch of science, in the plainly observable realities of life, and in the processes of common sense there is no place for the picture of a God; the idea doesn't fit in with a calmly reasoned and realistic view of life. The atheist, therefore, denies the assumptions of theism, because they are mere assumptions and are not proved; whereas the contrary evidences against the idea of theism are overwhelming. He takes a clear-cut position. To proclaim himself an agnostic, while to some it might appear more respectable and cautious, would be to say in effect that he hadn't decided what to believe.

We can understand, of course, why many prefer to call themselves agnostics. They don't wish to appear bigoted. Or they are honestly in doubt and feel that the idea of God may or may not be true; yet with scarcely an exception the attitude of the agnostic is the same as that of the atheist—he denies the assumptions of theism—his disbelief in God, as an agnostic, is quite as strong really as the atheist's disbelief.

But atheism is not in the least bigoted. It is a conclusion reached by the most reasonable methods and one which is not asserted dogmatically but is explained in its every feature by the light of reason. The atheist does not boast of knowing in a vainglorious, empty sense. He understands by knowledge the most reasonable and clear and sound position one can take on the basis of all the evidence at hand. This evidence convinces him that theism is not true, and his logical position, then, is that of atheism.

We repeat that the atheist is one who denies the assumptions of theism. He asserts, in other words, that he doesn't believe in a God because he has no good reason for believing in a God. That's atheism— and that's good sense.

Atheism Is the Realistic Answer to the God Idea

We are not fanatics on the subject of religion. If it were merely a matter of abstract argument, we should not be so interested. Ideas, if they could be quite separated from actual influence in living issues, might be regarded with an air of detachment. They might in such case be discussed mildly and dismissively. One might be indifferent to such ideas or only amused by them.

But religion has always asserted and it does yet assert a very direct and commanding interest in the conduct of men. It is true that, fortunately, there are old terrors and powers that religion no longer can exercise so effectively as it did only a few score years ago. But the atmosphere and the attitude of bigotry remain. If religion cannot ordinarily invoke the armed force of law to punish heretics, it still plays upon the psychology of fear, and predominantly its influence is to frighten men and distort their views and poison every process of their reasoning.

The remnant of religion that is cherished by a few educated and urbane men—the philosophical or poetic religion that one observes here and there—does not concern us so acutely. Such a provisional or partial belief in religion is baseless logically, and it is confusing; but we may grant that it is relatively harmless; we can point out its fallacy and continue cheerfully on our way about other things. But this philosophical or poet religion is not, after all, the religion of the masses.

There are many cultured people who do not realize that among the masses—among millions of honest but deluded people—the most extravagant, fanatical, and obviously dangerous notions about religion are prevalent. One of the malign emotional and prejudicial influences that helped to lend menacing strength to the late Ku Klux Klan, for example, was the spirit of religious prejudice. We all know how that vicious organization was strengthened by a Protestant tone of creedal fanaticism. On the other hand, the Catholics have their own extreme tone of fanaticism; and they still assert, moreover, that the Catholic religion should be and rightfully is supreme in belief and power—Catholicism, that is to say, is definitely opposed to the modern principles of political liberty and intellectual freedom.

Protestantism is not, in its definite official statements, so brazenly intolerant. Probably this is because Protestantism includes so many creeds—and these religious people feel that they must be protected against one another. They are not so kindly toward atheists.

In a number of American states atheists cannot testify in a court of law. Blasphemy laws are still on the statute books; and occasionally they are enforced. Our laws regarding marriage and sex are sadly distorted by religious prejudice; and a few of these distortions and absurdities are ably summarized by Anthony M. Turano. Bible reading (which means Bible teaching) in the public schools is compulsory in Pennsylvania, Arkansas, and other states. In Tennessee and Mississippi a medieval law bans the teaching of evolution—the teaching, in a word, of the most serious principle of truth in modern science—in the public schools. The circulation of a responsible, scholarly, important sex questionnaire at the University of Missouri was followed by a ridiculous campaign of prejudice in which the chief element, plainly enough, was a religious attitude of obscurantism on the sex question.

Our laws and customs are still deplorably handicapped and corrupted by the ideas of religion. These ideas are no longer of valid currency in the intellectual world. They are centuries behind the times. They are not insisted upon with such vicious and perilous persistency as was the case a few centuries ago. But they remain—these terribly wrong and menacing ideas—and it is the part of a civilized program of enlightenment to combat these ideas with all the force possible.

We, of course, believe in the force of reason and argument and persuasion; yes, and the force of ridicule and denunciation, all legitimate and free weapons which we can employ against religion; in short, we believe in the clarifying conflict of ideas, and as region cannot be defended intelligently we know that in the long run it must he conquered. It remains yet, however, as a serious and major issue in the thoughts and actions of men. Granting, we naturally do, the fullest right of every man to believe in any theory of religion or politics or social conduct which is preferred by him, we do not forget that we have an equal right to promote our own ideas and to attack, relentlessly and clearly, ideas which we recognize as vicious in theory and inevitably vicious also in practice.

We are well aware that religion is not as bad an influence as it was a short time ago, as history is counted. But it is a sufficiently bad influence even in modern times; and its reduced viciousness (in practice) is due plainly enough to its reduced power. We want to reduce that power to an absolute nullity. We want religion to be entirely outgrown by the advancing intelligence of mankind. Universal education is our ideal; and this means, in our convinced opinion, that the philosophy of atheism (which is also the philosophy of realism) will displace with complete sanity and wholesomeness the dark and morbid and unintelligently fanciful ideas of religion.

We advocate the atheistic philosophy, because it is the only clear, consistent position which seems possible to us. As atheists, we simply deny the assumptions of theism; we declare that the God idea, in all its features, is unreasonable and unprovable; we add, more vitally, that the God idea is an interference with the interests of human happiness and progress. We oppose religion not merely as a set of theological ideas; but we must also oppose religion as a political, social, and moral influence detrimental to the welfare of humanity.

We attack religion, because religion is not true—because religion is an obstacle (or a set of obstacles) in the way of progress—because religion foments strife and prejudice—because religion is the breeding ground of intolerance—because, in short, religion is essentially hostile to mankind.

Religion glorifies the dogma of a despotic, mythical God. Atheism ennobles the interests of free and progressive Man. Religion is superstition. Atheism is sanity. Religion is medieval. Atheism is modern.

Preacher Urges the Establishment of Religious Despotism

That religious fanaticism is a modern menace and not merely a medieval memory, that steady propaganda on behalf of freedom of thought is a most serious necessity, we have proved again for our warning in the sermon of Rev. W.D. Lewis, pastor of the Second Presbyterian Church of Wheeling, West Virginia. This preacher, who occupies the pulpit of an important city church, declares that religious liberty must be ended in America and that a system of compulsory religion must be established. "I shall never be in full sympathy with our system of compulsory education," he said, "until there is set up side by side with it a system of compulsory religion."

In suggesting a course of despotic religious procedure for modern times, Rev. Lewis goes way back to the days of ancient Israel. He turns to the Bible and its Old Testament code of theocratic laws. Modern Americans, he says, must be compelled to acknowledge the sovereignty of a personal, autocratic, all-ruling God, even as did the ancient Israelites—and, according to the scheme of this preacher, this God of Bunk must be worshipped by all and no argument permitted.

"The whole scheme of things in Israel," says Rev. Lewis, "revolved around the idea of a personal God. The first leaders of the Jews saw that it would never do to attempt to create a national solidarity without the establishment of a fixed authority. . . . So those first leaders of Israel did the wisest thing ever done by any group of men aspiring to bring forth a nation: they invested all authority in God. They took neither responsibility nor credit for themselves. . . . They were simply his mouthpieces and his agents."

That the priests and rulers of Israel "took neither responsibility nor credit for themselves" is of course a ridiculous bit of sophistry. They had a very imposing prestige and very profitable revenues in their role as the "mouthpieces and agents" of their mythical God. Clearly it was a great stroke of clever exploitation (clever enough to deceive primitive tribes and clever enough to fool many moderns who nevertheless do not live intellectually in the modern age) for the priests to put over the faction that a big, strong, mysterious, and fearsome God was behind their words and actions; that piece of fiction made the priests seem far greater than mere men, greater than merely human rulers, and they have fought and schemed jealously through the centuries to retain that advantage.

It is the prestige and power of clericalism that Rev. Lewis is eager to have restored fully in America. This is clear in what he says about the specific command to worship (i.e., to patronize the clerical shops of superstition). "One day in seven, the Sabbath," he says, "was made holy unto God and set aside solely for his worship (in ancient Israel). There was no choice about it. In those first days there was no such thing as religious liberty in Israel. A man had to go to worship whether he liked it or not. The fact that he didn't like the priests didn't matter. . . . The excuse that he was intellectually superior to the congregation of Israel didn't work. . . . Religious liberty was given no thought in Israel. I some- times wonder if it isn't given too much thought in our own America."

We might indeed remind Rev. Lewis that in modern America we have many features of life which were unknown in ancient Israel. We have not only religious liberty but also political liberty, and the two are inseparable. The Old Testament Jews, that primitive and superstitious tribe, had no conception of modern democracy. They had no glimmer- ing of the materials of modern education. For instance, those old Jews whom Rev. Lewis would have us follow in their system of religious des- potism had the most ridiculous notions of life—they believed in crea- tion by a God and in all the farrago of legends which are sprawlingly conspicuous in the Old Testament. They believed that the earth was the center of a very small universe (they had really no conception of a universe) and that the sun, moon, and stars were merely conveniences to illuminate the earth. They had the most absurd, strangely twisted, cruelly barbaric, and superstitious ideas of morality—the conception of moral law as social law, while it was necessarily followed by them to some extent, was not fully understood by them. Crude indeed were the ideas prevalent in ancient Israel about religion and about government and about morality and about the earth and man. If we were really compelled to follow the ways of ancient Israel, as this West Virginia preacher insists we should, we have should have to scrap our system of education and embrace the system of despotic religion in its stead.

It may be doubted if Rev. Lewis has much concern for education, save as it can be used spuriously as a support for religion. His fixed idea seems to be the importance of compulsory religion. "I shall never be in full sympathy with our system of irreligious education. Why should we be compelled to attend and support our schools if there is nothing that can be done to compel us to attend and support our churches? . . . If education is absolutely necessary for our community life so is religion. Or yet why should we be compelled to support the idea of government if we are at liberty to treat the idea of God with contempt? . . . You will never make a full success of a compulsory government or a compulsory education until you give the same dignity to religion and make it compulsory; at any rate compulsory enough to make it respected throughout the land. The nation that plays fast and loose with its idea of God will soon or late play fast and loose with its idea of education and its idea of government. . . . If God doesn't matter, then nothing else matters, and all the compulsions of life might just as well be set aside."

What Rev. Lewis does not understand (and presumably does not care about) is the truth, well illustrated in history, that no system of education can survive as educationally free and genuine if it is loaded with the chains of a compulsory religion. A religious despotism is utterly incompatible with the freedom and dignity and progressive achievements of social life. As a matter of fact, religion is an eccentric revival from ignorant earlier periods in the life of mankind. It is not in sympathy with modernism (of course not), and it cannot be reconciled with modernism. The right to believe in religion and practice its forms of worship as an individual affair is one that, on modern principles, we must grant. Religion, however, must be kept in its place as a private matter. It is too dangerous when it goes beyond that and presumes to command or threaten the state. Rev. Lewis is an exponent, bold yet typical, of a sentiment of religious bigotry which we cannot afford lightly to dismiss nor to ignore. We must expose these bigots and fight them with a sternness that is uncompromising and a sweep of propaganda that is irresistible.

The Problem of Evil

The problem of evil has always been a mischievous, difficult trap of tormented logic for theologians. They have affirmed dogmatically the existence of an all-powerful and omniscient and benevolent God—but in explaining the evil things in the world they have been not at all deft but rather desperate.

We have been told that God created only the good and not the evil—but that doesn't jibe with the theory of a God who has complete power. If he can't prevent evil, then he is a limited God with a grave element of weakness.

Others have argued that God permitted the evil for purposes of his own, which were really good purposes but beyond man's finite comprehension. But that is a harassed recourse of a man who is in a corner and can think of nothing better to say. It is an argument that admits of no demonstration. It assumes something that can't be proved. It isn't satisfactory.

Again, we are told that there is no evil in the world—that when we regard certain phenomena as evil it is only because we have a distorted view—that all things are good if we could only understand them truly. And that again is wild assertion without even the appearance of logic.

Yes, the problem of evil is too much for theologians. It can't be reconciled with the God idea. It is understandable only in a naturalistic, atheistic view of things.

After all, the principle objection which a thinking man has to religion is that religion is not true—and is not even sane.

The fear of gods and devils is never anything but a pitiable degradation of the human mind.

Can God Lie?

This question is put to Christians who believe that the Bible unerringly describes God and reports the commands and the characteristics of God. If there is a God, it is natural that we should wish to be quite correct in our understanding of that God's nature. So we ask: Can and does God lie?

Looking this point up in the mazes of Holy Writ, we discover confusion. In Numbers 23:19, we are told: "God is not a man, that he should lie." This is put even mere strongly in Hebrews 6:18, where we read: "It was impossible for God to lie."

But do these citations settle the matter? Ah, no, we are upset in our calculations the moment we turn to 2 Thessalonians 2:11, where we read: "For this cause God shall send them strong delusions, that they should believe a lie." And in I Kings 22:23, God is thus reported: "Now, therefore, behold, the Lord hath put a lying spirit in the mouth of all these thy prophets, and the Lord hath spoken evil concerning thee."

Can God lie? Can the Bible lie? Anyway, there is a mistake somewhere. The big mistake is in entertaining the idea of a God.

When we read that some minor scientist (usually a skilled technical worker but not a thinker in science) has "found God" somewhere, we are not excited. We know this is only a form of words, meaning only that the scientific worker, turning away from science, has redis-covered the stale old assumption of theology, "There is a God." We find invariably (as we should expect) that there is no satisfactory defini-tion or description or identification or location or proof of a God. "God" is merely a word, whether it is used by a preacher or a mystic in a laboratory.

The fact that millions of people still believe in a hell of eternal pun-ishment for sinners and unbelievers is a drastic reminder of the need for persistent, progressive education of the masses. We have as yet only begun to realize the possibilities of progress. But science, rationalism, and humanism have pointed the way; they have taken the first great steps, and we must keep right ahead on the highway of modernism.

Don't take our word for it. Read the Bible itself. Read the state-ments of preachers. And you will understand that God is the most desperate character, the worst villain in all fiction.

Commonly, those who have professed the strongest motives of love of a God have demonstrated the deepest hatred toward human joy and liberty.

Theism tells men that they are the slaves of a God. Atheism assures men that they are the investigators and users of nature.

Belief in gods and belief in ghosts is identical. God is taken as a more respectable word than ghost, but it means no more.

Religion, throughout the greater part of its history, has been a form of "holy" terrorism. It still aims its terrors at men, but modern realism and the spread of popular enlightenment has progressively robbed those terrors of their old-fashioned effectiveness. Wherever men take religion very seriously—wherever there is devout belief—there is also the inseparable feeling of fear.

Christian theology has taught men that they should submit with unintelligent resignation to the worst real evils of life and waste their time in consideration of imaginary evils in "the life to come."

Priests and preachers have tricked, terrified, and exploited mankind. They have lied for glory of God." They have collected immense financial tribute for "the glory of God." Whatever may be said about the character of individuals among the clergy, the character of the profession as a whole has been distinctly and drastically anti-human. And, of course, the most sincere among the clergy have been the most dangerous, for they have been willing to go to the most extreme lengths of intolerance for "the glory of God."

Perhaps religion might be dismissed as unimportant if it were merely theoretical. It is difficult, however, if not impossible to separate theory and practice. Religion, to be sure, is full of inconsistencies between theory and practice; but there is and has always been sternly and largely a disposition of religion to enforce its theory in the conduct of life; religion has meant not simply dogmatism in abstract thinking but intolerance in legal and social action. Religion interferes with life and, being false, it necessarily interferes very much to the detriment of the sound human interests of life.

For centuries men have fought in the most unusual and devious ways to prove the existence of a God. But evidently a God, if there were a God, has been hiding out. He has never been discovered or proved. One would think a God, if any, should have revealed himself unmistakably. Isn't this non-appearance of a God (the non-appearance of a God in the shape of a single bit of evidence for his existence) a pretty strong, sufficient proof of non-existence?

A God of love, a God of wrath, a God of jealousy, a God of bigotry, a God of vulgar tirades, a God of cheating and lying—yes, the Christian God is given all of these characteristics, and isn't it a wretched mess to be offered to men in this twentieth century? The beginning of wisdom, the beginning of humanism, the beginning of progress is the rejection of this absurd, extravagantly impossible myth of a God.

Hidden Gods

Look at the God idea from any angle, and it is foolish, it doesn't make sense but extravagantly proposes more mysteries than it assumes to explain. For instance, is it sensible that a real God would leave mankind in such confusion and debate about his character and his laws?

There have been many alleged revelations of God. There have, indeed, been many Gods as there have been many Bibles. And in different ages and different lands an endless game of guessing and disputing has gone on. Men have argued blindly about God. They still argue—just as blindly.

And if there is a God, we must conclude that he has willfully left men in the dark. He has not wanted men to know about him. Assuming his existence, then it would follow that he would have perfect ability to give a complete and universal explanation of himself, so that all men could see and know without further uncertainty. A real God could exhibit himself clearly to all men and have all men following his will to the last letter without a doubt or a slip.

But when we examine even cursorily the many contradictory revelations of God, the many theories and arguments, the many and diverse principles of piety, we perceive that all this talk about God has been merely the natural floundering of human ignorance.

There has been no reality in the God idea which men could discover and agree upon. The spectacle has been exactly what we should expect when men deal with theories of something which does not exist.

Hidden Gods—no Gods—all we see is man's poor guesswork.

Take Your Choice

If the Bible, which Christians believe is the word of God, is inspired and infallible, why does it have two distinctly opposite versions of many things? God's nature and God's opinions and God's wishes are contradictorily reported in Holy Writ.

It is stated, for example, in Genesis 1:31, as follows: "And God saw everything that he had made, and behold it was very good." But in Genesis 6:6, it is stated: "And it repented the Lord that he had made man on the earth, and it grieved him at his heart." Does the good Christian believe both statements?

In Chronicles 7:12, 16, we read: "And the Lord appeared to Solomon by night, and said unto him: I have heard thy prayer, and have chosen this place to myself for a house of sacrifice. . . . For now have I chosen and sanctified this house that my name may be there forever; and mine eyes and my heart shall be there perpetually." Then in Acts 7:48, we read: "Howbeit the Most High dwelleth not in temples made with hands."

Whether God preferred the darkness or the light seemed to be uncertain to the Hebrew prophets of the Most High; but if the Bible were thoroughly inspired there should have been perfect agreement. But in I Timothy 6:16, God is referred to in this manner: "Dwelling in the light which no man can approach." On the other hand, in I Kings 8:12, this reference is contradictorily made: "The Lord said that he would dwell in the thick darkness." And in Psalm 18, we are told about God:

"He made darkness his secret place." And in Psalm 47:2, we are told: "Clouds and darkness are round about him."

Such contradictions are common in the Bible. Naturally this happened, as the Bible was a collection of books written at different times by different men—a strange mixture of diverse human documents—and a tissue of irreconcilable notions. Inspired? The Bible is not even intelligent. It is not even good craftsmanship but is full of absurdities and contradictions.

"God's Will"

Thoughtful men have always observed that "God's will," as that amusing expression has been employed by theologians and by lay commentators, has been nothing more nor less than a reflection of human impulses and desires and fears and whimsicalities. Whoever interprets this so-called will of God always presents a picture of his own, the interpreter's, way of looking at things.

A sober, devout man will interpret "God's will" soberly and devoutly. A fanatic with bloodshot mind will interpret "God's will" fanatically. Men of extreme, illogical views will interpret "God's will" in eccentric fashion. Kindly, charitable, generous men will interpret "God's will" according to their character.

And, of course, this means that whatever happens in life and in the world of nature, entirely independent of the will of any supposed God, such happenings (of the most immensely variant and complex kind) are ascribed to the will of God—a blanket phrase and a bombastic one too, which explains absolutely nothing. Back of the phrase "God's will"—and back of the idea, such as it is, which is reflected by this phrase—there is the old, sound, and really (to the thinking man) obvious truth that gods and all that appertains to them are fashioned by man in his own image or, that is to say, by men in the images cast by their fancies and fears. What we have under observation, always, are human impulses and schemes of action: to say that "God's will" is behind them is to say exactly nothing.

Incredible Instances

As the Bible is regarded as a holy and inspired book by practically all Christians, a book absolutely without errors by many Christians, and the most important proof (through alleged revelation) of the existence of a God by many Christians, it is very important to point out incredible instances recorded in the Bible which no man can sensibly believe.

Colonel Robert G. Ingersoll did a very useful work in exposing the folly of believing that the Bible was inspired. "One can scarcely be blamed," he said, "for hesitating to believe that God met Moses at a hotel and tried to kill him [Exodus 4:24]; that afterward he made this Moses a god to Pharaoh and gave him his brother Aaron for a prophet [Exodus 7:1]; that he turned all the ponds and pools and streams and all the rivers into blood [Exodus 7:19] and all the water in vessels of wood and stone; that the rivers thereupon brought forth frogs [Exodus 8:3]; that the frogs covered the whole land of Egypt; that he changed dust into lice, so that all the men, women, children and animals were covered with them [Exodus 8:16–17]; that he sent swarms of flies upon the Egyptians [Exodus 8:21]; that he destroyed the innocent cattle with painful diseases; that he covered man and beast with blains and boils [Exodus 9:9]; that he so covered the magicians of Egypt with boils that they could not stand before Moses for the purpose of performing the same feat [Exodus 9:11]; that he destroyed every beast and every man that was in the fields, and every herb, and broke every tree with storm of hail and fire [Exodus 9:25]; that he sent locusts that devoured every herb that escaped the hail, and devoured every tree that grew [Exodus 10:15]; that he caused thick darkness over the land and put lights in the houses of the Jews [Exodus 10:22–23]; that he destroyed all of the firstborn of Egypt, from the firstborn of Pharaoh upon the throne to the firstborn of the maidservant that sat behind the mill [Exodus 11:5], together with the firstborn of all beasts, so that there was not a house in which the dead were not [Exodus 12:29–30]."

Do these marvels read like inspiration? Or do they read like superstition? Remember that millions of Christians still base their belief in a God upon the words of the Bible, which is a collection of the most flabbergasting fictions ever imagined—by men, too, who had lawless but very poor and crude imagination. Ingersoll and numerous other critics have shot the Christian holy book full of holes. It is worthless and proves nothing concerning the existence of a God. The idea of a God is worthless and unprovable.

Blind Alleys

> Myself when young did eagerly frequent
> Doctor and Saint and heard great argument
> About it and about evermore
> came out by the door as in I went.

This well-known stanza by Omar, the agnostic Persian poet, expresses the simple truth that he learned nothing from all the arguments about God—nothing, that is to say, except that the arguments were aimless and meaningless. The doctors and the saints were floundering amid unrealistic abstractions. God was merely a name. It had scarcely the solid dignity and comprehensibility of an idea—even a false idea.

This argumentation which taught nothing to Omar—which left him with as little evidence for a God as before he heard a word of the argumentation—was a vain, wordy repetition of fears, fancies, assumptions, dogmas, and whimsically elaborated nonsense. And so it has always been. The efforts of theism, intellectually speaking, have been a chasing up blind alleys. They have arrived nowhere—but, on the contrary, the more argument there has been about the idea of God, the more steadily have men grown in the conviction that the idea is obviously untrue and unrealistic.

Talk of God leads by a direct road to the conclusion of atheism. The only sensible attitude is to dismiss the idea of God—to get it out of the way of more important ideas. The wide dissemination of this intelligent atheistic attitude is one of the leading features of any program of popular education which is completely worthy of the name.

With its fears and superstitions and prejudices, religion poisons the mind of anyone who believes in it—and even the best man, under the influence of religion, cannot reason wholesomely. Atheism, on the contrary, opens the mind to the clean winds of truth and establishes a fresh air sanity.

Nobody has ever taken notable pains to locate the legendary heaven; but probably that is because nobody ever thought seriously of going to a heaven.

Is God a Joker?

A few weeks ago, a hurricane struck the little religious community of Bethany, Oklahoma. A number of pious citizens of the little town were killed. Houses were destroyed—homes in which prayer and devotion reigned. A church was demolished.

Only a few miles away is the large, wicked city of Oklahoma City—at least we can certainly assume that, from the religious viewpoint, many sinners live in Oklahoma City. Assuming also (which is a great deal riskier assumption) that there is a God, why should he perpetrate this grim and sardonic joke? The sinners in the big city were left untouched. The godly folk in the little nearby village were punished by the evidences of God's wrath. How do the religious people interpret this calamity? Often they explain such calamities as flood, fire, and storm by saying that God is angry at the sinful people and is warning them or destroying them for their sins. Was the hurricane in Bethany a sign of the love of God for his faithful worshipers?

And God missed an even better chance, if there were a God who wished to punish rebels against his majesty and inscrutability. Just a few hundred miles north and east of Bethany, Oklahoma, is Girard—the home of *The American Freeman* and *The Debunker* and *The Joseph McCabe Magazine* and the *Little Blue Books*—the center of American free thought where an enormous stream of atheistic literature and godless modern knowledge pours forth to enlighten the masses. If there were a God directing hurricanes and he wanted to really "get" an uncompromising foe, whom he has no chance of persuading in the ordinary way, it would have been a devastating stroke for him to send his howling punitive blasts through the town of Girard. It would be a more remarkable suggestion of the avenging act of a God if only the Haldeman-Julius plant were destroyed and the rest of the town left unhurt—and, as good neighbors, we shouldn't wish the Christian and respectable people of Girard or those who are respectable and not so Christian or those who are Christian and not exactly respectable to suffer from our proximity and our propaganda of atheism.

Is God a joker? No—let us whisper it—the joke is that there is no God. Hurricanes come upon the just and the unjust, the pious and the impious.

To be true to the mythical conception of a God is to be false to the interests of mankind.

God as a Gamble

One of the most amusing arguments frequently offered in defense of belief in the idea of a God is that such a belief is a way of playing safe.

It is said that even though a man is not sure of the existence of a God and a future life beyond the grave, it is the part of caution for him to believe; then, as the argument goes, the man believing is safe whether there is or is not a God and a future existence; if there is no God, the believer will be no more dead than the unbeliever; while if there is a God, the believer will have preferential treatment in the judgments of the celestial tribunal.

This queer argument makes the matter of belief in a God an intellectual gamble. It is, of course, an utter denial of intellectual integrity. Proceeding on this basis, the appeal to belief is not made on the score of truth. One is urged to consider the God idea not from the standpoint of its reasonableness but, rather, from the standpoint of blind faith and a chance bet on an idea.

Doesn't the religious person who uses this appeal to a particularly low form of intellectual cowardice? What men need is courage in their thinking. They need to be trained in facing facts frankly. They need to learn that all ideas should be judged with strict regard for the evidence. Instead religion harps on the emotion of fear and tells men that they should treat ideas merely as gambling chances, and that it is safer (not intellectually the better but the more craven part) to believe in a God.

This argument has other fallacious aspects. It assumes, for instance, that the evidence for and against the idea of a God is equal; whereas the vast preponderance of evidence is against the idea, there being, in fact, no genuine evidence for the idea. It is overlooked, too, that belief is genuine or it is not; and that a belief which is frankly grounded on a gamble—a belief affirmed for safety's sake—cannot be a real belief. One believes or one does not; real belief can only assert the truth of an idea. In short, the man who bases his belief on such a principle is bordering close to hypocrisy and is certainly revealing a striking lack of mental integrity.

Such weak arguments exemplify the decline of religion and show its utter intellectual bankruptcy. It has all the air of a desperate and last plea for a set of ideas which, ordinarily and reasonably, cannot be defended. It is, after all, a virtual admission of the charge of the atheist that the idea of a God is merely an assumption and has no ground of truth upon which firmly to plant itself.

Credulity—A Crime

Credulity is not a crime for the individual—but it is clearly a crime as regards the race. Just look at the actual consequences of credulity. For years men believed in the foul superstition of witchcraft, and many poor people suffered for this foolish belief. There was a general belief in angels and demons, flying familiarly, yet skittishly, through the air, and that belief caused untold distress and pain and tragedy. The most holy Catholic Church (and, after it, the various Protestant sects) enforced the dogma that heresy was terribly sinful and punishable by death. Imagine— but all you need do is to recount—the suffering entailed by that belief.

When one surveys the causes and consequences of credulity, it is apparent that this easy belief in the impossible, this readiness toward false and fanatical notions, has been indeed a most serious and major crime against humanity. The social life in any age, it may be said, is about what its extent of credulity guarantees. In an extremely credulous age, social life will be cruel and dark and treacherous. In a skeptical age, social life will be more humane. We assert that the philosophy of humanity—that the best interests of the human race—demands a strong statement and a repeated, enlightening statement of atheism.

"Spiritual Realities"

When preachers talk about "spiritual realities," what do they mean? They do not mean the emotions of men. At least they do not mean these emotions as realistically observed and interpreted human emotions. Love, hate, fear, greed, malice, envy, ambition, dreams, and desires— these are human emotions which the rational, scientific mind takes as themes for analysis. They are understood not in any "spiritual" sense but in terms of heredity and environment and constitutional (physical and mental) makeup. Their causes and their expressions are, so far as science has been able to trace them, essentially material.

All of mankind's art, mankind's morality, mankind's experiments with and yearning for beauty can be and are explained in terms of human cause and effect and are placed in the evolutionary pattern worked out by science. They are not mysterious in the theistic sense; they are not, that is to say, mystic. An emotion in human nature is as realistic a fact as an object in nature: and science deals with both emotions and objects materialisticly, experimentally, analytically.

"Spiritual realities" mean nothing to science. This is the special and unrealistic lingo of the clerical bunk shooters, who depend upon sweeping (but empty) phrases and pious dogmas and a large spooky and spoofy atmosphere of aimless mystery for the maintenance of their prestige. That their belief is often sincere does not affect the case.

By "spiritual realities," if you probe the phrase, you will discover that the preachers mean some mystic working of the mind of a God in the minds and motives of men. They intend us to believe that human emotions are something more than human—that back of them is the shadowed and obscure and awesomely immense loom on which is woven a divine pattern.

"Spiritual realities," according to the preachers, are the reflections of the most unreal of all myths, namely, the myth of a God. These so-called "realities," said to be the highest conceivable, are seen to be the most unreal and the most inconceivable.

Is God Fair?

That's a funny question. But still we ask it: Is God fair? The Christians say that God damns forever anyone who is skeptical about truth of bunkistic religion as revealed unto the holy haranguers. What this means is that a God, if any, punishes a man for using his reason.

If there is a God in existence, reasons should be available for his existence. Assuming that such a precious thing as a man's eternal future depends on his belief in a God, then the materials for that belief should be overwhelming and not at all doubtful.

Yet here is a man whose reason makes it impossible for him to believe in a God. He sees no evidence of such an entity. He finds all the arguments weak and worthless. He doubts and he denies.

Then is a God fair in visiting upon such a skeptic the penalty for his inevitable intellectual attitude? The intelligent man refuses to believe fairy tales. Can a God blame him? If so, then a God is not as fair as an ordinarily decent man. And fairness, we think, is more important than piety.

"Faith," said St. Paul, "is the evidence of things not seen." We should elaborate this definition by adding that faith is the assertion of things for which there is not a particle of evidence and of things which are incredible.

CHAPTER VII

How Christianity Grew Out of Paganism

Christianity and Slavery

and

Judeo-Christian Degradation of Woman

by Joseph McCabe

How Christianity Grew Out of Paganism

How the Creed Was Synthetically Formed

It is one of the ironies of the history of religion that what we call the great, historical, or organized religions took their rise from prophets whose mission in life was to denounce religion in the sense in which these organized bodies use the word. The very corrupt and hypocritical Buddhism of Japan and its less offensive but equally elaborate counterpart in China and other Asiatic countries takes the name of a moralist, Buddha, who was, according to all the leading authorities, an atheist and urgently warned folk to keep clear of priests, temples, and idle speculations about a future life. The vast army of Buddhist priests and monks, the most sordid priesthood in the modern world, now make a gorgeous living chiefly by inspiring simple folk for the next world.

I do not include Confucianism, because it never was a religion, and it has therefore consistently preserved the atheism and high moral code of its founder. Taoism, the second religion of China, pretends to have been founded by Lao Tzu, a contemporary of Confucius, who, though inclined to mysticism, equally warned his followers against organized religion with its ceremonies and devil dodging. What is broadly called Zoroastrianism in Persia takes the name of another prophet, Zoroaster or Zarathustra, who set out to purify religion by stripping it of all that the modern Zorastrians call religion. Even Mohammed was a rebel against all organized and priestly religion, yet Islam, while rejecting the title of priests and remaining comparatively simple in its services, really has a powerful and tyrannical body of priests.

But the most notable instance of this, shall we say, ingenuous development in the religious world is Christianity. As I said, if there is one thing that we may on sound historical principles consider probable about Jesus, it is that he was an independent moral preacher—as hundreds of the Essenes were in Judea at the time—who so angered the Jewish priests, presumably by his criticisms of them and their temple religion, that they had him put to death as what we now call a Bolshevik. When that fine leader of the French Revolution Camille Desmoulins was asked his religion, he said: "The same as that of the sansculotte Jesus." If you want me to give the proper American equivalent of the French expression, I shall have to paraphrase it: "ragged seat of the pants." Fortunately, we have no quarrel here with those who think that the Gospels are real biography. Except for a ridiculous, late interpolation about his "church," they uniformly represented Jesus as a violent opponent of priests, temples, services, set prayers, and every element of sacerdotal and ritual religion. Paul has the same idea.

We have nothing to do here with modern explanations of how or why this iconoclastic Gospel, which is still read in church (in the midst of the most gorgeous and elaborate ceremonies) every Sunday, became the basis of the Episcopal or the Roman Church. One of the funniest explanations, which you often hear today, is that Jesus took his fishermen lieutenants up one of those high mountains of which he was so fond and explained to them that he "spoke in parables to the multitude so that they would not understand"—in the next page you read that he spoke to the multitude in parables, because it was the simplest and most beautiful way to get his ideas over to them—but he would tell them something. What he said to the people about an approaching end of the world was—well, anything you like to call it. The world was going to last for thousands of years, and for security of Christian morality they must found a great Church with buildings and choirs (including soprano eunuchs), bishops, archbishops, cardinals, priests, etc., vestments, incense, and dog collars, the power to kill heretics and dictate to princes and presidents. . . . Tens of millions of Christians believe that. But there is no need for any guessing about what happened. Early Christian literature makes it clear. In one of the most important, yet one of the least frequently quoted, documents of the first century is a "Letter from the Christians of Rome to those of Corinth," which we may confidently date about the year 96. That "Letter to the Corinthians" says that the Romans have just simple meetings—in each other's houses, for we know that they had no sort of chapel until after 200 AD—at which they said prayers and sang a hymn (probably Jewish) or two. To keep order they had an overseer (which in Greek is the word we have corrupted into bishop) and a few assistants (deacons). The "Letter" says nothing about priests, who were pagan officials, much less a pope. Pliny's letter to the emperor about Christians in Bithynia suggests the same simplicity.

Before the end of the second century, the simple supper they had periodically held had grown into "the Mass," and the priests who performed this very august ceremony were, of course, a special and consecrated caste. The word Mass is taken from a Latin phrase which the priest still addresses to the people at the end of the ceremony. It means, "off you go: dismissal." Now we know that in ancient Rome this formula was used (in Greek) at the end of the service in the temples of Mithra and of Isis, and the temple of Mithra particularly interests us. At Rome it was almost next door to the Christian quarter, and it was a fierce rival. To be brief, if you will look up the English translation (*The Mysteries of Mithra*, 1903) of the smaller work on Mithraism of Franz Cumont, the highest authority on the subject, you will find that in the underground temples of Mithra, blazing with candles and stuffy with incense, priests in vestments consecrating bread and wine at an altar and communicating them to the people. The evolution of the Mass out of the Lord's Supper is clear enough, and it gave a mighty lift to the priestly caste over the laity.

The Christians still, and until the fourth century, refused to celebrate Christmas . . . or pay any honor to Mary. The reason again is clear. All the pagan religions celebrated either one or the other or both. If you want the details and the references in the writings of the Fathers, I must refer you to my *Little Blue Books* 1102 and 1104, since I must confine myself here to an outline.

Take Mithraism. The simpleminded Christian Father Firmicus Maternus says candidly—he explains that it is all a trick of the devil to seduce Christians—that Cumont has verified from the inscriptions that Mithra was a Savior God who brought "eternal life" to his votaries (especially through baptism and communion). They celebrated his birth in a cave, with great pomp and blaze of lights, at midnight (Midnight Mass) December 25—the date when the Romans themselves celebrated "The Birthday of the Unconquered Sun"; and Mithra was a solar god. In the spring they celebrated the death and resurrection of Mithra with equal solemnity, as Firmicus describes in detail. The image of the dead god was exhibited on a bier in the temple and the worshipers mourned. Then—Firmicus does not say how long the mourning lasted—the priests bade them rejoice for the god had risen again.

In another part of Rome was the temple of Isis, and the early Christian Paschal chronicle tells us that in midwinter the temple of Isis used to exhibit a sort of tableau (as Catholic churches still do at Christmas) of the mother Isis and her newborn divine child, Horus, lying in a manger. The Greeks at the same time made great parade of their god Dionysos (or Bacchus), represented by the statue of a newborn infant lying in a basket (some say manger). At Alexandria, another early Christian writer tells us, there was a cult of a virgin mother Kore, who was particularly honored as giving birth to a divine child in midwinter. In other words, since these Greek, Persian, and Egyptian religions had temples in all cities, and December 25 was a gold-letter day in the Roman calendar as the birthday (virtually the resurrection) of the sun, there is not much doubt how the simple early Christian religion came (when it suppressed all its rivals by force) to have its most popular and characteristic festival and its cult of a virgin mother and divine babe.

But the celebration of the death and resurrection of a god was even more familiar to the Greeks and Romans. I have told how the Mithraists, who were for three centuries more numerous than the Christians and spread from Persia to Britain, celebrated annually the death and resurrection of their god. Even more familiar to the Romans was the annual celebration of the violent death and resurrection of Athis, son of the Great Mother (Cybele), because the devotees were permitted to hold their picturesque processions in the streets. The ceremonies lasted a week, which is very clearly the model of the later Holy Week. St. Augustine saw them in Rome and described them. It is enough here to say that on the first day the priests carried reeds (compare palms) in procession; the fifth day—remember that Good Friday is the fifth day from Palm Sunday—was "the Day of Blood," when the eunuch priests gashed themselves with knives (in the East they publicly emasculated themselves) and howled as they bore a statue of the dead young god bound on a pine tree; and the last day was the Day of Rejoicing, because he had come to life again. All over the East that was one of the most famous religious ceremonies, the god being variously called Athis, Adonis, and Tammuz. The prophet Ezekiel (8:15) refers to it: "And behold there sat women weeping over Tammuz," and as late as the fourth century, Jerome, Augustine, Cyril, and other Church Fathers speak of it.

This covers most of the ancient world, from Rome to Mesopotamia, but the Egyptians had another version of what we may almost call the universal myth. Firmicus says that "they buried a statue of Osiris in the temple and honored it with an annual lamentation," and a few days later "they lay aside their grief and rejoiced." Frazer's masterly *Adonis, Attis, Osiris* will give you all details. And—to complete the circle of the ancient world—the Greeks, besides having a legend (Demetese Persophone) of their own that comes near to the common myth, borrowed the mourning festivals over both Osiris and Tammuz (Attis). Plutarch describes them holding the ceremony as early as 415 BC (*The Life of Alcibiades*, XV:111), and the Roman writer Ammianus Marcellinus (*Res Gestae*, XXII) describes it in Antioch, in 362 AD.

The birth, death, and resurrection of a god, which simpleminded believers imagine to be so characteristic of Christianity, were almost as familiar in the Greek-Roman world for two or three hundred years before Christ as the Fourth of July is in America. There is not the least obscurity about the matter. In midwinter, the sun begins to wax strong again and, as the Roman writer Macrobius says, these temple representations of the birth (obviously rebirth or resurrection) of a divine infant refer to the solar deity (Mittra, Horus, etc.). At the beginning of winter, the spirit of vegetation, the divine son of Mother Earth, is stricken and dies. It is interesting that often in the myth and ceremony he dies by losing his testicles or penis, figuring the earth's loss of fertility. But he rises to full vitality again in the spring. On these great phenomena of the year, pre-civilized man built his winter and spring nature festivals and, for convenience and greater effect, later priests compressed the death and resurrection festivals into three days.

These are by no means all the cults of the ancient world that influenced Christianity. The city of Tarsus had its own god, Sandan, who died and rose again annually. Late Babylonia and Phoenicia had a savior god, Esmun, whose cult could give spiritual features to the new religion. But what I have said will suffice to illustrate how the austere creed of Paul, which was developed out of late Jewish ideas of what the Messiah was to do for them, and the still simpler religion ascribed to Jesus in the Gospels, once it won power to stay all its rivals by imperial decrees, borrowed their myths and services, their art and temple paraphernalia (vestments, incense, holy water, etc.), and attracted the old pagan worshipers.

The Facts About Early Christianity

For several centuries the early Christians, especially those who lived in the first century after the death of Jesus, would have none of these pagan robes and trimmings. Paul was the real founder of this early Church, and his grim spirit haunted it for a century. But a change occurred before the second century was out, and the myth that for several centuries these early Christians remained shining examples of virtue in a wicked world, ready at all times to sit on red-hot gridirons or meekly face the lions for their faith, is another element that must be set aside if you want to get a correct attitude to Christianity. It is the first point to which those who talk about our Christian civilization would appeal, and it has to be flatly and comprehensively denied.

Although, as Paul's letters to the Corinthians plainly tell, some of the new communities were by no means solid in virtue, we are pleased to learn from his other letters and from the letter of the Romans to the Corinthians that the latter community was exceptional; and it must have been particularly difficult to sustain the Christian sex code in gay Corinth. Anyhow, we find the Roman Christians still virtuous in the year 96 AD. You may, of course, suggest that if they expected the end of the world at any moment and the alternatives being an eternity in boiling oil or amongst cool clouds, it ought not to have been difficult for a man to be satisfied with one bed; but we have nothing to do with those things. Temptation was, as a matter of fact, not as alluring in the early Church at Rome as the preachers seem to think. Apparently, they do not know that the Christians did not live in Rome at all but outside the walls in a poor foreign settlement, and that their language was Greek. On the other hand, the common picture of them as a communistic body is a libel. I say libel, because this would bring them into line with those dreadful Bolsheviks. Some of them were rich and some poor. Some had slaves, and some were slaves. Paul sends his kind regards to two of them who were high officials in the imperial palace, and later Christian historians claim that the community included cousins of the Emperor Vespasian.

But the luster of their virtue was very much dimmed before the end of the second century. A learned man arose in the Christian Roman community—the only one in six or seven centuries—and, as he is a "saint" in the Roman calendar, we must read him with respect. In his *Refutation of All Heresies,* this Hippolytus has a few chatty pages about the life of the Roman Christians. Pope Victor, the first pope who tried to be papal and got very nastily rapped on the knuckles by the other bishops, was, it seems, a friend of a lady named Marcia, who lived in the Emperor Commodus's palace. Not to put too fine a point on it, Marcia was the lewdest concubine in the spacious harem (which also included three hundred handsome boys) of Commodus, who could have given lessons to Nero in sex matters. However, Marcia and her friend and tutor in vice, Hyacinth, who is claimed to have been a Christian, got many favors for the Christians when Pope Victor went for tea or something to the palace.

Hippolytus broadens the picture. One of the rich Christians directs his Christian slave Callistus to open a bank in the city, and the faithful, although the Christian code declared all interest on money to be usury and a mortal sin, all rushed to put their money in it and make a bit. Callistus embezzled the lot and went to jail, and a few years later he became pope and applied his talents to the humanization (and enrichment) of the Church. It was, he said, time they abolished this musty old idea that if a Christian sinned after baptism he or she must be expelled and considered damned forever. He and his priests could forgive sins, he said. So by this and other humane measures he opened the door of the Church to rich Roman women, and they brought in a good many things besides money. In fact, anybody who represents the Roman community after this time as an oasis of virtue in a desert of sin ought to be on the staff of a Ministry of Information.

Documents of the third century show that the dry rot spread quickly and very thoroughly to the whole Church. About the middle of the century, St. Cyprian, a very stern man, was leader of the African Church, and his letters to the pope describe how a large part of his clergy and bishops were unmitigated scoundrels: fornication, murder, embezzlement, and all the rest of it. For the Spanish Church, we have, about the end of the century, the canons, and, my word, the women were as gay as the cigar girls of modern Seville. For the East, we have a letter (in Bishop Eusebius's *History*) of the bishop of the place describing the behavior by the Christians of Alexandria when the general persecution opened. With mordant irony, the bishop describes how, when his Christians were summoned to the tribunal, they provoked the jeers of the crowd by nervously disowning the faith. Of course, the bishop himself, being a very necessary person, had had to avoid martyrdom.

This question of martyrdoms gives you a general indication of the character of the Christians of the thirteenth century, when the only two real general persecutions of Christians occurred, and at the same time gives you the measure of the fairy tales that are still told about the early Church—told, that is to say, to the people and cherished by politicians and editorial writers, though Catholic scholars who have specialized in martyr literature (the Jesuit Father Delehaye, the Austrian Professor Ehrhard, Bishop Gregg, etc.) have to admit that it is the finest collection of forgeries that we have. For instance, Catholic historians claim that by the middle of the third century, when the Decian persecution occurred, the Roman Christians numbered about 30,000 or more. But in his special study of this persecution, Bishop Gregg finds that only half a dozen of them won the golden crown of martyrdom. Of about 150 priests and clerics of the Church, only 6 were arrested. And in the next and greatest general persecution, under Diocletian, the Catholic historian Duchesne can find only a score of genuine martyrdoms in the whole Church, and only 2 of these were at Rome.

The African very orthodox Bishop Optatus has a pleasant little story about what happened in his *History of the Donatist Schism* (of the fourth century). A bunch of the African bishops met to discuss the appalling general apostasy of their Christians when the persecution was over. They fell to violent quarreling, and it transpired that they had all dodged the golden crown. One had, presumably with a wink at the presiding pagan official who was bribed, handed in a medical work pretending that it was the Bible. Another of the bishops was accused by his brothers in Christ of murders. "Yes," he said—and Optatus is copying a stenographic report of the proceedings, "I did, and I'll knock off anybody who gets in my way." In short, modern experts on this literature find that only a few dozen of the supposed "acts" (accounts of trial and execution) of the martyrs are not blatant forgeries, and beyond these we just have the vague reports of local bishops that a number of the more zealous of their people—generally enthusiasts who regarded martyrdom as a sure ticket to paradise—were executed. Delehaye has shown in a special study that all stories of Christians being exposed to lions in the Roman amphitheater (which so moved Mr. George Bernard Shaw that he based a play on them) are bogus. Of three generations of Christians in the third century—certainly at least six or seven million—only a hundred or two did not deny the faith or take to flight; and the learned Origen himself says that for the first two centuries you could count the martyrs on your fingers.

That will give you some idea of the colossal fabrication of the early Middle Ages, on which the first part of the myth of our Christian civilization—the character of the early Church—is based. Naturally the corruption deepened when, after the conversion of the Emperor Constantine, the Church became rich. The legend is that the Christians were now able to build churches in Rome and attract the pagans by their virtuous lives. Let me state, very briefly, three notorious facts.

In the year 366, there was an election for the papacy, which was now very rich. The successful candidate was "St." Damasus, and his methods were such that in one day his men left the corpses of 160 of his rival's supporters on the floor of a small church. The war lasted a week and was so furious that the Roman "police" were swept aside and the prefect driven out of the city. The second fact is that St. Jerome, who then lived in Rome as a sort of secretary to Pope Damasus, has left us a large number of letters in which he describes the character of the Christians of Rome. In almost incredible language, he insists that clergy, monks, consecrated virgins, widows, etc. are monstrously and, with very few exceptions, comprehensively corrupt. "St." Damasus himself was denounced by his priests to the civil power for adultery and was only saved by the emperor. And the third undisputed fact is that there was no "attraction" of the pagans at all. In the extant Theodosian Code we have ten decrees which the bishops got from the emperors suppressing all rival religions and sects under pain of fine, imprisonment, or death.

The corruption of character was general in the Church. St. Augustine in his sermons and letters describes it in North Africa, which was then more flourishing and populous than it now is. St. John Chrysostom in his sermons paints an equally dark picture of the people of Constantinople and Antioch. At Antioch, he says, there are one hundred thousand Christians but he doubts if one hundred of them will ever see heaven. They laugh, he says, when he preaches on chastity. St. Gregory of Nyssa in two extant letters forbids Christian women of his diocese to make the pilgrimage to Jerusalem, because it is, he says, a hotbed of crime and vice. And so on. The Christian world was sinking into the Dark Age in which not only all attempts at restoring the shattered Greek-Roman civilization were suspended for seven centuries, but Europe fell to a level which most historians describe as barbarism.

That is [but] part of the reply to those who glibly talk about our Christian civilization. In its primitive purity Christianity was, like Paul and (possibly) Jesus, quite indifferent to what we call civilization.

Christianity and Slavery

Paganism and Slavery

About the year 100 AD, a remarkable lecture on slavery was delivered in Rome. The central part of Rome was a very broad open space, the Forum, crowded with statues and works of art, lined with beautiful marble temples and public halls. In these halls lectures were delivered, just as they are in New York and Chicago today; and, as the Romans knew and practiced shorthand as well as we do, many of the lectures have been preserved for us.

The orator to whom I now refer was the eloquent Greek Stoic, Dion Chrysostom, or "Dion of the Golden Mouth." He was no demagogue. At times you would see him driving about Rome with the great emperor, Trajan, of whom he was an intimate friend. He was the idol of the thoughtful section of the Roman nobility. And for the two days—the subject was too large for one day—Dion had announced as his subject "Slavery": a delicate topic, one would imagine, if pagan Rome were quite the slave driving city it is commonly supposed to have been, unless the aristocratic orator intended to justify the institution for his aristocratic audience, every member of which owned many slaves.

But Dion, as we read in the extant lectures, denounced slavery as unjust. But no religious writer in the world seems ever to have heard of Dion Chyrsostom and his denunciation of slavery.

It is quite formal, explicit and lengthy. It fills two lectures. Here is an express and honorable condemnation of slavery by a well-known friend of the emperor in the most public and effective circumstances, at a time when the Christians were a mere handful of obscure folk, mumbling a Greek liturgy and debating whether the end of the world was not at hand.

It is the reverse of the truth to say that Christianity abolished slavery and gave the world education; and I say this knowing well that H.G. Wells has endorsed the Christian claim. No one admires Wells's ability and service to this generation more than I do, but here he made, or borrowed, a statement which he had never examined. The undisputed historical facts are that:

1) The Greek and Roman moralists perceived the injustice of slavery, often denounced it, and rendered great services to the slave.
2) No Christian leader denounced slavery until the ninth century, when the age of slavery was over.
3) In the Christian Middle Ages the workers were far worse off, because nearly everyone was a serf, and serfdom was slavery under another name.
4) The betterment of the condition of the workers has been won quite independently of religion and to an enormous extent in spite of the churches.

Let me underline a truth which is a simple historical fact. There have in history been two great periods of benevolence and social services: one was under the pagan Stoics and the other is under modern paganism. The Christian Era lies between these two paganisms, and it has as poor a record of social service as one can imagine. By the first century, the Stoics openly condemned slavery. Other Greek moralists besides the Stoics condemned it. Plutarch condemned it. Epicurus had come near to condemning it three centuries earlier when he had defined the slave as "a friend in an inferior condition"; and the Epicurean Hegesias had maintained that slaves were the equals of free men. Florentinus and Ulpian, the two famous Stoic jurists, declared that the enslavement of a man was against the law of nature, the supreme standard of the Stoic. Seneca insisted that the slaves were our "lowly friends," and he pleaded repeatedly and nobly for them. Pliny shows us in his letters that by the second century the slaves were very humanely treated, even on provincial estates. Juvenal fiercely attacked inhumanity to slaves.

Yet I presume that all that any religious reader is likely to know about Roman slavery is that the rich patricians had large armies of slaves on their estates and treated them like cattle. He is never told that this refers to the early period of Roman expansion, and that before the end of the first century the slaves were protected by law.

He has probably heard how Cato made some callous remark about his slaves; and he is not told that the pagan writer who has preserved it for us gives it expressly as an instance of "a mean and ungenerous spirit."

The Gospel and the Slave

There can be no doubt that if the Roman Empire had continued and developed normally slavery would have been abolished. Abolition would, as every American knows, have been a colossal task. It would have been far more terrible in Rome than in the southern [United] States, because the entire empire rested to a great extent upon slave labor. The immense privileges even of the Roman working men were based upon the labor of slaves in the provinces.

Yet public feeling was profoundly affected by the Stoic principle, and the "manumission" of slaves—the grant or sale of freedom to them—was a daily occurrence. Even before Christ this liberation proceeded on so large a scale that the Emperor Augustus checked it for a time, on political grounds. The Stoics urged it and facilitated it, and the final term of the movement was certain.

Rome, however, fell upon evil days just at the time when the humanitarian gospel was accepted. The manhood of Italy, then of the provinces, was almost exhausted in war. The empire was so vast, its frontiers so far-flung, that the military burden was terrible; and frontier wars naturally increased as the military forces weakened. The third century was one of great poverty and confusion. In the fourth century there was a recovery, but the empire was bleeding to death, and new formidable forces were advancing upon it.

Early in the fifth century it fell. The great slaveowners, the imperial estates, and the wealthy Romans were ruined. The whole economic system was shattered. The old slaves were not "freed": they found themselves free. No one "broke their fetters." They had no fetters. But the barbarians slew or sent into exile the owners, destroyed the connection of the provinces with Rome, and wrecked the administration of the estates. The slaves dispersed and there were now no Roman troops to prevent them.

Thus, we can write the history of ancient slavery without any reference to Christianity. If it were not for this religious controversy which perverts the facts of history, the Christian religion would hardly be noticed in any complete and impartial study of Roman slavery. All that would be noted would be that some of the Christian emperors of the fourth century issued edicts about the condition of slaves; though they are much less important than the great measures of the pagan emperors. It would then be recorded that the new Christian masters of Europe—petty princes, bishops, abbots, and landowners—continued to use slave labor. But it was comparatively easy to deal with this new kind of slavery, and Christendom, tardily recognizing a little of the Stoic ethic, turned it into serfdom: which would have horrified the Stoics.

How, then, has this persistent belief that Christianity broke the fetters of the slave originated and been maintained? Naturally, in the same way as the belief that the Church emancipated woman. It is a quite modern belief. Until recent times nobody cared two pins about the social services of religion. Its business was to save souls. When men could no longer be prevented from attaching importance to social interests, however, the cry arose that religion was just the thing to serve us. The history of the past was caricatured. Already everybody believed that the era before Christ was dark and impotent, and the Christian Era brought a wonderful transformation. Part of this transformation, it was now said, was the uplifting of woman, the emancipation of the slave, the opening of schools, the purification of morals, the beginning of charity, and so on. Neither preachers nor their hearers read the facts of ancient history.

What is there in the Bible that even tends to discourage or condemn slavery? Not a word from cover to cover. Apologists manage to find a word or two which they can twist into a desperate defense of woman, but there is not a single phrase of Jehovah or Jesus or Paul that they can, with all their ingenuity, represent as a condemnation of slavery or war, the two most colossal evils of the ancient world.

As I have said, one of the ablest of the apologists actually turns this silence of the Bible into a piece of high diplomacy. Jesus did not want to cause the economic ruin of the empire, so he did not condemn slavery! How religious readers permit such stuff to be presented to them one cannot imagine.

Throughout the Bible slavery is as cheerfully and leniently assumed as are war, poverty, and royalty. In the English Bible there is frequent mention, especially in the parables, of "servants." The Greek word is generally "slaves." Jesus talks about them as coolly as we talk about our housemaids or nurses. Naturally, he would say that we must love them: we must love all men (unless they reject our ideas). But there is not a syllable of condemnation of the institution of slavery. Fornication is a shuddering thing; but the slavery of fifty or sixty million human beings is not a matter for strong language. Paul approves the institution of slavery in just the same way—he is, in fact, worse than Jesus. He saw slaves all over the Greco-Roman world and he never said a word of protest.

As to the customary quibble, that these reforms were "implied" in the teaching of Jesus, it reminds me of Disraeli's famous joke. Asked his religion, he (being a rationalist, yet a politician) said that he held "the religion of every sensible man." And to the question what that was, he replied that no sensible man ever tells. It reminds me also of the great achievement of Pope Leo XIII, who at last (in the eighteenth century of papal power) found the courage to declare that the worker was entitled to "a living wage." But when the clergy found that working men of the nineteenth century were not so easily duped by phrases and wanted to know what was a living wage, the pope refused to answer the questions privately submitted to him.

Here is another historical truth to underline: for eight hundred years no Christian leader condemned slavery. And here is one for the Roman Catholic: no pope ever condemned slavery. In Rome, the pope saw more slavery than in any other city in the world. The life of Rome was based upon the labor of millions of slaves in the provinces. All the dreadful things quoted about pagan slavery are from Roman writers. And no pope ever uttered a syllable of condemnation of slavery.

Negative statements are a little dangerous. I borrowed this statement—that no Christian writer condemned slavery until the ninth century—from Ingram's *A History of Slavery and Serfdom*, which is the best authority on the subject. Then I waited for the reply. It came in a shabby booklet or pamphlet from the Christian Evidence Society; and it reminded me of the Irishman's complaint about his sandwich, that there was "so much mustard for so little meat." In quite a fury of righteous indignation the clerical writer exposed my "lies" to the contempt of the Christian world. He had found—or he confessed that some industrious theologian had found for him—one Christian condemnation of slavery in those eight hundred years!

Now, I did not profess to have read every page of every Christian work for eight centuries. I know the Migne collection of this literature as well as anybody and have spent, in all, many weary months over it. But it was fair to assume that theologians would long ago have quoted Christian condemnations of slavery if there were any; and none had appeared. The great search now yielded a sort of condemnation of slavery in a work ascribed to Gregory of Nyssa, one of the least influential of the Fathers. How I would have treasured that solitary gem; but, alas, it was spurious. The authorship of the work is disputed, and the author, whoever he is, does not so much condemn slavery as an unjust institution but attacks all holding of property, including slaves.

The true and typical attitude of the churchman is seen in Pope "St. Gregory the Great." Possibly some Catholic may be surprised at my effrontery in quoting Gregory. Did he not say in one of his letters that all men are "born free," that slaves are only such by "the law of nations," and that it is proper to free slaves? Oh, yes. I know the letter well: much better than the Catholic writers (and even Ingram, who, being a positivist, favors the Church when he can) who quote it. The pope is writing to two of his slaves. He is giving them their freedom. But this is the little suppressed fact—they have inherited money, and Gregory secures the money for the Church!

Pope Gregory, my Catholic friend, was the greatest slaveowner in the world in the sixth century. Announcing that the end of the world was to come in 600 AD, he kindly allowed landowners and slaveowners to hand over their property to the Church—God would not damn the Church for its wealth—and enter monasteries. The papacy soon had an income from land of about two million dollars a year; a stupendous sum in those impoverished days. Enormous numbers of slaves tilled the 1,800 square miles of the Church's property. Gregory freed them occasionally: when they got money. He never condemned slavery. He would not allow any slave to become a cleric, and he expressly reaffirmed (Epp. 7:1) that no slave could marry a free Christian.

Judeo-Christian Degradation of Woman

Woman could not hold any property, either earned or inherited. If unmarried, she was obliged to place it in the hands of a trustee, to whose will she was subject. If she contemplated marriage, and desired to call her property her own, she was forced by law to make a contract with her intended husband by which she gave up all title or claim to it. A woman, either married or unmarried, could hold no office of trust or power. She was not a person. She was not recognized as a citizen. She was not a factor in the human family. She was not a unit but a zero, in the sum of civilization. . . . The status of a married woman was little better than that of a domestic servant. By the English Common Law [in force in Boston] her husband was her lord and master. He had the sole custody of her person and of her minor children. He could punish her "with a stick no bigger than his thumb," and she could not complain against him. . . . The common law of the State held man and wife to be one person, but that person was the husband. He could by will deprive her of every part of his property, and also of what had been her own before marriage. He was the owner of all her real estate and her earnings. The wife could make no contract and no will, nor, without her husband's consent, dispose of the legal interest of her real estate . . . . She did not own a rag of her clothing. She had no personal rights and could hardly call her soul her own. Her husband could steal her children, rob her of her clothing, neglect to support the family; she had no legal redress. If a wife earned money by her labor, the husband could claim the pay as his share of the proceeds.

—Elizabeth Cady Stanton on the situation of women in Boston, 1850

Woman Before Christ

In the year 586 BC, King Nebuchadnezzar of Babylon destroyed Jerusalem and carried away most of the Jews of the better class to his great city on the Euphrates. Let us imagine the dark-eyed maid Rebecca or the portly matron Susannah blinking in the light of the brilliant metropolis and then inquiring what the position of woman was.

We know well what the position of woman was in Judea. It is pithily put in Leviticus 7:1–5. This book had, in the year 586, not yet been forged, it is true, but it clearly gives an old law:

> And the Lord spake unto Moses, saying, Speak unto the children of Israel, saying, if a woman have conceived seed, and borne a man child; then she shall be *unclean seven days;* according to the days of the separation for her infirmity shall she be unclean. And on the eighth day the flesh of his foreskin shall be circumcised. And she shall then continue in the blood of her purifying *three and thirty days;* she shall touch no hallowed thing, nor come into the sanctuary, until the days of her purifying be fulfilled. But if she bear a maid child, then she shall be unclean *two weeks*, as in her separation; and she shall continue in the blood of her purifying *threescore and six days.* (emphasis added)

It's ironic to describe this bit of primitive tribal barbarism and superstition as a special revelation from the Most High! It just expresses woman's position under this "foregleam of Christianity."

The female was an inferior creature. She never had a lover or chose a husband. Her parents handed her over to a youth who became her very despotic lord and master. She was "unclean" about ten times in twenty years, as a rule, to say nothing of shorter periods. She had no property, no personality. Her husband could divorce her when he willed; she could not divorce him when she willed. Her husband could take a second wife or a concubine or dally with painted ladies. Rebecca had to disguise herself as a prostitute if she wanted a change (Genesis 38:14). And when she had fulfilled the whole Law, she was peppered with spiteful aphorisms (Proverbs, Ecclesiasticus, etc.) about her malice and odiousness.

Rebecca would not find this inspired code in Babylon. She would see the women living under the code of King Hammurabi, which the old monarch refused to ascribe to any god. And, as laws are very solid documents, let us quote at once a few clauses about woman's position, to contrast with the Jewish law:

127. If a man has pointed the finger against a priestess or the wife of another man unjustifiably, that man shall be thrown before the judge, and his brow shall be branded.

134. If a man has been taken prisoner, and there is no food in his house, and his wife enters the house of another; then that woman bears no blame.

137. If a man has set his face to divorce a concubine who has borne him children, or a wife who has presented him with children, then he shall give back to that woman her dowry, and he shall give her the usufruct of field, garden, and property, and she shall bring up her children.

138. If a man divorce his spouse who has not borne him children, he shall give to her all the silver of the bride-price, and restore to her the dowry which she brought from the house of her father.

139. If there was no bride-price, he shall give her one Mina of silver for the divorce.

142. If a woman hate her husband, and says, "Thou shalt not possess me," the reason for her dislike shall be inquired into. If she is careful and has no fault, but her husband takes himself away and neglects her; then that woman is not to blame. She shall take her dowry and go back to her father's house.

171b. The spouse shall take her dowry, and the settlement which her husband made her and wrote in a tablet for her and she shall dwell in the domicile of her husband. While she lives she shall enjoy it; she may not sell it for silver, but after her it is her children's.

Not bad for the year 2100 BC is it? In fact, immeasurably superior to the Christian law under which Christian women were living in England and New England four thousand years afterward and far better than the Jewish law of 500 BC.

Yet this is the oldest law of Babylon. Rebecca would, in short, find women as free and respected in Babylon in 586 BC as they are in Boston today. I show in another book how the deciphering of the literature of ancient Babylon has completely discredited those picturesque ideas of the vice of the great city which are still used to give purple patches to sermons. So far were the Babylonians from enjoying a remarkable looseness in sexual relations that they incurred sentence of death by adultery. We will hope that their practice was not as savage as their law. And there was not one law for the man and one for the woman (as in Christendom). The man and woman were bound together and thrown into the Euphrates. A man was burned alive for rape. A mother and son were burned alive for incest. A man was drowned for intercourse with his daughter-in-law. No woman was forced to prostitute herself at the temple, and there was probably no temple of that kind in Babylon.

In other words, if we were to return tomorrow to the "morals of ancient Babylon," as preachers somberly announce that we may if their income is cut off, a woman would find herself protected from man's "lust" by a series of drastic laws which no section of Christendom ever knew!

Woman was, at any rate, quite free in ancient Babylonia. Her rights were splendidly protected by law. She held property as legally as man did. She was not an inferior creature; she had no periods of uncleanness. She did not miss the Christian Mary, because Ishtar was one of the greatest deities of Babylonia and Assyria, and, at least in later Babylon, was an ethical deity. Woman had, of course, no vote, as there were no votes for either sex. In a word, she was in every respect the equal of man, free to own and control her own property and therefore be independent, able to divorce an unworthy or even merely neglectful husband at any time, protected against any encroachments upon her rights by other women. That is what Rebecca, coming from the female slavery of Judea, would find in benighted Babylon.

And woman was just as free, equal, independent, and respected in ancient Egypt. Every single authority on ancient Egypt will tell you that. Flinders Petrie even observes that in the home the husband was merely "a sort of boarder, a visitor, who had to keep up the establishment." Maspero, another of the chief authorities, puts it that the husband was "a privileged guest": that the many tomb inscriptions we have show that the wife was "the beloved of her husband and the mistress of the house." There was no "stick as thick as a man's thumb" in the corner, no exploitation or bullying, no appropriation of her earnings or property. In the *Maxims of Ptah-Hotep*, a middle-class treatise [written] four thousand years ago or more, it is said: "She will be doubly attached if the chain is sweet to her." Of course there was a chain, a contract of marriage; but it was mutual. "Make glad her heart during the time that

thou hast," the counsel to the husband ran; and even in case of mis-
conduct he was urged: "Be kind to her for a season, send her not away,
let her have food to eat."

Polygamy was permitted in Egypt, but a wife could, and did, stipu-
late in her marriage contract that there should be none. It is one of the
"higher religions," Mohammedanism (in this respect borrowing from
Judaism), which has brought degradation upon the woman of Egypt.
For the four thousand years of life of the old pagan civilization, she
was the equal of man in all respects. She could not only bring an action
on her own account in court, but she could plead. She could practice
medicine. She had a great career as priestess; and the female deity Isis
was one of the most famous and revered, and in later times one of the
most ethical, in the pantheon. The Christian Madonna and child is
based most particularly upon the popular Egyptian representation of
Isis and Horus. Mary is an understudy of Isis and Ishtar.

As in Babylonia, there was no political opportunity for either sex,
since the form of government was a despotic monarchy, so that woman
had no special injustice here. In the palace she was treated as an equal,
and there were queens who made great names in Egyptian history.
It was most probably Queen Tu, the mother of Amen-Hotep IV, who
brought about the religious revolution which substituted the worship
of one God for the polytheism of the Egyptian temples.

The beginning of civilization is dated by different authorities at
various periods between 3000 and 4000 BC. This means that the stretch
of time during which Egypt and Babylon were the chief representatives
of civilization is far greater than the whole of subsequent history; and
during all that time woman was free, independent, and the equal of
man. She was "treated with justice and respect."

The only other civilizations were those of the Cretans, the Hittites,
and the Chinese. The Cretan is the most interesting, since it began as
early as the great kingdoms of Egypt and Mesopotamia. We have not
yet discovered the key to the Cretan language, and our knowledge is
therefore imperfect; but if there is one point on which the authorities
are agreed and upon which they feel justified in expressing an opinion,
it is the position of woman. The fact that Crete had no male deity but
only the Mother Earth goddess would dispose us to expect to find
woman in an excellent position. That sex cannot be held inferior which
is the sex of the deity.

But we have ample indications of the fact. The frescoes on the walls of the Knossos palace plainly show that there was no oriental confinement of women. They are depicted enjoying themselves on the terrace of the great palace just as ladies do on the terrace of the modern mansion. The impression of every student of Cretan remains is that women probably had in the Cretan civilization an even better position than they had in Egypt and Babylonia.

[Here] we are concerned with that particular evolution of the human race into which Christianity entered as an influence. Looking back, in the light of what I have said, upon that evolution, and taking the position of woman as a test of civilization, we should have to divide the whole into two eras, the era of light and justice and the era of darkness and injustice; and it is an elementary historical truth to say that the era of light is the period before Christ and the era of darkness the time which we proudly call the *Christian Era*.

It is also an elementary and uncontroverted historical truth that the recovery of woman, the removal of her wrongs, did not begin until the Christian domination of the world was profoundly shaken and reduced; it made progress in proportion as the churches grew weaker; it received no assistance whatever from Christianity; and it was brought to a triumphant issue only when the majority of men in the cities of the world had thrown off their allegiance to Christianity. These are statements of fact, not rhetoric. I have shown this for the period before Christ, and later chapters will establish the rest. And it would hardly be possible to frame a more deadly reply than these facts give to the claim that Christianity has been "woman's best friend."

There is only one qualification to be made in this general statement. Egypt and Babylon did not bring the story of woman's equality down to the beginning of the Christian Era; and the influence of Christianity, on the other hand, did not begin until about the end of the fourth century. This leaves a period of eight or nine centuries between what I have called the era of light and the era of darkness. That period is filled with the stories of Greece and Rome, and we have next to see whether it may not have been these which inaugurated the degradation of woman, and whether the Church did not simply inherit an unjust social order for which it was not responsible. The further question, what the effect of the destruction of the Roman civilization by the northern barbarians was likely to be, will be considered in a later chapter.

The Greek and Roman Woman

Let us say at once that in the Greek and Roman civilizations woman had not the position of equality and freedom which she had had in Egypt, Mesopotamia, and, apparently, Crete.

The earlier attitude of the Greeks toward woman does not concern us much. She was in a position of dependence and inequality but certainly not of degradation. Polygamy was abandoned before the historical period opened, and another change of which we have some trace improved the lot of the wife. Originally it had been the custom, as in many savage and barbaric tribes, for the wooer to make a present to the girl's father. Very early this was changed into a gift from her father, so that she was no longer a chattel, an article to be bargained for and bought.

In the earliest Greek literature, in fact, woman already has a position of respect, if not honor. Some noble types of wives are described in the Homeric poems, and the great tragedians of the earlier part of the brilliant career of Athens have given the world some of the finest types of womanhood in all literature: not scheming assassins like Judith, not bloodless and loveless automata like the Christian saints and ascetics, but normal women bearing their part in life bravely and honorably and sweetly.

When the full light of history falls upon the Greek community we find woman in a position that certainly would not accord with modern standards. A special and secluded part of the home was set apart for the women, and while their excursions from the home were restricted, the men had full liberty. Athens and most of the Greek city-states were democracies, yet woman had no part whatever in the political life. Her place was the home.

Girls, it is true, had a life of comparative freedom and, one feels that they would say, happiness. They had excellent athletic training, music, games, and graceful dancing. The old idea that a woman was a man's property to be carefully guarded from a defilement that lowered her value persisted; but there was no note of contempt, no insinuation, as in Judea, that she was unclean and useful only as a breeder of men. She was the companion of man; but it was understood that politics and war were not her concern. She was excluded from public life.

Quite early in Greek life, however, a movement began for the removal of whatever wrongs and disabilities she had. The *Medea* of the great tragedian Euripides is one of the most poignant presentments of the case for woman that was ever given to the world. Its exaggeration is so great, yet so sincerely and profoundly felt, that no woman genius could have penned a more formidable complaint. Already, also, the Greeks had the poetry of Sappho, a brilliant practical demonstration of woman's independence. The historian Herodotus also shows, Mahaffy says, a "fair and gentle attitude toward women."

In fact, in the best days of Athenian prosperity there was a "women's movement" akin to that of modern times.

It seems, as we should expect, to have been connected with the famous Aspasta, one of the most brilliant and most respected ladies of antiquity, a friend of the leading writers and statesmen of Athens. The comedian Aristophanes ridiculed the movement, but the philosopher Plato defended it, as, apparently, Socrates had done before him. We may, in fact, infer that this "women's rights" movement of 2,200 years ago had very solid support amongst the educated men of Athens, and it was clearly of sufficient importance for the greatest of the comedians to devote two plays to it, the *Lysistrate* and the *Ecclesiazusae* (a word which might almost be translated "suffragettes"). In the latter play Aristophanes ironically describes the women of Athens donning male dress, taking over the work of making laws, and reforming the "man-made" state.

Thus, the fight which agitated England and America in the last part of the nineteenth and early part of the twentieth century really began and reached important proportions in Athens in the fourth century before Christ! It was the mass of the people who ridiculed the movement, as modern crowds ridiculed the suffragettes. Educated men realized that, although it was unquestionably part of the ideal of a Greek gentleman to see that his wife was happy, the position of woman was unjust. Plato eloquently pleaded that woman had, though in a less developed form, the same faculties as man and ought to have the same education. Her supposed unfitness for political life he caustically ridiculed. Epicurus, who closes the long line of Greek thinkers, had no interest in politics. He urged both men and women to avoid the corrupt and turbulent life of politics and cultivate a sober tranquility. Within the limits of his own ideal, however, he welcomed men and women on equal terms.

Thus, Greece, to which religious writers appeal as an example of the antagonism of the most brilliant of the pagan civilizations to woman, proves to be exactly the contrary. For three or four thousand years, in Crete, Egypt, and Mesopotamia, woman had been free and respected. Then for a few centuries we find her in Greece, not degraded or vilely used, for nearly every great Greek writer treats her with respect, but certainly in a position of dependence and inferiority. But at the very dawn of the Golden Age of Athens, a movement for her emancipation begins, and it has the support of all the best elements of Greek life.

Unfortunately, Athens was ruined before the movement could reach a successful issue. Yet its ideals continued. The chief Greek writer about the time of Christ, Plutarch, maintained that woman was mentally and morally equal to man and ought to have, as Plato had said, the same education. He denied that the moral law should be interpreted more liberally in the case of man than of woman. And the last glimpse that we have in history of Greek culture before it is entirely lost in a Christianized and barbarized world is a picture of the philosopher Hypatia taking a leading part in the life of the great city of Alexandria, and by her culture and personality rising high above all her contemporaries.

The murder of Hypatia by a Christian mob is a fitting allegory of the murder of the new hope of women by the new religion. That may seem a harsh sentence, but even the broad historical facts must give the modern Christian woman ground for reflection. A movement for the emancipation of woman from grievances far lighter than those of a century ago began in Greece nearly 2,300 years ago. It gathered force and was endorsed by the most influential Greek writers. But it completely disappeared when Christianity became the religion of Europe, and it did not reappear until skepticism about Christianity spread through the civilized world.

We shall see that the prejudice which this broad fact creates against the new religion is fully confirmed by a study of Christian teaching. First, however, we must carefully consider the position of woman in the Roman civilization with which Christianity came into actual contact.

It is usual in religious literature to divide Roman history into two parts: a first part, until a century or two before the birth of Christ, in which woman was very virtuous but a slave, and a later part, in which she was free but very wicked.

This generalization is as false as most of the other "historical" statements upon which the supposed service to the race of the new religion is based. The women of the Roman Republic (in its earlier centuries) were assuredly very chaste and virtuous. The names of some of them rank with the names of Christian saints. But just as the chastity of the saint is a kind of commercial venture, the price of a colossal reward in heaven, so the virtue of the early Roman maid or matron may be attributed to fear of the lash or the knife. The women were the property of the men. They ranked with the children. The law did not enter a Roman's house. He had power of life and death over his wife, his children, and his slaves. Small wonder that the wife and daughters were very "virtuous."

Yet even here woman was far better treated than she was in Judea. One of the Roman historians, Valerius Maximus, makes the almost incredible claim that there was no divorce in the Roman Republic for 520 years after its foundation! The Jewish civilization—the real, not the legendary, civilization of the Hebrews—was practically a contemporary of the Roman, and a record of woman's experience in the two would be an instructive document. Roman women were not confined in special quarters of the house, were not forbidden to go out to dine or to the theater, and had not separate places in the temple. They were treated with the greatest respect at home and abroad.

Moreover, the tyranny of the older Roman custom broke down long before the time of Christ. Greece had been civilized only a few centuries—not 1,500 years, like Christian Europe—when it started a movement for the emancipation of woman. Rome, similarly, was civilized only some three or four centuries when its women began a formidable movement for emancipation and admission to political life.

In the second century before Christ scenes curiously like those of the suffrage struggle of modern times were witnessed in Rome. Crowds of women obstructed the way of the reactionary senator and loudly demanded their rights. And I may add that their greatest opponent, Cato the Elder, the personification of the old Roman discipline, is nevertheless reported to have said: "A man who beats his wife or his children lays impious hands on that which is most holy and most sacred in the world." As to property, Roman women had already, in 215 BC, become so wealthy that a law—a special war measure—was passed restricting their property.

The suffrage, or a share in political life, was not won in Rome, because long before the birth of Christ the men themselves lost or surrendered their political power. The Republic became an Empire. There were still municipal elections, and, as "election addresses" which were found in the ruins of the buried city of Pompeii informed us, women took an active part in these. In the provinces, the inscriptions show, women sometimes held high municipal offices. At Rome there were "women's clubs" (*conventus matronarum*) where the affairs of the city and the state were keenly discussed. A Roman woman could hold property just as well as a man and was often very rich and independent. Men, in fact, grumbled (as in ancient Egypt) that their wives charged an excessive interest on the money they lent their husbands!

Not only the later and more liberal ideas of the Greek philosophers but the humanitarian precepts of the Stoic ethic had entered into the blood of Rome and softened the harshness of its old discipline. "The old law," says the famous jurist Sir Henry Maine, "had fallen into complete discredit and was verging on extinction." The end of the first century and greater part of the second century of the Christian Era were a well-recognized "Stoic Period" at Rome, and the emperors, a splendid series of monarchs, allowed the Stoic lawyers to infuse their humanitarian ideals into the law concerning woman and the slave. Education was, as we shall see, organized on a most generous basis, and philanthropy covered Italy with orphanages and homes for the aged and ailing. "Anyone who knows the inscriptions," says Sir Samuel Dill, "may be inclined to doubt whether private benefactions under the Antonines were less frequent and generous than in our own day." (Samuel Dill, *Roman Society from Nero to Aurelius* [London: Macmillan and Co., 1925], 234).

We will return to this later. But this "great Stoic doctrine of the brotherhood and equality of men," as Sir Samuel Dill calls it, completed the work of the emancipation of woman from the tyranny of the old institutions. Sir Henry Maine, perhaps the highest authority on Roman law, says of Gaius, one of the famous Stoic lawyers of the time:

> The great jurisconsult himself scouts the popular apology offered for it [the old law] in the moral inferiority of the female sex, and a considerable part of his volume is taken up with descriptions of the numerous expedients, some of them displaying extraordinary ingenuity which the Roman lawyers had devised for enabling women to defeat the ancient rules. Led by their theory of

> Natural Law the jurisconsults had evidently at this time assumed
> the equality of the sexes as a principle of their code of equity.
> —Henry Maine, *Ancient Law* (New York: Henry Holt and Company,
> 1906), 154

Woman had, in short, just been freed from the grievances which older Greek and Roman tradition had laid on her at the time when the Christian Church was spreading through the Roman world. By the end of the second century she was, socially and legally, as free as the modern woman; and she remained free to the end of the Empire. When the influence of Christianity began in the fourth century, paganism had recovered from its temporary injustice to woman. Throughout the range of Roman law, which means throughout civilization at the time, there was no degradation or subjection of woman. Yet fifteen centuries of degradation and subjection followed.

Could there be a more ironic comment on the preacher's eloquent and constant plea that Christianity brought into the world the doctrine of the brotherhood of men? It was precisely the great Stoic doctrine of the brotherhood and equality of men (as the Protestant historian calls it) which had emancipated woman. It was the new Christian doctrine of the *inequality* of the sexes which degraded her. The Christian scholars who claim that at least the new religion taught men a "reverence" for woman are almost completely ignorant of the facts. They rely only on the usual rhetoric about the vices of the pagans and the virtues of the Christians.

All this rhetoric is based upon the most scandalously loose quotation of particular instances. Even the best Christian writers ask us to blush at the crimes of Nero or Elogabalus, and never mention that during three-fourths of the Empire its rulers were good men. They say dark and vague things about the vices of Messalina and Faustine (which are grossly exaggerated), and they never tell that there were ten good pagan empresses for every bad one. They quote St. Jerome about the virtue of his score of Christian pupils, and they entirely ignore his assurance, in the same letters, that the Christian world generally was vicious and corrupt.

There was no such general contrast of pagan vice and Christian virtue; and the notion that at the adoption of Christianity the world passed from an era of vice to one of virtue, from a period in which woman was the toy of "brutal lusts" to a period in which she was respected because of her Christian virtues, is, as we shall see, one of the most fantastic and unjustifiable beliefs that zeal ever engendered.

The Effect of Christianity

Let me at once oppose to this frothy rhetoric, this fanciful construction of history by men who will not take the trouble to study the facts, the sober and deliberate testimony of a great lawyer, based upon the solid foundation of the actual tenor of the law.

I have quoted Sir Henry Maine's recognition of the position of justice and freedom won for women by the Stoic lawyers. "Christianity," he says (p. 156), "tended somewhat from the very first to narrow this remarkable liberty"; and "the latest Roman law, so far as it is touched by the Constitutions of the Christian Emperors, bears some marks of a reaction against the liberal doctrines of the great Antonine jurisconsults."

I try always to let my reader know what the best-informed religious writer or scholar would at each step say to my arguments and facts. For the mass of popular Christian literature, I have too much disdain to answer it. It is appallingly untruthful; and, unfortunately, it is just from this literature that preachers and the great bulk of the faithful derive their ideas. Yet even the more scholarly Christian writer is apt to betray an inaccuracy of knowledge and a straining of the evidence which deprive his conclusions of value and entitle them to little or no respect. Here he would remind me that the new liberty of the Roman women was won by weakening the institution of marriage, and that Christianity strengthened marriage and so fortified and uplifted the position of woman.

It is true that the freedom and the right to own property of the Roman women were won by an attack upon the old form of marriage (*confarreatio*). This ancient ceremony conferred upon the husband his despotic power over the wife, and no enlightened generation would preserve it. But Roman law and religion were, as they always are, conservative, and the ceremony was evaded rather than replaced. Looser forms of marriage were introduced. They were, however, recognized in law, and were as valid as a modern marriage. All that the Christian writer can mean, if he knows the facts, is that divorce was comparatively easy and frequent, and that the Church now came forward with the doctrine that the union of man and wife was a holy thing, a sacrament, an indissoluble association. Sir Henry Maine has this in mind chiefly when he speaks of the "reaction" caused by the Church.

And the distinguished Christian lawyer calls the change, in so far as there was any change—there was very little in the fourth century— a "reaction" not an "advance," because he knows well that it tended to restrict the rights of women without in the least securing for them greater respect.

Sir Henry Maine was no theologian. In point of fact, marriage was not a sacrament to the Christians of the fourth century. An ascetic priest here and there might publish the speculations of his dreamy hours about "sacraments," the Christian leaders generally might pour their disdain upon the flesh and its joys, but the great mass of the Roman people, even after their conversion to Christianity, regarded marriage and divorce as civic and human affairs and did not listen to the clergy. The Church did not obtain control of marriage until the eleventh century. Until that time the clergy themselves were commonly married, and the laity had almost as much liberty of divorce as the pagans had had. I have written a special work on this subject, *The Influence of the Church on Marriage and Divorce* (London: Watts & Co., 1916) and carefully studied every phase of the transition.

The only meaning, therefore, that one can read into this common claim that the Church won respect for woman is that the religious writer supposes that the Church induced women to be more chaste and thus earn the respect of men.

This, as I amply show in other books, is a double untruth. It is a repetition of the threadbare legend of pagan vice and the discredited legend of Christian virtue. I have, I trust, amply shown that the charge against the Romans rests on vague and unsatisfactory grounds. I will merely give here one or two authoritative opinions. Dr. Ludwig Friedlander is one of the highest authorities on the morals of the Romans. He was a Christian and a Puritan, yet in his classical *Darstellungen aus der Sittengeschichte Romo*, he says:

> There is nothing to show that in imperial Rome shamelessness ever went so far as it did in parts about the middle of the last [eighteenth] century.

Whatever the proportion of virtue and vice in this pagan world was, there is not one single bit of evidence of improvement when

Christianity triumphed. There is, on the contrary, ample evidence of actual deterioration. On the one hand, the pagan ideas so far remained that we find St. Augustine himself permitting a man to take a concubine into his home if his wife proves barren *(De Bono Conjugali,* XV— Augustine, of course, refuses a corresponding right to the wife of an impotent man); we find Paulinus of Pella boasting that he guarded "the treasure of chastity" and was "content with the enjoyment of the female slave of the house" *(Eucharisticos,* line 166); we find the First Synod of Toledo under the archbishop laying it down in its seventeenth canon that a man who has a mistress but not a wife also may be admitted to communion. On the other hand, every contemporary Christian authority assures us that from the fifth century onward the morals of Europe suffered a swift, appalling deterioration.

Thus, the main plea of the writers who try feverishly to show that the new religion improved the position of woman is demonstrably false. Neither men nor women became more virtuous. We should, in fact, find any such service to woman reflected in the legislation of the Christian Emperors, and, as Sir Henry Maine says, every innovation in their laws tends to restrict woman's rights and liberties. I have in my work on marriage and divorce collected and analyzed such innovations as there were, and they constitute, as Professor J. Muirhead says *(Historical Introduction to the Private Law of Rome,* [London, A & C Black, Ltd., 1916], 356), "a miserable chapter in the history of law."

After the severe verdicts of two such experts it is needless to dilate on the various changes of the law by Christian emperors. Constantine restricted the grounds of divorce to three, but his successors allowed his law to lapse. Theodosius, the brutal and superstitious soldier who, as I describe in *The Triumph of Christianity* (*Little Blue Book,* no. 1110, [Girard, KS: E. Haldeman-Julius Company, 1926]), bludgeoned the rival religions out of existence, applied the ideas of the clergy; and certainly no modern American will see anything but the most cruel harshness to woman in his enactments. He forbade the marriage of cousins; he imposed severe disabilities on any woman who married again after the death of her husband; he forbade a woman to remarry for five years, and then restricted her right to inherit if she had divorced her husband for a very grave cause; and, if she divorced her husband for one of the lighter causes recognized in the law, she lost her dowry, she was strictly forbidden to marry again, and she was liable to a sentence of banishment. The husband, I may add, was, in the same circumstances, permitted to marry again!

This is the new "fairness" to woman, as seen in the legislation of the most priest-ridden of all the Roman emperors. His laws were so brutal that his successors were compelled to repeal them, yet each in turn attempted some new interference with the right of divorce. In practice, during the whole of this period the people followed the old Roman custom of divorce by mutual consent or for any of a dozen serious reasons. In the west the ruin of the Empire reduced everything to a chaotic condition. Synods of bishops repeatedly attempted to impose indissoluble marriage, but they failed. The prayer books of the Anglo-Saxon Church as late as the ninth century recognize several grounds of divorce, and it was the same in France.

In the east, where Roman law continued in force, it was remodeled by Justinian, and six or seven specific grounds of divorce were admitted. It was not until the eleventh and twelfth centuries that the clergy got control of marriage: with what awful results you may read elsewhere.

In point of historical fact, therefore, we find little more than the failure of the Church during seven or eight centuries to achieve what it proposed to do: to set up indissoluble marriage. Its real influence was apart from legislation, and we must ask how far its teaching was calculated to improve or did in fact improve the position of woman.

The crop of feminist literature which the rapid progress of the women's movement brought into existence a few years ago contains more than one work of a Christian character. As I will tell in the last chapter, this task had been for decades left almost entirely to non-Christian writers and agitators. In their books—the works of Mrs. Cady Stanton, Mrs. Gage, A. Bebel, etc.—the grievance against the Christian religion was very frankly, if not very vehemently, expressed. Neither Jesus nor any follower of Jesus before the nineteenth century had helped woman; and even in three-quarters of the nineteenth century, in spite of the flagrant degradation of woman's position, very few Christians—and the world was still overwhelmingly Christian—and no clergymen would open their lips. In spite of them the movement throve, and then Christian accounts of the evolution of woman's position and her debt to Christianity began to appear.

I have one of the most orthodox of these before me, and I seek with some interest the page in which the lady describes woman's indebtedness to Christ. It is amusing. Jesus, it seems, insisted that man and woman were equal, because he described them as "twain in one flesh." I should have thought that Christian delicacy would prevent any lady from trying to read a mystic meaning into that very broad remark.

Next, we are reminded that after his resurrection Jesus appeared first to a woman: which is one of the least historical statements in the latest parts of the Gospels. Thirdly, and this completes the case, we are reminded that Jesus saved an adulterous woman from death and bade her "go, and sin no more," which is one of the most flagrantly apocryphal stories in the New Testament; for any such interference with the course of Jewish law would have been drastically resented. The writer discreetly omits to notice that in text after text Jesus speaks harshly of his mother, and in no single text has he a tender or affectionate word for her.

Jesus, the dreamer who saw the end of the world close at hand, the ascetic who saw in the sweet charm of woman only a snare of the devil, never troubled for a moment about woman's position. Not one word of his was calculated to affect it. The Gospel writers, it is true, attribute to him certain words about divorce (not mentioned by the Protestant lady to whom I have just referred) which have had a profound influence on woman; but these words are given in two contradictory versions, and this plainly shows that they are merely the interpolated opinions of two rival schools in the early Church. The Jews themselves in the time of Jesus were divided as to whether divorce should be permitted for adultery or entirely forbidden. The quarrel passed on into Christianity. What the devout Christian ought to ask himself is why Jesus, who (he believes) foresaw all things, permitted this ambiguity on a fundamental issue to be given to the world in his name?

On this, however, we will not linger. Protestant America in practice rejects both versions of the words of Jesus. The indissolubility of marriage, or even the restriction of divorce to adultery, is so patent a cause of immorality that whether Jesus said it or not, the good Protestant demands a more proper and humane and less disastrous rule of life.

I have said that Jesus never gave a thought to the question of woman's position, and it is usual to blame Paul for the profoundly mischievous spirit which got into the early Church. But Paul, here at least, does not differ from Jesus. It is the asceticism or puritanism of both that led to the degradation of woman. She is the chief implement used by the devil in his scheme of temptation. The gentle touch of her hair upon your cheek, the ripe lips that draw you, the tender pressure of her breasts, the white rounded limbs and finely molded neck—the devil smiles cynically in every one of her allurements, and the ascetic sees only that imaginary smile.

What Paul adds to this general asceticism is a reminder of the childish, yet fateful, references to woman in Genesis. She was made out of man and for man; and she at once dragged him down from a state of semi-divine bliss to all the horrors and labors of earthly life. Man, says Paul, not only may, but must, remove his hat in church, "for as much as he is the image and glory of God"; but woman must veil her head, for she was made from man and for man, not in the image and likeness of God (I Cor. 11:5–10). There is no need to quote Paul's other depreciations of woman; though, if there is anything in Christian tradition, he found the devoted attentions of maids like Thecla very comforting amidst his labors.

We have only to glance over the works of the Fathers to see how these two ideas—the ascetic scorn of woman's sweetest ministry in life, her love, and the belief in her inferiority on account of her origin and her primary share in the fall—brought into the life of Europe the element which caused and explains the degradation of woman. Scores of these quotations from the Fathers are given in feminist histories, while even the Christian historians can find no pleasant or tender sentiment to put in the scale against these profoundly mischievous aphorisms.

Already in the second century, Justin pronounced that "a man who marries a divorced woman is guilty of adultery," and Athenagoras sneered at a second marriage as "a decorous sort of adultery." St. Basil said: "The wife will take back her husband when he returns to her from his whoring, but the husband will cast forth a sinful wife from his house." Origen said that "bigamists are saved in the name of Christ, but are no means crowned by him."

Contempt of marriage is associated with contempt of woman. St. Gregory of Nazianzum, supposed to be the most tender and emotionally the least flinty, I should say, of the Fathers, gives counsel in poetic form to the maid Olympias. She is not to study philosophy, for "Woman's philosophy is to obey the laws of marriage." She must take no interest in public affairs or attend even innocent entertainments. She may marry, but "blessed is the man who soils not the divine image within him with the filth of concupiscence." And at last it comes: "Fierce is the dragon, cunning the asp: but woman has the malice of both."

Tertullian is almost as eloquent. For Christian women he writes a book, *De Cultu Feminarum* [On the Adornment of Women]. "What do they want with finery?" he asks.

> If, my beloved sisters, your faith were as firm as its eternal reward, no one of you, after learning of the living God and her own condition as a woman, would dare to seek gay apparel, but would dress in rags and remain in dirt as a sorrowful and penitent Eve.

And a few lines later he hisses this fine Christian sentiment: "Thou art the devil's gate, the betrayer of the tree, the first deserter of the divine law." Marriage, even, he says, is "a sort of fornication."

The learned Clement of Alexandria said: "It brings shame to a woman even to reflect of what nature she is." Gregory the Wonder-Worker said: "You may find one chaste man among a thousand, but not a woman." St. Ambrose said: "It becomes not the modesty of a maid to choose a husband." Paulinus of Nola invented the phrase "weaker vessel" on the ground that the devil found woman easier to tempt.

St. Augustine said, in his *Commentary on Genesis* (XIX), that "man was made to rule, woman to obey"; and in a second *Commentary* he asks with portentous seriousness why woman was created at all and can find no decent answer. Possibly, he reflects, it was just part of the divine scheme to create a being of inferior personality so as to insure that the fall would take place!

His contemporary, St. Jerome, who was the spiritual director of the prettiest and wealthiest young ladies of the Roman Church, habitually scorned woman and all tender sentiment. Woman is "the root of all evil," and marriage is "good for those who are afraid to sleep alone at night." In one beautiful letter, which his lady pupils learned by heart, he says: "Though thy father cling to thee, and thy mother rend her garments and show thee the breasts thou hast sucked, thrust them aside with dry eyes to embrace the cross."

These were the sentiments which the great interpreters of the Christian message gave to the world. At first, it is obvious, the world at large took little or no notice of them. But to say, in the face of them, that the new religion uplifted woman and taught man a respect for her which the pagans had not known is worse than empty rhetoric. It is stupid.

It is very little use to remind us how the Church exalted Mary. She was not placed even so high as Isis and Cybele. But the main point is that the special treatment of Mary did not affect women generally. There was to be no second Mary. Woman was the devil's gate, the cause of the curse and of Christ's death, the weaker vessel, the worst occasion of sin and damnation, and so on, except in one special case which no other woman could imitate.

Nowhere else is Christian rhetoric quite so insincere. I have shown that from Paul to Augustine all the Christian leaders used contemptuous language about woman, and no language, either of Jesus or any distinguished follower of his can be quoted in the opposite sense. On the other hand, as we shall now see, the historical facts are as plain as facts can be. Woman was not uplifted, but she sank, when Europe became entirely and thoroughly Christian, to a position which she had not known throughout the whole history of civilization.

The Middle Ages and Woman

There is no need to attempt here to trace the gradual descent of woman. Her position at the beginning of the nineteenth century is enough. It was a legacy from the Middle Ages. Pagan Rome had made of her a personality. Christian Rome degraded her to a chattel, a dependent, a weaker vessel, a wholly inferior creature. From the fifth century onward she sank steadily, though differently in different countries.

In England women had a good deal of political influence—I mean women of the noble families—almost down to the Reformation, though the position of the mass of the women throughout the Middle Ages was vile. In most countries, the days of chivalry, which were plainly due to the old pagan spirit of the Teutons, maintained for a time the position of the aristocratic women. Incautious Catholic writers sometimes quote this age of chivalry as one of the proofs that their religion won respect for woman. All that they know about it, as a rule, is from Tennyson's puritanical version of the legendary King Arthur and his legendary knights. Chivalry was a glorification of lust, the lust of fighting and the lust of love. If a woman was pretty and aristocratic, she met very courtly deference. If she was aristocratic and not pretty, she had a worse time than the Greek matron had had. If she was pretty and not aristocratic—well, the adventures of Rebecca in Scott's *Ivanhoe*, which comes nearer to the historical truth than Tennyson's pretty *Idyls*, fairly illustrate her chances in life.

In short, this argument from chivalry is one more good illustration of the feebleness and carelessness of all religious arguments. As I said, a beautiful and noble woman had quite a good time. Knights fought for her "favors." You may or may not trace the influence of Jesus of Nazareth either in the fight—which was a real deadly combat—or in the tender reward of the victor, but it is more important to keep this clearly in mind: not one woman in tens of thousands during the age of chivalry got the least advantage from its amorousness. You pick out the baron's pretty wife or daughter and remind us of the knights bowing to the dust before her; and you say nothing whatever about the wives and daughters of the ten thousand serfs or yeomen, or even craftsmen and merchants. *Their* life could be hell. *They* were protected neither by law nor religion against the "lusts" of these very hot-blooded and masterful knights. And then you boast about the religion of the brotherhood and equality of men!

There has been a good deal of talk about the medieval *fits primae noctis:* the right of the lord to have the peasant bride in his own bed for the first night, or the first few nights, after the wedding. Someone discovered that there was such a right in medieval Europe, and for a time it figured as an important item in the indictment of the Christian Middle Ages. Now, religious writers say it has all been exploded. "Modern historians" find that there was no such right. The Church has been libeled, as usual.

There was no libel whatever. The *jus primae noctis* was for centuries, and over a large part of Europe, a recognized institution. Sometimes it was the bishop or abbot who had the right to the bride for a night—if his retainers reported her a virgin and attractive to the episcopal palate. As late as the sixteenth century we find the French peasantry rebelling against the odious custom. It was well-known in medieval England. It was not generally a formal law for the simple reason that barons and abbots did not dream, as a rule, of waiting until the peasant's daughter married. She was rarely a virgin when she did marry. Bede, the English clerical chronicler, tells us that in his time in England it was the custom for the lord to take to his harem any attractive peasant girl on his lands, then sell her when she became pregnant. There was hardly such a thing as chastity in Europe during the Middle Ages. A wench was a wench.

Does anybody imagine that a peasant or a smith would "go to court" in the Middle Ages when a soldier or a noble manhandled his daughter?

Mrs. Cady Stanton hardly exaggerates when she says that "mankind touched the lowest depths of degradation" in the medieval treatment of women. The brutality and grossness which the Church suffered to spread over Europe were bound to degrade woman when the strong arm of Roman law no longer protected her. Europe had undergone one of the most amazing transformations in history. Streams of barbaric Goths and Vandals had poured all over it. Their fertility seems to have been stupendous. They crossed into Africa and swamped the Roman province of North Africa as well as Spain. Law and justice and education disappeared. The barbaric chief became a feudal noble and was a law to himself. His women became as loose and vicious as any wealthy Roman woman who had ever lived. "Conjugal morals returned to brutality," says Legouve, the historian of female morality (*Histoire morale des femmes* [Paris: Librairie Académique Didier et Cie, 1869], 183).

No one questions that several centuries of moral chaos, of the densest ignorance and most unbridled license and violence, followed the Christianization of Europe. But how, I am asked, could one expect the Church to tame at once these myriads of hot-blooded barbarians from the north and the mixed population they bred everywhere in Europe? The answer is quite easy, as far as the treatment of woman is concerned. The pagan myths of these barbarians had persuaded them to treat woman with respect. If you hold that the Christian myth was even more favorable to women, how is it that it entirely failed where paganism had succeeded? The plain truth is that the old Teutonic religion had taught men that woman is a superior being, and Christianity taught exactly the opposite. One modern historian has gone so far as to say that the Goths and Vandals embraced Christianity because it taught the inferiority of woman! They now had a free run.

It is at all events clear that the teaching of the Fathers continued to be the belief of the bishops; that is to say, when they happened to be really religious, which was not often. It was precisely the best Christians, the men most eager to apply Christian doctrine to life, who damned woman. All through the period of chaotic transition from Roman civilization to the later civilization of Europe, we find gatherings of bishops depreciating women, like the Council of Auxerre, in 578, which said that women must not, like men, take the sacramental cup in their own hands, because they are "impure."

The decrees of these councils of bishops and of the popes make up what is called canon law or Church law. When Europe settled down again to a rudimentary sort of civilization, its law consisted of fragments of the old Roman law and the native laws of the barbarians with a good deal of canon law. The Church was all powerful. Abbots and bishops were dispensers of justice.

Now both the Roman and the barbaric laws bad been favorable to woman, yet the new law of Europe was grossly unjust to her. It was then that she was legally and socially degraded; that she lost control of her person and property, lost her legal personality, and lost all respect except that which a man pays to the woman whose caresses he desires. Sir Henry Maine and every other authority trace the degradation to the Church law. Maine says:

> No society which preserves any tincture of Christian institutions is likely to restore to married women the personal liberty conferred on them by the middle Roman law; but the proprietary disabilities of married females stand on quite a different basis from their personal incapacities, and it is by the tendency of their doctrines to keep alive and consolidate the former that the expositors of the Canon law have deeply injured civilization.

Sir Henry shows that the British law, which, through colonial days, was responsible for the state of things in Boston as late as 1850, owes all its enormities to Church law, and therefore to Christianity. And no one with the least authority on the subject questions this. One of the recent feminist historians who certainly does not write from an anti-clerical point of view, Mrs. Georgiana Hill, says:

> Although women appear to have had a wider field of activity than they afterwards enjoyed when social life became more complex, there was a counteracting influence which told against the development and free exercise of their energies. This was the influence of the Church. It was the policy of the Church to keep women in a subordinate position.
> —*Women in English Life,* [London: Richard Bentley & Sons, 1896], vii)

The "wider field of activity" in the Middle Ages means that all sorts of trades were open to women. Some, like brewing, were almost monopolized by them. As the population was kept almost stationary by war, famine, and disease, there was no sex rivalry in work. Women have always had liberty to work. Let us grant man that.

When Mrs. Hill and others remind us that women might become abbesses—a new trade opened by Christianity—one must again deplore the lack of sense of proportion. For every abbess who had a little power, there were tens of thousands of women whom the Church had degraded to the level of children or cattle. It is as if the world had discovered what Genesis really taught. "Male and female created he them," says the English Bible. But the Hebrew word for "female" is, literally, "A thing to be perforated." That was all woman had become. You may say that the Church provided an escape from all the brutality: the nunnery. Alas, most nunneries during the Middle Ages were totally corrupt. In any case, it is a rather curious service to the race to make a country desolate and then provide one or two quiet retreats amidst the desolation.

But it is needless to brood any longer over the period of woman's degradation. It was in every respect except art a foul period, a state of semi-barbarism; and, while the Church can be indicted only for permitting the hourly violence, the fearful cruelty, the sordid ignorance, the universal exploitation, the incredible filth and disease, and the almost equally incredible growth of prostitution and monastic hypocrisy, it has a direct and clearer responsibility for the injustice to woman.

The Clergy and the Modern Struggle

After about the year 500, "human life was suspended for a thousand years," says a brilliant French writer. Something like that certainly will be the unanimous verdict of historians when our scholars have shed the last trace of subservience to the clergy. At present, some of them have an affectation of showing that the Middle Ages were not quite so bad as the older historians had said. It is wrong, it appears, to call the early Middle Ages the Dark Ages, because, by diligent search, we can find a lamp in it here and there!

But we may see enough about the Middle Ages in other books. As far as our present subject, the degradation of woman, is concerned, no one is quite so foolish as to try to defend the Church. By the year 300

AD, woman was in a position of freedom and respect. She had enjoyed that position throughout nearly the whole four thousand years of civilization. After the year 500 AD—allowing two centuries for the application of the principles of the new religion—woman fell to a state of degradation which has no parallel in the history of any pagan nation. For more than a thousand years, during which Christianity absolutely dominated the life of man, she remained in that condition of degradation. That requires a good deal of explaining—if you are reluctant to admit the obvious fact that Christianity degraded woman.

And there is no room here for the familiar quibble that it was not Christianity but the men who professed it that injured woman. It was quite plainly the doctrine. It was the morbid puritanism about love and the legends of Genesis. The men who most drastically relegated woman to an inferior position were the men whom the Churches regarded as their religious heroes and oracles.

The true story of woman's recovery of the position she had held under paganism can be told in a few lines, and it is actually more significant and instructive when it is so told. From the fifth to the fifteenth century, from the death of Hypatia to the time of Petrarch at least, no one had a good word to say for woman. Not a scholar in Christendom, not a priest or writer, was inspired to make a syllable of protest against the disgraceful injustice of the system. It was the literary men of the Renaissance who began to raise woman—the woman of their class—to a position of equality; and the Renaissance was, notoriously, the rebirth of paganism and skepticism.

Then came the Reformation and what Catholics humorously call "the Christian Renaissance," or a half-hearted attempt to reform the morals of Rome under the lash of Protestantism. Europe became again intensely interested in religion. Many millions of people cut each other's throats in the name of religion. The civilization of Europe was put back a hundred years by the zeal for religion. And the attempt to emancipate woman was at once crushed.

Luther gave a shrewd and healthy blow at the Catholic glorification of virginity and all the hypocrisy caused by it—but he also said such things as: "No gown worse becomes a woman than the desire to be wise." To say that he robbed women (how many?) of opportunities by suppressing nunneries is fatuous; but he certainly provided no other opportunities for them. The "three Ks" (Kinder, Küche, Kirche—children, kitchen, church) were stereotyped as the ideal of the German woman.

The Reformation did nothing for women on the continent of Europe. In England, in the Elizabethan age, educated women (a tiny minority) had more freedom socially, though they lost their last hold on public life. But their new freedom was plainly due to the fact that in England the Reformation and the Renaissance occurred together. The Reformers, through a statute of Henry VIII, forbade "women and others of low condition" to read the Bible. The humanist's invited them to read.

But the historical facts are clear enough. Protestantism of a pure or puritanical type was as deadly to woman as Catholicism. What did she get from the Puritans of England or New England? From the Calvinists of Switzerland? From the Lutherans of Germany and Scandinavia? Nothing whatever. Protestant divines were as blind to the injustice of the system as Catholic divines were. The service of Protestantism was indirect; and I would stress that in this sense it was mighty. It smashed the tyranny of Rome and could not set up a lasting tyranny of its own. Yet to use a phrase of Emerson's in a different connection, "Luther would, if he had foreseen the revolt of the women, have cut off his right hand rather than nail his theses to the door of the cathedral."

This is the stark truth about the redemption of woman from all the injustices which Christianity had brought upon her. *Not one single Christian clergyman the world over raised a finger in the work until it had so far succeeded that the clergy had to save their faces by joining it.* No amount of pulpit rhetoric, no amount of strained apology from Christian feminist writers, can lessen the significance of that fact. And to it you must add another of equal significance. The men and women who started the revolt against the injustice and carried it to the stage of invincibility were non-Christian in the proportion of at least five to one.

Take the movement in America. Three of its greatest leaders, Mrs. Cady Stanton, Mrs. Gage, and Miss Susan B. Anthony, have described it minutely and conscientiously in their monumental *History of Woman Suffrage.* It began in 1820, when Frances Wright, a deist, a pupil of the British agnostic Robert Owen, invaded the [United] States. She was joined by the brilliant Ernestine L. Rose, a Polish Jewess who had cast off all theology; by Lucretia Mott, a Quaker whose views were regarded as "heresy" even in the Society of Friends; by Abby Kelly, another rationalistic Quaker; and by the sisters Grimke, also Quakers. I have shown in my *Biographical Dictionary of Distinguished Rationalists* that Mrs.

Cady Stanton, Mrs. Gage, and Miss Anthony, who led the fight in the next generation, were all agnostics. And for fifty years, as this detailed history shows, the clergy of America were the most deadly enemies of the movement, basing their opposition expressly upon the Bible.

I smiled when, in 1917, 1 was invited to speak for the movement in New York. It was then respectable. Parsons were available by the score. Few in the movement had ever heard of Fanny Wright or Abby Kelley or Ernestine Rose and the other splendid pioneers.

None knew of the time when pastoral letters had circulated amongst the American clergy calling their attention to "the dangers which at present seem to threaten the female character with widespread and permanent injury." That was all over. Preachers were now assuring them that Christianity was the best friend, the only friend, that woman had ever had!

It was the same everywhere. In Britain, the pioneers were Mary Wollstonecraft, Fanny Wright, George Eliot, Harriet Martineau—all rationalists—supported by Godwin, Robert Owen, Jeremy Bentham, G.J. Holyoake, and J.S. Mill—all agnostics or atheists. In Germany, the work was done by Max Stirner, Karl Marx, Büchner, Engels, Bebel, and Liebknecht—all atheists. In France, it was Sieyès and Condorcet—atheists—who first pleaded for the emancipation of woman, and George Sand, Michelet, Saint-Simon, and Fourier—all deep-dyed heretics—who raised the plea again in the nineteenth century. In Scandinavia, Ibsen and Bjørnsen and Ellen Key—all rationalists—led the protest.

Let the women of the world read their remarkable story once more, with open eyes.

CHAPTER VIII

Why Science Leaves Religion in the Dust

and

Twenty Reasons to Abandon Christianity

by Chaz Bufe

Why Science Leaves Religion in the Dust

Know-nothingism has become fashionable on the religious right. Many right-wing fundamentalists insist that assertions contained in an ancient mishmash of a book are every bit as valid as carefully arrived at, repeatedly tested scientific theories and conclusions.

In a striking bit of irony, some go even further and (unconsciously) mimic academic postmodernists, insisting that all "opinions" (including scientific conclusions) are equal. Thus, willful ignorance among the least educated mirrors willful ignorance among the most educated.

Given all this, it's good to remind ourselves of why facts matter and why science is superior to religious faith.

Failure to take facts into account has real-world consequences. To cite a trivial example, if you believe you're invulnerable because you believe you are, test your hypothesis by stepping in front of a truck. To cite a sadder, all too real example, science has established that the similarities between human beings vastly outweigh the differences, and that there's no basis for assertions that any race is superior to any other. So, are the opinions of racists just as valid as the scientific conclusion that the differences between racial groups are trivial?

To cite still another example of why facts matter, in the Middle Ages in Europe, with science at a standstill, many believed that disease and bad weather were caused by witchcraft. End result? Tens, perhaps hundreds, of thousands of "witches" were brutally murdered for "causing" storms and disease.

There are innumerable other examples demonstrating why facts matter. And, yes, you can't absolutely prove anything, but probabilities are so high in so many cases that it's reasonable to act as if the probability is 100 percent.

So, facts do matter. But why does science trump religion?

1. The scientific method is the only reliable way to arrive at the most probably correct explanation of almost *anything*. Scientists reach conclusions by formulating hypotheses, checking those hypotheses against observed phenomena, devising experiments to test the hypotheses, checking them for internal consistency, and checking to see if the hypotheses can generate accurate predictions. Then doing all this over and over again, with different scientists repeatedly testing the hypotheses ("theories" if they consistently pass all these tests over a prolonged period of time) through experiment, observation, and analysis. This is a bit different than pointing to a hoary book written by iron-age slaveholders and asserting, "This is a fact! It says so here!"

2. Science is self-correcting. Religion isn't. Science continually tests and refines hypotheses and theories to arrive at more accurate explanations. Religion doesn't.

A good example of this is provided by scientific exploration of racial differences between humans. In the nineteenth century, some scientists asserted that whites were superior to other races. By the middle of the twentieth century, other scientists had definitively debunked those assertions through observation, experiment, and analysis. (Yes, there are still a few racist scientists, but their assertions are knocked down almost as soon as they make them, and the vast majority of scientists now accept, in line with scientific research, that assertions of racial superiority or inferiority are baseless.)

The overt racism of the Book of Mormon slightly predates the racist assertions of some nineteenth-century scientists, with the Book

WHY SCIENCE LEAVES RELIGION IN THE DUST

of Mormon referring to Caucasians as "white and exceedingly fair and delightsome" (2 Nephi 5:20–21); and as late as 1935, Mormon prophet Joseph Fielding Smith asserted that "because of [Cain's] wickedness he became the father of an inferior race" (*The Way to Perfection* [Salt Lake City: Genealogical Society of Utah, 1931], 101).

Finally, in 1978, in response to widespread social condemnation (and undoubtedly a desire to increase the number of potential converts), then prophet Spencer W. Kimball announced a new "revelation" that the church should abandon its racial restrictions on the priesthood (but not the "revealed" racist passage in 2 Nephi, nor the racist statements of previous "prophets"). That's a bit different than the way science handled the matter, eh?

3. Science improves daily life. Religion doesn't. One clear example of this is in the field of medicine. Scientists discovered the microbial nature of disease. That discovery led to use of antiseptics and the later development of antibiotics, which have saved the lives of untold millions. In contrast, religion has led to no developments that improve daily life. (And please don't start talking about the power of prayer and the peace it supposedly brings—we're speaking here of demonstrable physical improvement.)

4. Science leads. Religion lags. A good example of this is our understanding of the universe beyond the earth. Early scientists (Copernicus, Galileo et al.) led the way to accurate description of the physical universe. At the same time, the Church was insisting that the sun revolves around the earth, and hauling scientists who dared to state the opposite before the Inquisition.

Another example is the scientific versus religious attitude toward women. Science has established that while there are obvious and not so obvious differences between men and women, their intellectual abilities are almost identical (with a few "end of the bell curve" differences in a few specific areas). In contrast, religion has insisted on the inferiority and consequent subordination of women from antiquity. To cite but two of a great many Bible verses denigrating women, "How then can man be justified with God? or how can he be clean that is born of a woman?" (Job 25:4) and "These [redeemed] are they which were not defiled with women" (Revelation 14:4).

Today, some religions have acknowledged reality and accept the equality of men and women. Others have dug in their heels and still insist upon female subordination, though most are now wary of openly stating that women are inferior. And it's safe to say that the more conservative the religion—that is, the more literally its members take their scriptures—the more likely they are to insist upon the inferiority and subjugation of women.

5. Finally, science opens doors and religion closes them, as Neil deGrasse Tyson famously remarked. Science not only leads to improvement in daily life but to broader intellectual horizons; it encourages people to think for themselves, to question everything; it leads to one question after another. Religion insists that all the answers are contained in ancient holy books, and that it's wrong, even dangerous, to question those answers—that you have an intellect, but you shouldn't use it. It's hard to conceive of anything more stultifying.

Twenty Reasons to Abandon Christianity

This essay looks at many of the reasons that Christianity is undesirable from both a personal and a social point of view. All of the matters discussed here have been dealt with elsewhere at greater length, but that's beside the point: the purpose of "Twenty Reasons to Abandon Christianity" is to list the most outstanding misery producing and socially destructive qualities of Christianity in one place. When considered in toto, they lead to an irresistible conclusion: that Christianity must be abandoned, for the sake of both personal happiness and social progress.

As regards the title, "abandon"—rather than "suppress" or "eliminate"—was chosen deliberately. Attempts to coercively suppress beliefs are not only ethically wrong, but in the long run they are often ineffective—as the resurgence of religion in the former Soviet Union demonstrates. If Christianity is ever to disappear, it will be because individual human beings wake up, abandon their destructive, repressive beliefs, and choose to be here now in the only life we have.

1. Christianity is based on fear. While today there are liberal clergy who preach a Gospel of love, they ignore the bulk of Christian teachings, not to mention the bulk of Christian history. Throughout almost its entire time on earth, the motor driving Christianity has been—in addition to the fear of death—fear of the devil and fear of hell. One can only imagine how potent these threats seemed prior to the rise of science and rational thinking, which have largely robbed these bogeys of their power to inspire terror. But even today, the existence of the devil and hell are cardinal doctrinal tenets of almost all Christian creeds, and many fundamentalist preachers still openly resort to terrorizing their followers with lurid, sadistic portraits of the suffering of nonbelievers after death. This is not an attempt to convince through logic and reason; it is not an attempt to appeal to the better nature of individuals; rather, it is an attempt to whip the flock into line through threats, through appeals to a base part of human nature—fear and cowardice.

2. Christianity preys on the innocent. If Christian fearmongering were directed solely at adults, it would be bad enough, but Christians routinely terrorize helpless children through grisly depictions of the endless horrors and suffering they'll be subjected to if they don't live obedient Christian lives. Christianity has darkened the early years of generation after generation of children, who have lived in terror of dying while in mortal sin and going to endless torment as a result. All of these children were trusting of adults, and they did not have the ability to analyze what they were being told; they were simply helpless victims, who, ironically, victimized following generations in the same manner that they themselves had been victimized. The nearly two thousand years of Christian terrorizing of children ranks as one of its greatest crimes. And it's one that continues to this day.

As an example of Christianity's cruel brainwashing of the innocent, consider this quotation from an officially approved, nineteenth-century Catholic "children's" book, *Tracts for Spiritual Reading*, by Rev. John Furniss, C.Ss.R.:

> Look into this little prison. In the middle of it there is a boy, a young man. He is silent; despair is on him. ... His eyes are burning like two burning coals. Two long flames come out of his ears. His breathing is difficult. Sometimes he opens his mouth and breath of blazing fire rolls out of it. But listen! There is a sound just like that of a kettle boiling. Is it really a kettle which is boiling? No;

then what is it? Hear what it is. The blood is boiling in the scald-ing veins of that boy. The brain is boiling and bubbling in his head. The marrow is boiling in his bones. Ask him why he is thus tormented. His answer is that when he was alive, his blood boiled to do very wicked things.

There are many similar passages in this book. Commenting on it, William Meagher, vicar-general of Dublin, states in his approbation:

I have carefully read over this Little Volume for Children and have found nothing whatever in it contrary to the doctrines of the Holy Faith; but on the contrary, a great deal to charm, instruct and edify the youthful classes for whose benefit it has been written.

3. Christianity is based on dishonesty. The Christian appeal to fear, to cowardice, is an admission that the evidence supporting Christian beliefs is far from compelling. If the evidence were such that Christianity's truth was immediately apparent to anyone who consid-ered it, Christians—including those who wrote the Gospels—would feel no need to resort to the cheap tactic of using threats to inspire "belief" (more accurately, "lip service"). That the Christian clergy have been more than willing to accept such lip service (plus the money and obedience that go with it) in place of genuine belief is an additional indictment of the basic dishonesty of Christianity.

How deep dishonesty runs in Christianity can be gauged by one of the most popular Christian arguments for belief in God: Pascal's wager. This "wager" holds that it's safer to "believe" in God (as if belief were *volitional!*) than not to believe, because God might exist, and if it does, it will save "believers" and condemn nonbelievers to hell after death. This is an appeal to pure cowardice. It has absolutely nothing to do with the search for truth. Instead, it's an appeal to abandon honesty and intellectual integrity and to pretend that lip service is the same thing as belief. If the patriarchal God of Christianity really exists, one wonders how it would judge the cowards and hypocrites who advance and bow to this particularly craven "wager."

4. Christianity is extremely egocentric. The deep egocentrism of Christianity is intimately tied to its reliance on fear. In addition to the fears of the devil and hell, Christianity plays on another of humankind's most basic fears: death, the dissolution of the individual ego. Perhaps Christianity's strongest appeal is its promise of eternal life. While there is absolutely no evidence to support this claim, most people are so terrified of death that they cling to this treacly promise insisting, like frightened children, that it must be true. Nietzsche put the matter well: *"salvation of the soul*—in plain words, the world revolves around *me*." It's difficult to see anything spiritual in this desperate grasping at straws, this desperate grasping at the illusion of personal immortality.

Another manifestation of the extreme egotism of Christianity is the belief that God is intimately concerned with picayune aspects of and directly intervenes in the lives of individuals. If God, the creator and controller of the universe, is vitally concerned with your sex life, you must be pretty damned important. Many Christians take this particular form of egotism much further and actually imagine that God has a plan for them, or that God directly talks to, directs, or even does favors for them.[1] If one ignored the frequent and glaring contradictions in this supposed divine guidance and the dead bodies sometimes left in its wake, one could almost believe that the individuals making such claims are guided by God. But one can't ignore the contradictions in and the oftentimes horrible results of following such "divine guidance." As "Agent Mulder" put it (perhaps paraphrasing Thomas Szasz) in a 1998 *X-Files* episode, "When you talk to God it's prayer, but when God talks to you it's schizophrenia. . . . God may have his reasons, but he sure seems to employ a lot of psychotics to carry out his job orders."

In less extreme cases, the insistence that one is receiving divine guidance or special treatment from God is usually the attempt of those who feel worthless—or helpless, adrift in an uncaring world—to feel important or cared for. This less sinister form of egotism is commonly

---

1   A friend who read the first draft of this essay notes: "My moronic sister-in-law once told me that God found her parking spots near the front door at Walmart! Years later, when she developed a brain tumor, I concluded that God must have gotten tired of finding parking places for her and gave her the tumor so that she could get handicapped plates." As Nietzsche put it in *The Anti-Christ*: "That little hypocrites and half-crazed people dare to imagine that on their account the laws of nature are constantly broken—such an enhancement of every kind of selfishness to infinity, to impudence, cannot be branded with sufficient contempt. And yet Christianity owes its triumph to this pitiable flattery of personal vanity."

found in the expressions of disaster survivors that "God must have had a reason for saving me" (in contrast to their less worthy of life fellow disaster victims, whom God—who controls all things—killed). Again, it's very difficult to see anything spiritual in such egocentricity.

5. Christianity breeds arrogance, a chosen-people mentality. It's only natural that those who believe (or playact at believing) that they have a direct line to the Almighty would feel superior to others. This is so obvious that it needs little elaboration. A brief look at religious terminology confirms it. Christians have often called themselves "God's people," "the chosen people," "the elect," "the righteous," "the saved," etc., while nonbelievers have been labeled "heathens," "infidels," and "atheistic Communists" (as if atheism and Communism are intimately connected). This sets up a two-tiered division of humanity, in which "God's people" feel superior to those who are not "God's people." That many competing religions with contradictory beliefs make the same claim seems not to matter at all to the members of the various sects that claim to be the only carriers of "the true faith." The carnage that results when two competing sects of "God's people" collide—as in Ireland, the Indian subcontinent, and Palestine—would be quite amusing but for the suffering it causes to the innocent.

6. Christianity breeds authoritarianism. Given that Christians claim to have the one true faith, to have a book that is the Word of God, and (in many cases) to receive guidance directly from God, they feel little or no compunction about using force and coercion to enforce "God's Will" (which they, of course, interpret and understand). Given that they believe or pretend that they're receiving orders from the Almighty, who would cast them into hell should they disobey, it's little wonder that they feel no reluctance, and, in fact, are eager, to intrude into the most personal aspects of the lives of nonbelievers.

This is most obvious today in the area of sex, with Christians attempting to deny women the right to abortion and—ignoring overwhelming scientific evidence—to mandate ineffective abstinence-only sex "education" in the public schools. It's also obvious in other areas of education, with Christians attempting to force biology teachers to teach their creation myth (but not those of Hindus, Native Americans et al.) in place of (or as being equally valid as) the very well-established theory of evolution. But the authoritarian tendencies of Christianity reach much further than this.

Up until well into the twentieth century, in the United States and other Christian countries (notably Ireland), Christian churches pressured governments into passing laws forbidding the sale and distribution of birth control devices, and they also managed to enact laws forbidding even the description of birth control devices. This assault on free speech was part and parcel of Christianity's shameful history of attempting to suppress "indecent" and "subversive" materials (and to throw their producers in jail or burn them alive). This anti–free speech stance of Christianity dates back centuries, with the cases of Galileo Galilei and Giordano Bruno (who was burnt alive) being good illustrations of it. Perhaps the most colorful example of this intrusive Christian tendency toward censorship is the Catholic Church's Index of Prohibited Books, which dates from the sixteenth century and which was abandoned only in the latter part of the twentieth century—not because the Church recognized it as a crime against human freedom, but because it could no longer be enforced (not that it was ever systematically enforced—that was too big a job even for the Inquisition).

Christian authoritarianism extends, however, far beyond attempts to suppress free speech; it extends even to attempts to suppress freedom of belief. In the fifteenth century, under Ferdinand and Isabella, at about the time of Columbus's discovery of the New World, Spain's Jews were ordered either to convert to Christianity or to flee the country; about half chose exile, while those who remained, the "conversos," were favorite targets of the Inquisition. A few years later, Spain's Muslims were forced to make a similar choice.

This Christian hatred of freedom of belief—and of individual freedom in general—extends to this day. Up until the late nineteenth century in England, atheists who had the temerity to openly advocate their beliefs were jailed. Even today in many parts of the United States laws still exist that forbid atheists from serving on juries or from holding public office. And it's no mystery what the driving force is behind laws against victimless "crimes" such as nudity, sodomy, fornication, cohabitation, and prostitution.

If your nonintrusive beliefs or actions are not in accord with Christian "morality," you can bet that Christians will feel completely justified—not to mention righteous—in poking their noses, often in the form of state police agencies, into your private life.

7. Christianity is cruel. Throughout its history, cruelty—both to self and others—has been one of the most prominent features of Christianity. From its very start, Christianity, with its bleak view of life, its emphasis upon sexual sin, and its almost impossible to meet demands for sexual "purity," encouraged guilt, penance, and self-torture. Today, this self-torture is primarily psychological, in the form of guilt arising from following (or denying and, thus, obsessing over) one's natural sexual desires. In earlier centuries, it was often physical. W.E.H. Lecky, in *The History of European Morals*, relates:

> For about two centuries, the hideous maceration of the body was regarded as the highest proof of excellence. . . . The cleanliness of the body was regarded as a pollution of the soul, and the saints who were most admired had become one hideous mass of clotted filth. . . . But of all the evidences of the loathsome excesses to which this spirit was carried, the life of St. Simeon Stylites is probably the most remarkable. . . . He had bound a rope around him so that it became embedded in his flesh, which putrefied around it. A horrible stench, intolerable to the bystanders, exhaled from his body, and worms dropped from him whenever he moved, and they filled his bed. . . . For a whole year, we are told, St. Simeon stood upon one leg, the other being covered with hideous ulcers, while his biographer [St. Anthony] was commissioned to stand by his side, to pick up the worms that fell from his body, and to replace them in the sores, the saint saying to the worms, "Eat what God has given you." From every quarter pilgrims of every degree thronged to do him homage. A crowd of prelates followed him to the grave. A brilliant star is said to have shone miraculously over his pillar; the general voice of mankind pronounced him to be the highest model of a Christian saint; and several other anchorites [Christian hermits] imitated or emulated his penances.

Given that the Bible nowhere condemns torture and sometimes prescribes shockingly cruel penalties (such as stoning and burning alive) and that Christians so wholeheartedly approved of self-torture, it's not surprising that they thought little of inflicting appallingly cruel treatment upon others. At the height of Christianity's power and influence, hundreds of thousands of "witches" were brutally tortured and burned alive under the auspices of ecclesiastical witch finders, and the Inquisition visited similarly cruel treatment upon those accused of heresy. Henry Charles Lea, in *A History of the Inquisition of the Middle Ages*, reports:

> Two hundred wretches crowded the filthy gaol and it was requisite to forbid the rest of the Conversos [Jews intimidated into converting to Christianity] from leaving the city [Jaen, Spain] without a license. With Diego's assistance [Diego de Algeciras, a petty criminal and kept perjurer] and the free use of torture, on both accused and witnesses, it was not difficult to obtain whatever evidence was desired. The notary of the tribunal, Antonio de Barcena, was especially successful in this. On one occasion, he locked a young girl of fifteen in a room, stripped her naked and scourged her until she consented to bear testimony against her mother. A prisoner was carried in a chair to the auto da fé with his feet burnt to the bone; he and his wife were burnt alive.... The cells in which the unfortunates were confined in heavy chains were narrow, dark, humid, filthy and overrun with vermin, while their sequestrated property was squandered by the officials, so that they nearly starved in prison while their helpless children starved outside.

While the torture and murder of heretics and "witches" is now largely a thing of the past, Christians can still be remarkably cruel. One current example is provided by the Westboro Baptist Church of Topeka, Kansas. Its members picket the funerals of victims of AIDS and gay bashings, brandishing signs reading, "God Hates Fags," "AIDS Cures Fags," and "Thank God for AIDS." The founder and long-time pastor of this church reportedly once sent a "condolence" card to the bereaved mother of an AIDS victim, reading "Another Dead Fag."[2] Christians are

---

2 The Westboro Baptist Church directly addresses the question of its hatefulness and cruelty on its website (www.godhatesfags.com): "Why do you preach hate? Because the Bible preaches hate. For every one verse about God's mercy, love, compassion, etc., there are two verses about His vengeance, hatred, wrath, etc." Unfortunately, they're right about this.

also at the forefront of those advocating vicious, life destroying penalties for those who commit victimless "crimes," as well as being at the forefront of those who support the death penalty and those who want to make prison conditions even more barbaric than they are now.

But this should not be surprising coming from Christians, members of a religion that teaches that eternal torture is not only justified, but that the "saved" will enjoy seeing the torture of others. As St. Thomas Aquinas put it:

> In order that the happiness of the saints may be more delightful and that they may give to God more copious thanks for it, they are permitted perfectly to behold the sufferings of the damned.... The saints will rejoice in the punishment of the damned.

Thus, the vision of heaven of Christianity's greatest theologian is a vision of the sadistic enjoyment of endless torture.

8. Christianity is anti-intellectual, anti-scientific. For over a millennium Christianity arrested the development of science and scientific thinking. In Christendom, from the time of Augustine until the Renaissance, systematic investigation of the natural world was restricted to theological investigation—the interpretation of biblical passages, the gleaning of clues from the lives of the saints, etc.; there was no direct observation and interpretation of natural processes, because that was considered a useless pursuit, as all knowledge resided in scripture. The results of this are well-known: scientific knowledge advanced hardly an inch in the over one thousand years from the rise of Orthodox Christianity in the fourth century to the 1500s, and the populace was mired in the deepest squalor and ignorance, living in dire fear of the supernatural—believing in paranormal explanations for the most ordinary natural events. This ignorance had tragic results: it made the populace more than ready to accept witchcraft as an explanation for everything from illness to thunderstorms, and tens, maybe hundreds, of thousands of women paid for that ignorance with their lives. One of the commonest charges against witches was that they had raised hailstorms or other weather disturbances to cause misfortune to their neighbors. In an era when supernatural explanations were readily accepted, such charges held weight—and countless innocent people died horrible deaths as a result. Another result was that the fearful populace remained very dependent upon Christianity and its clerical wise men for protection against the supernatural evils which they believed surrounded and constantly menaced them. For men and women of the Middle Ages, the walls veritably crawled with demons and witches, and their only protection from those evils was the Church.

When scientific investigation into the natural world resumed in the Renaissance—after a thousand-year-plus hiatus—organized Christianity did everything it could to stamp it out. The cases of Copernicus and Galileo are particularly relevant here, because when the Catholic Church banned the Copernican theory (that the earth revolves around the sun) and banned Galileo from teaching it, it did not consider the evidence for that theory: it was enough that it contradicted scripture. Given that the Copernican theory directly contradicted the Word of God, the Catholic hierarchy reasoned that it must be false. Protestants shared this view. John Calvin rhetorically asked, "Who will venture to place the authority of Copernicus above that of the Holy Spirit?"

More recently, the Catholic Church and the more liberal Protestant congregations have realized that fighting against science is a losing battle, and they've taken to claiming that there is no contradiction between science and religion. This is disingenuous at best. As long as Christian sects continue to claim as fact—without offering a shred of evidence beyond the anecdotal—that physically impossible events ("miracles") occurred or are still occurring, the conflict between science and religion will remain. That many churchmen and many scientists seem content to let this conflict lie doesn't mean that it doesn't exist.

Today, however, the conflict between religion and science is largely being played out in the area of public school biology education, with Christian fundamentalists demanding that their creation myth be taught in place of (or along with) the theory of evolution in the public schools. Their tactics rely heavily on public misunderstanding of science. They nitpick the fossil record for its gaps (hardly surprising given that we inhabit a geologically and meteorologically very active planet), while offering absurd interpretations of their own which we're supposed to accept at face value—such as that dinosaur fossils were placed in the earth by Satan to confuse humankind, or that Noah took baby dinosaurs on the ark.

They also attempt to take advantage of public ignorance of the nature of scientific theories. In popular use, "theory" is employed as a synonym for "hypothesis," "conjecture," or even "wild guess," that is, it signifies an idea with no special merit or backing. The use of the term in science is quite different. There, "theory" refers to a testable, well-developed, logically consistent explanation of a phenomenon and an explanation that is consistent with observed facts and that has withstood repeated testing. This is very different from a wild guess. But fundamentalists deliberately confuse the two uses of the word in an attempt to make their religious myth appear as valid as a well-supported scientific theory.

They also attempt to confuse the issue by claiming that those non-specialists who accept the theory of evolution have no more reason to do so than they have in accepting their religious creation myth, or even that those who accept evolution do so on "faith." Again, this is more than a bit dishonest.

Thanks to scientific investigation, human knowledge has advanced to the point where no one can know more than a tiny fraction of the whole. Even the most knowledgeable scientists often know little beyond their specialty areas. But because of the structure of science, they (and everyone else) can feel reasonably secure in accepting the theories developed by scientists in other disciplines as the best possible current explanations of the areas of nature those disciplines cover.

They (and we) can feel secure doing this because of the structure of science and, more particularly, because of the scientific method. That method basically consists of gathering as much information about a phenomenon (both in nature and in the laboratory) as possible, then developing explanations for it (hypotheses), and then testing the hypotheses to see how well they explain the observed facts and whether or not any of those observed facts are inconsistent with the hypotheses. Those hypotheses that are inconsistent with observed facts are discarded or modified, while those that are consistent are retained, and those that survive repeated testing are often labeled "theories," as in "the theory of relativity," "the theory of gravity," and "the theory of evolution."

This is the reason that nonspecialists are justified in accepting scientific theories outside their disciplines as the best current explanations of observed phenomena: those who developed the theories were following standard scientific practice and reasoning—and if they deviate from that, other scientists will quickly call them to task.

No matter how much fundamentalists might protest to the contrary, there is a world of difference between "faith" in scientific theories produced using the scientific method and subject to near continual testing and scrutiny and faith in the entirely unsupported myths recorded three thousand years ago by slaveholding goat herders.

Nearly five hundred years ago Martin Luther, in his *Table Talk*, stated: "Reason is the greatest enemy that faith has." The opposite is also true.

9. Christianity has a morbid, unhealthy preoccupation with sex. For centuries, Christianity has had an exceptionally unhealthy fixation on sex, to the exclusion of almost everything else (except power, money, and the infliction of cruelty). This stems from the numerous "thou shalt nots" relating to sex in the Bible. That the Ten Commandments contain a commandment forbidding the coveting of one's neighbor's wife but do not even mention slavery, torture, or cruelty—which were abundantly common in the time the Commandments were written—speaks volumes about their writer's preoccupation with sex (and women as property).

Today, judging from the pronouncements of many Christian leaders, one would think that "morality" consists solely of what one does in one's bedroom. The Catholic Church is the prime example here, with its moral pronouncements rarely going beyond the matters of birth control and abortion, and with its moral emphasis seemingly entirely on those matters.

Also note that the official Catholic view of sex—that it's for the purpose of procreation only—reduces human sexual relations to those of brood animals. For more than a century the Catholic Church has also been the driving force behind efforts to prohibit access to birth control devices and information—to everyone, not just Catholics.

The Catholic Church, however, is far from alone in its sick obsession with sex. The current Christian hate campaign against homosexuals is another prominent manifestation of this perverse preoccupation. Even at this writing, condemnation of "sodomites" from church pulpits is still very, very common—with Christian clergymen wringing their hands as they piously proclaim that their words of hate have nothing to do with gay bashings and the murder of gays.

10. Christianity produces sexual misery. In addition to the misery produced by authoritarian Christian intrusions into the sex lives of non-Christians, Christianity produces great misery among its own adherents through its insistence that sex, except the very narrow variety it sanctions, is evil, against God's law. Christianity proscribes sex between unmarried people, sex outside of marriage, homosexual relations, bestiality,[3] and even "impure" sexual thoughts. Indulging in such things can and will, in the conventional Christian view, lead straight to hell.

Given that human beings are by nature highly sexual beings, and that their urges very often do not fit into the only officially sanctioned Christian form of sexuality (monogamous, heterosexual marriage), it's inevitable that those who attempt to follow Christian "morality" in this area are often miserable, as their strongest urges run smack-dab into the wall of religious belief. This is inevitable in Christian adolescents and unmarried young people in that the only "pure" way for them to behave is celibately—in the strict Christian view, even masturbation is prohibited. Philip Roth has well described the dilemma of the religiously/sexually repressed young in *Portnoy's Complaint* as "being torn between desires that are repugnant to my conscience and a conscience repugnant to my desires." Thus, the years of adolescence and young adulthood for many Christians are poisoned by "sinful" urges, unfulfilled longings, and intense guilt (after the urges become too much to bear and are acted upon).

Even after Christian young people receive a license from Church and state to have sex, they often discover that the sexual release promised by marriage is not all that it's cracked up to be. One gathers that in marriages between those who have followed Christian rules up until marriage—that is, no sex at all—sexual ineptitude and lack of fulfillment are all too common. Even when Christian married people do have good sexual relations, the problems do not end. Sexual attractions ebb and flow, and new attractions inevitably arise. In conventional

3   The repeated mention of this sin in medieval ecclesiastical writings leads one to wonder how widespread this practice was among the Christian faithful, including the Christian clergy. One eighth-century penitential (list of sins and punishments) quoted in Arthur West Hadden, *Councils and Ecclesiastical Documents*, 3 vols. (Oxford: Clarendon Press, 1869–1878) states: "If a cleric has fornicated with a quadruped let him do penance for, if he is a simple cleric, two years, if a deacon, three years, if a priest, seven years, if a bishop, ten years." Similar lists of sins and penalties can be found in many other types of penance.

Christian relationships, one is not allowed to act on these new attractions. One is often not even permitted to admit that such attractions exist. As Sten Linnander puts it, "with traditional [Christian] morality, you have to choose between being unfaithful to yourself or to another."

The dilemma is even worse for gay teens and young people, in that Christianity *never* offers them release from their unrequited urges. They are simply condemned to lifelong celibacy. If they indulge their natural desires, they become "sodomites" subject not only to earthly persecution under religion-inspired laws but to being roasted alive forever in the pit. Given the internalized homophobia Christian teachings inspire, not to mention the very real discrimination gay people face, it's not surprising that a great many homosexually oriented Christians choose to live a lie. In most cases, this leads to lifelong personal torture and gross unfairness to their spouses, who deserve someone who desires them sexually, but it can have even more tragic results.

A prime example is Marshall Applewhite, "John Do," the guru of the Heaven's Gate religious cult. Applewhite grew up in the South in a repressive Christian fundamentalist family. Horrified by his homosexual urges, he began to think of sexuality itself as evil, and eventually underwent castration to curb his sexual urges.[4] Several of his followers took his anti-sexual teachings to heart and likewise underwent castration before, at Applewhite's direction, killing themselves.

11. Christianity has an exceedingly narrow, legalistic view of morality.
Christianity not only reduces, for all practical purposes, the question of morality to that of sexual behavior, but by listing its prohibitions, it encourages an "everything not prohibited is permitted" mentality. So, for instance, medieval inquisitors tortured their victims, while at the same time they went to lengths to avoid spilling the blood of those they tortured, though they thought nothing of burning them alive. Another very relevant example is that until the latter part of

---

4   Given his religious background, and that his cult mixed Christianity with UFO beliefs, Applewhite was quite probably aware of the divine approbation of self-castration in Matthew 19:12: "For there are some eunuchs, which were so born from their mother's womb: and there are some eunuchs, which were made eunuchs of men: and there be eunuchs, which have made themselves eunuchs for the kingdom of heaven's sake. He that is able to receive it, let him receive it."

the nineteenth-century Christians engaged in the slave trade, and Christian preachers defended it, citing biblical passages from the pulpit.

Today, with the exception of a relatively few liberal churchgoers, Christians ignore the very real evils plaguing our society—poverty; homelessness; hunger; militarism; a grossly unfair distribution of wealth and income; ecological despoliation; corporate greed; over-population; sexism; racism; homophobia; misogyny; freedom denying, invasive laws against victimless "crimes"; an inadequate educational system; etc., etc.—unless they're actively working to *worsen* those evils in the name of Christian "morality" or "family values."

12. Christianity encourages acceptance of real evils while focusing on imaginary evils. Organized Christianity is a skillful apologist for the status quo and all the evils that go along with it. It diverts attention from real problems by focusing attention on sexual issues, and when confronted with social evils like poverty glibly dismisses them with platitudes such as: "The poor ye have always with you." When confronted with the problems of militarism and war, most Christians shrug and say, "That's human nature. It's always been that way, and it always will be." One suspects that two hundred years ago their forebears would have said exactly the same thing about slavery. This regressive, conservative tendency of Christianity has been present from its very start. The Bible is quite explicit in its instructions to accept the status quo: "Let every soul be subject unto the higher powers. For there is no power but of God: the powers that be are ordained of God. Whosoever therefore resisteth the power, resisteth the ordinance of God; and they that resist shall receive to themselves damnation" (Romans 13:1–2).

13. Christianity devalues the natural world. In addition to its morbid preoccupation with sex, Christianity creates social myopia through its emphasis on the supposed afterlife, encouraging Christians not to be concerned with "the things of this world" (except, of course, their neighbors' sexual practices). In the conventional Christian view, life in this "vale of tears" is not important—what matters is preparing for the next life. (Of course, it follows from this that the "vale of tears" itself is quite unimportant—it's merely the backdrop to the testing of the faithful.)

The Christian belief in the unimportance of happiness and well-being in this world is well illustrated by a statement by St. Alphonsus:

> It would be a great advantage to suffer during all our lives all the torments of the martyrs in exchange for one moment of heaven. Sufferings in this world are a sign that God loves us and intends to save us.

This focus on the afterlife often leads to a distinct lack of concern for the natural world, and sometimes to outright anti-ecological attitudes. Ronald Reagan's fundamentalist secretary of the interior, James Watt, went so far as to actively encourage the strip mining and clear-cutting of the American West, reasoning that ecological damage didn't matter because the "rapture" was at hand.

14. Christianity models hierarchical, authoritarian organization. Christianity is perhaps the ultimate top-down enterprise. In its simplest form, it consists of God on top, its "servants," the clergy next down, and the great unwashed masses at the bottom, with those above issuing, in turn, thou shalts and thou shalt nots backed by the threat of eternal damnation. But a great many Christian sects go far beyond this, having several layers of management and bureaucracy. Catholicism is perhaps the most extreme example of this, with its laity, monks, nuns, priests, monsignors, bishops, archbishops, vicars general, cardinals, and popes, all giving and taking orders in an almost military manner.

This type of organization cannot but accustom those in its sway—especially those who have been indoctrinated and attending its ceremonies since birth—into accepting hierarchical, authoritarian organization as the natural if not the only form of organization. Those who find such organization natural will see nothing wrong with hierarchical, authoritarian organization in other forms, be they corporations, with their multiple layers of brownnosing management, or governments, with their judges, legislators, presidents, and politburos. The indoctrination by example that Christianity provides in the area of organization is almost surely a powerful influence against social change, a powerful influence against freer, more egalitarian forms of organization.

15. Christianity sanctions slavery. In the eighteenth and nineteenth centuries, the African slave trade was almost entirely conducted by

Christians. (Today, it's almost entirely conducted by Muslims.) Christian slavers transported their victims to the New World in slave ships with names such as "Mercy" and "Jesus," where they were bought by other Christians, both Catholic and Protestant. Organized Christianity was not silent on this horror: it actively encouraged it and engaged in it. From the friars who enslaved Native Americans in the Southwest and Mexico to the Protestant preachers who defended slavery from the pulpit in Virginia, the Carolinas, and Georgia, the record of Christianity as regards slavery is quite shameful.

(Those who point out that many abolitionists were Christians should remember that the abolitionists were a very small group and were well hated by most of their fellow Christians.)

The Christians who defended slavery and engaged in it were amply supported by the Bible, in which slavery is accepted as a given, as simply a part of the social landscape. There are numerous biblical passages that implicitly or explicitly endorse slavery, such as Exodus 21:20–21: "And if a man smite his servant, or his maid with a rod, and he die under his hand; he shall be surely punished. Notwithstanding, if he continue a day or two, he shall not be punished: for he is his money." Other passages that support slavery include Ephesians 6:5, Colossians 3:22, Titus 2:9–10, Exodus 21:2–6, Leviticus 25:44–46, 1 Peter 2:18, and 1 Timothy 6:1. Christian slave owners in colonial America and the preachers who provided them with "moral" guidance were well acquainted with these passages.

16. Christianity is misogynistic. Misogyny is fundamental to the basic writings of Christianity. In passage after passage, women are commanded to accept an inferior role and to be ashamed of themselves for the simple fact that they are women. Misogynistic biblical passages are so common that it's difficult to know which to cite. From the New Testament we find "Wives, submit yourselves unto your own husbands, as unto the Lord. For the husband is the head of the wife, even as Christ is the head of the church" (Ephesians 5:22–23) and "These [redeemed] are they which were not defiled with women" (Revelation 14:4); and from the Old Testament we find "How then can man be justified with God? Or how can he be clean that is born of a woman?" (Job 25:4). Other relevant New Testament passages include Colossians 3:18; 1 Peter 3:7; 1 Corinthians 11:3, 11:9, and 14:34; and 1 Timothy 2:11–12 and 5:5–6. Other

Old Testament passages include Numbers 5:20–22 and Leviticus 12:2–5 and 15:17–33.

Later Christian writers extended the misogynistic themes in the Bible with a vengeance. Tertullian, one of the Early Church Fathers, wrote:

> In pain shall you bring forth children, woman, and you shall turn to your husband and he shall rule over you. And do you not know that you are Eve? God's sentence hangs still over all your sex and His punishment weighs down upon you. You are the devil's gateway; you are she who first violated the forbidden tree and broke the law of God. It was you who coaxed your way around him whom the devil had not the force to attack. With what ease you shattered that image of God: Man! Because of the death you merited, even the Son of God had to die. . . . Woman, you are the gate to hell.

One can find similarly misogynistic—though sometimes less venomous—statements in the writings of many other Church Fathers and theologians, including St. Ambrose, St. Anthony, Thomas Aquinas, St. Augustine, St. John Chrysostom, St. Gregory of Nazianzum, and St. Jerome.

This misogynistic bias in Christianity's basic texts has long been translated into misogyny in practice. Throughout almost the entire time that Christianity had Europe and America in its lock grip, women were treated as chattel—they had essentially no political rights, and their right to own property was severely restricted. Perhaps the clearest illustration of the status of women in the ages when Christianity was at its most powerful is the prevalence of wife beating. This degrading, disgusting practice was very common throughout Christendom well into the nineteenth century, and under English Common Law husbands who beat their wives were specifically exempted from prosecution. (While wife beating is still common in Christian lands, at least in some countries abusers are sometimes prosecuted.)

At about the same time that English Common Law (with its wife beating exemption) was being formulated and codified, Christians all across Europe were engaging in a half millennium–long orgy of torture and murder of "witches"—at the direct behest and under the direction of the highest Church authorities. The watchword of the time was

Exodus 22:18: "Thou shalt not suffer a witch to live," and at the very minimum tens of thousands of women were brutally murdered as a result of this divine injunction and the papal bulls amplifying it (e.g., *Spondit Pariter*, by John XXII, and *Summis Desiderantes*, by Innocent VIII). Andrew Dickson White notes:

> On the 7th of December, 1484, Pope Innocent VIII sent forth the bull *Summis Desiderantes*. Of all documents ever issued from Rome, imperial or papal, this has doubtless, first and last, cost the greatest shedding of innocent blood. Yet no document was ever more clearly dictated by conscience. Inspired by the scriptural command, "Thou shalt not suffer a witch to live," Pope Innocent exhorted the clergy of Germany to leave no means untried to detect sorcerers. . . . [W]itchfinding inquisitors were authorized by the Pope to scour Europe, especially Germany, and a manual was prepared for their use [by the Dominicans Heinrich Krämer and Jacob Sprenger]—"The Witch Hammer," *Malleus Maleficarum*. . . . With the application of torture to thousands of women, in accordance with the precepts laid down in the *Malleus*, it was not difficult to extract masses of proof. . . . The poor creatures writhing on the rack, held in horror by those who had been nearest and dearest to them, anxious only for death to relieve their sufferings, confessed to anything and everything that would satisfy the inquisitors and judges. . . . Under the doctrine of "excepted cases," there was no limit to torture for persons accused of heresy or witchcraft.

Given this bloody, hateful history, it's not surprising that women have always held very subservient positions in Christian Churches. In fact, there appear to have been no female clergy in any Christian Church prior to the twentieth century (with the exception of those who posed as men), and even today a great many Christian sects, most notably the Catholic Church, continue to resist ordaining female clergy. While a few liberal Protestant Churches have ordained women in recent years, it's difficult to see this as a great step forward for women; it's easier to see it as analogous to the Ku Klux Klan's appointing a few token blacks as Klaxons.

As for the improvements in the status of women over the last two centuries, the Christian Churches either did nothing to support them or actively opposed them. This is most obvious as regards women's control over their own bodies. Organized Christianity has opposed this from the start, and as late as the 1960s the Catholic Church was still putting its energies into the imposition of laws prohibiting access to contraceptives. Having lost that battle, Christianity has more recently put its energies into attempts to outlaw the right of women to abortion.

Many of those leading the fight for women's rights have had no illusions about the misogynistic nature of Christianity. These women included Mary Wollstonecraft, Victoria Woodhull, Elizabeth Cady Stanton, and Margaret Sanger, whose slogan "No God, No Masters" remains relevant to this day.

17. Christianity is homophobic. Christianity from its beginnings has been markedly homophobic. The biblical basis for this homophobia lies in Genesis, in the story of Sodom, and in Leviticus. Leviticus 18:22 reads: "Thou shalt not lie with mankind, as with womankind: it is abomination," and Leviticus 20:13 reads: "If a man lie with mankind as he lieth with a woman, both of them have committed an abomination: they shall surely be put to death; their blood shall be upon them."

This sounds remarkably harsh, yet Leviticus proscribes a great many other things, declares many of them "abominations," and prescribes the death penalty for several other acts, some of which are shockingly picayune. Leviticus 17:10–13 prohibits the eating of blood sausage; Leviticus 11:6–7 prohibits the eating of "unclean" hares and swine; Leviticus 11:10 declares shellfish "abominations"; Leviticus 20:9 prescribes the death penalty for cursing one's father or mother; Leviticus 20:10 prescribes the death penalty for adultery; Leviticus 20:14 prescribes the penalty of being burnt alive for having a three-way with one's wife and mother-in-law; and Leviticus 20:15 declares, "And if a man lie with a beast, he shall surely be put to death: and ye shall slay the beast" (which seems rather unfair to the poor beast). (One suspects that American Christians have never attempted to pass laws enforcing Leviticus 20:15, because if passed and enforced such laws would decimate both the Bible Belt and the cattle industry.)

Curiously, given the multitude of prohibitions in Leviticus, the vast majority of present-day Christians have chosen to focus only upon Leviticus 20:13, the verse calling for the death penalty for homosexual acts. And at least some of them haven't been averse to acting on it. (To be fair, some Christian "reconstructionists" are currently calling for institution of the death penalty for adultery and atheism, as well as for "sodomy.")

Throughout history, homosexuality has been illegal in Christian lands, and the penalties have been severe. In the Middle Ages, strangled gay men were sometimes placed on the wood piles at the burning of witches. One member of the British royalty caught having homosexual relations suffered an even more grisly fate: Edward II's penalty was being held down while a red-hot poker was jammed through his rectum and intestines. In more modern times, countless gay people have been jailed for years for the victimless "crime" of having consensual sex. It was only in 2003 that the Supreme Court struck down the felony laws on the books in many American states prescribing lengthy prison terms for consensual "sodomy." And many Christians would love to reinstate those laws.

Thus, the current wave of gay bashings and murders of gay people should come as no surprise. Christians can find justification for such violence in the Bible and also in the hate filled sermons issuing from all too many pulpits in this country. If history is any indication, the homophobic messages in those sermons will continue to be issued for many years to come.

18. The Bible is not a reliable guide to Christ's teachings. Mark, the oldest of the Gospels, was written twenty to forty years after Christ's death, at a time when historical records were exceedingly rare and the vast bulk of the population was illiterate. Worse, the authors of the Gospels had no direct knowledge of Christ—they never met him; they almost certainly relied exclusively upon oral tradition. That's analogous to a contemporary author writing a history of the Reagan Administration while having no access whatsoever to research materials and having never even seen Reagan on television. In fact, it's worse than that, given that the other Gospels were written decades after Mark. As well, the Gospel texts have been amended, translated, and retranslated so often that it's extremely difficult to gauge the accuracy of current editions, even aside from the matter of the accuracy of texts written decades after the death of their subject. This is such a problem that the Jesus Seminar, a colloquium of over two hundred Protestant Gospel scholars mostly employed at religious colleges and seminaries, undertook in 1985 a multiyear investigation into the historicity of the statements and deeds attributed to Jesus in the New Testament. They concluded that only 18 percent of the statements and 16 percent of the deeds attributed to Jesus had a high likelihood of being historically accurate. So, in a very real sense fundamentalists—who claim to believe in the literal truth of the Bible—are not followers of Jesus Christ; rather, they are followers of those who, decades or centuries later, put words in his mouth.

19. The Bible, Christianity's basic text, is riddled with contradictions. There are a number of glaring contradictions in the Bible, in both the Old and New Testaments, including some within the same books. A few examples:

> ...God cannot be tempted with evil, neither tempteth he any man (James 1:13).
> And it came to pass after these things, that God did tempt Abraham" (Genesis 22:1).

> ...for I am merciful, saith the Lord, and I will not keep anger for ever (Jeremiah 3:12).
> "Ye have kindled a fire in mine anger, which shall burn forever. Thus saith the Lord" (Jeremiah 17:4).

> If I bear witness of myself, my witness is not true (John 5:31; Jesus speaking).
> "I am one that bear witness of myself... (John 8:18; Jesus speaking).

And last but not least:

> I have seen God face to face, and my life is preserved (Genesis 32:30).
> No man hath seen God at any time (John 1:18).
> And I [God] will take away mine hand, and thou shalt see my back parts... (Exodus 33:23).

Christian apologists typically attempt to explain away such contradictions by claiming that the fault lies in the translation, and that there were no contradictions in the original text. It's difficult to see how this could be so, given how direct many biblical contradictions are; but even if these Christian apologetics held water, it would follow that every part of the Bible should be as suspect as the contradictory sections, thus reinforcing the previous point: that the Bible is not a reliable guide to Christ's words.

20. Christianity borrowed its central myths and ceremonies from other ancient religions. The ancient world was rife with tales of virgin births, miracle working saviors, tripartite gods, gods taking human form, gods arising from the dead, heavens and hells, and days of judgment. In addition to the myths, many of the ceremonies of ancient religions also match those of that syncretic latecomer, Christianity.

To cite but one example (there are many others), consider Mithraism, a Persian religion predating Christianity by centuries. Mithra, the savior of the Mithraic religion and a god who took human form, was born of a virgin; he belonged to the holy trinity, he was a link between heaven and earth, and he ascended into heaven after his death. His followers believed in heaven and hell, looked forward to a day of judgment, and referred to Mithra as "the Light of the World." They also practiced baptism and ritual cannibalism—the eating of bread and the drinking of wine to symbolize the eating and drinking of the god's body and blood. Given all this, Mithra's birthday should come as no surprise: December 25; this event was, of course, celebrated by Mithra's followers at midnight.

Mithraism is but the most striking example of the appearance of these myths and ceremonies prior to the advent of Christianity. They appear—in more scattered form—in many other pre-Christian religions.

A Final Word

These are but some of the major problems attending Christianity, and they provide overwhelming reasons it should be abandoned. Even if you discount half, two-thirds, or even three-quarters of these arguments, the conclusion is still irresistible.

CHAPTER IX

May the Farce Be with You: A Lighthearted Look at Why God Does Not Exist

by Pamela Sutter

Introduction

Atheist. The word has shock value, but it simply means "without belief in God." Unlike agnostics, who suggest that God is unknowable, and that they cannot or do not know whether God exists, atheists discount any and all supernatural entities. Atheists are not waiting for evidence of God any more than they are waiting for evidence of purple unicorns.

It is no coincidence that humans are the only species that practices religion, for we are also the only species that is aware of death. Soon after evolving the ability to think (and to think about death), we began to believe in gods: sun gods, fertility gods, volcano gods, animal gods, and the god of special interest to atheists, the monotheistic Judeo-Christian, omnipotent, universe creating God of the Bible. God belief seems to be an inevitable cultural byproduct of self-awareness.

We may be smart enough to believe in (more accurately, hope for) a higher power, but our unique human brain is also stubborn enough to continue believing/hoping despite the discoveries of science that pretty much put God out of a job. Recent polls indicate that roughly 10 percent of Americans consider themselves to be atheists, making nonbelievers a larger minority than Jews or Mormons. That still leaves 90 percent of citizens claiming to believe in God.

God's existence, it is said, cannot be disproven. In fact, *anything* that the mind can imagine can never be disproven. Think up something fanciful, something you know can't possibly exist, such as an invisible elf that resides in your refrigerator or a table with ten thousand legs. "*Poof!*" it automatically has an above zero chance of existing, because it cannot be proven absolutely that this invention of your mind doesn't, hasn't, or won't exist somewhere at some time in the universe. All of space and time would have to be searched to prove it 100 percent false.

The logic seems absurd, but it's a necessary disclaimer. A believer who says "prove God doesn't exist" could just as easily demand, "Prove there isn't a colony of Flatlanders living in Planet X's core." God's existence is more problematic than that of Flatlanders, for God is supernatural, not physical. The whole cosmos could be searched atom by atom and He'd never be found. Because of this, atheists consider belief in the supernatural, and hence in God, to be irrational—as irrational as backwards time travel or claiming to know the final digit of pi.

Paradoxical Prayer

A comatose young boy hovers near death. Family and friends pray he'll survive. The boy dies. The family muses that God needed him; he's been called "home" and is being embraced by all his loved ones that preceded him. Perhaps his parents ask, "Why God, why?!" and then concede that the answer would be beyond their understanding. Suppose the child survives. It's a miracle; their prayers were answered! Now let's say the boy survives, but with a severe handicap. Were the prayers only partially answered? No, the boy becomes an inspiration to others as part of God's grand plan. What about a patient down the hall who dies. Not enough prayers? God needed her more? (And for that matter, how could God "need" anyone?)

Notice that no matter what the outcome, believers twist events to justify their sense of hope. No matter what happens, God comes out smelling like a rose.

A glance at the newspapers reveals God's odd prayer answering priorities. Apparently, He favors granting record-breaking home runs over saving a doomed commuter train. He allows a planeload of praying passengers to smash into the ocean while He puts someone's multiple sclerosis into remission. He looks the other way when a toddler is kidnapped and murdered but gladly answers a farmer's prayers for rain.

When planes don't crash or when a person doesn't get a disease, prayer again gets the credit, and God gets points for allowing life to proceed normally.

Praying before a sporting event is among the most ridiculous forms of "worship" imaginable. To think that the Creator of the universe would care about the outcome of a high school football game is ludicrous. Did God favor the winning team? Was He angry with the player who made the losing fumble? Many believe so: one in four Americans believe that God intervenes in sporting events.

He must have really had fun with Superbowl 49 (Seahawks vs. Patriots), especially in the final minute. That God—what a prankster!

The motive behind prayer is especially revealing. Prayer begs God to intervene. Isn't that second-guessing God's intent? Isn't prayer a suggestion to God that this present course might not be the best way to handle things? "Do you really need to take little Timmy now?" Praying implies that God's divine plan is in error, and that we have useful advice for him.

Why interfere with the Lord's plan for us? Don't pray for a loved one's cancer to be cured, for it's God's will that this disease will claim her, after which she'll be on her way to heaven. Might unanswered prayers be a test of faith? "God won't give me more than I can handle." My, what a nice God, always testing us, always toying with our emotions.

The September 11, 2001 terrorist attacks on the World Trade Center and the Pentagon spawned a surge of prayers, though all too late to have changed God's mind about allowing the tragedy. Inevitably, the "Where was God?" question surfaced. Clergy answered, "It's not a question of where was God or why did He let it happen, but rather, why wasn't it worse?" So, if we can imagine something worse, we then praise God for not letting it happen? Religious believers used every excuse in the book. The alternative was notably absent: "Maybe there is no God."

The fact is no prayers are answered. No prayers go unanswered. People are simply seeking meaning in otherwise inexplicable events, in much the same way that they see shapes in clouds. Prayer can be used as a form of calming meditation, which in turn can aid the body to heal, but there's nothing divine behind this placebo effect. Scientific studies show similar results from petting cats and watching fish swim in an aquarium.

Prayer is simply a human reaction to apparently meaningless physical and emotional pain.

Murky Miracles

A horrible accident took place in December 2000 in which an eight months pregnant woman was hurled through the windshield of a truck onto the pavement; the jackknifing vehicle then sliced her body in half. This caused the expulsion of the baby, still attached by the umbilical cord and very much alive. The child's survival was hailed as a miracle by the woman's husband, the driver of the truck. "Something else must be at work here besides luck," he commented.

A miracle? It was a miracle that the mother died an ugly death by being cut in half by a truck? A miracle that the baby will grow up without his mother and, when old enough, will be saddened by the horrible way she died? A miracle that the baby was jettisoned onto cold asphalt as his father became a widower?

Sorry, there was no miracle here. The human trait of seeking comfort is a strong one. Notice that the father focused only on the good: the baby survived the freak accident. People look for reasons to maintain their faith in God, and they will convince themselves they've found it, no matter what.

Time and again folks overlook the negative and latch on to whatever is left. An infertile couple praises the Lord for the miracle He bestowed when the fertility drugs kicked in to give them septuplets. Why was the couple plagued by infertility to begin with? Why weren't they content with the destiny He chose for them? Maybe they were meant to adopt a special needs child instead? No. Truth be told, all "miracles" are miracles only in hindsight.

A tornado skips along a residential neighborhood, wiping out some houses, sparing others. Those with intact houses will praise the Lord, while the neighbor next door standing amidst rubble demands, "Why me?!" Random happenstance is assigned meaning by pattern seeking humans. The result is a "miracle." No god need apply, for the human mind has filled the position.

A man has a near fatal encounter with (insert your own mayhem). In an interview he humbly explains, "It wasn't my time." Has he forgotten about all the people who were snuffed out in the prime of life and infants who never got to know life at all?

Watch what happens when trouble befalls a church. An earthquake in El Salvador destroyed the church in a small town and also killed hundreds under a landslide of dirt and rubble. Survivors quickly declared, "God loves us, He left some of us alive to rebuild the church!" Huh?! God let people die horrible, claustrophobic deaths in order for the others to see themselves as "survivors"? This is a good thing? Why wasn't the church spared? Come to think of it, why did the quake occur at all? Was God busy curing someone's canker sore?

"God only knows why this happened" is another common utterance, often spoken in dismay. Indeed, He must be one sinister God to allow or to create a natural disaster. Or maybe He's a nice God, taking whole families up to heaven at once so they can discuss his "acts of God."

"It's a miracle that more people weren't killed." Uh, it was a miracle that the earthquake killed a lot of people, but not everyone?

Miracles are in the eye of the beholder.

Illogical Heaven

"Everybody wants to go to heaven, but nobody wants to die." What's the matter, do we have doubts? We should, for the concept of heaven is a nightmare.

Take free will, the decision-making capability that lets us make personal choices and gives us our sense of self. As nice as free will is, it has the potential to lead to crime, lying, cheating, and other unheavenly behavior. Will we retain our free will in the afterlife?

It's a Catch-22 situation. Without free will, we become sheep. Keep our free will, and heaven would have all the problems found on earth. Either way, what's the point?

Perhaps spirits won't want to rebel? Ever hear of the fallen angel Satan? And look at Adam and Eve, the first humans given a shot at paradise; they blew it. Apparently, God didn't even see that one coming.

Then there's the slew of sticky social situations. The murder victim who sees her "born-again" attacker stroll through the Pearly Gates. Families waiting for their earthbound loved ones to die so they can all be reunited. Spouses sitting on a cloud *Family Circus*–style who spy their mates remarrying or pawning heirlooms.

And boredom. With death out of the picture and without goals or purpose, we are going to be a restless bunch. Humans like to overcome obstacles. We thrive on new challenges and on the unexpected events of a physical world. An eternity is a very long time, and the prospect of forced immortality will have winged residents wishing they could hang themselves with their halos.

Some believers claim boredom will be unheard of, that our souls will be free to embark on any endeavor in the universe. Hmmm, as long as we're making it up, might as well make it sound good, right? But, given infinite time, *anything* would wear thin eventually.

What about the Bible's own easy way of achieving eternal life, by believing in Christ (John 3:16)? Under this premise, a repentant rapist/serial killer who has "found religion" at the last moment will get his own harp, while any of his victims who rejected Christ will be doomed to eternal torture in the fiery pit. It seems that God cares more about the flattery of His own ego than the unfairness of a killer getting into heaven while his victims do not.

Heaven is nothing more than invention, false hope to make the living feel better. "Frank Sinatra is now singing for a heavenly audience" sounds a lot better than "He's six feet under and never coming back," doesn't it?

Observe the contradiction when dealing with the death of a loved one. In between sobs, people state the deceased has gone to a better place, and that there was a reason he died in the manner in which he did. Then shouldn't we be happy? We'll see them again someday? Right?

Heaven has a way of making a mockery out of life. So what if Grandma died? She's with Jesus now. One little girl even stepped in front of a train to "join" her recently deceased mom up in heaven. If heaven is so great, you'd think "believers" would enthusiastically welcome death for themselves and everyone they know who is "saved."

To underline what a selfish, fabricated notion heaven is, consider those who believe their pets are "crossing over" too. Not former chicken nuggets or last year's Christmas ham, but Fluffy, Fido, and Polly. Just because they own it, the creature must be deserving of heaven. How convenient to overlook dinosaurs, gazelles, and every trout that ever lived. But, by George, Poopsie will be there waiting for me. Hopefully not that mean pit bull next door, but Poopsie for sure. No doubt the owner of the pit bull is wishing the same thing for Fang.

Evolution and God: Incompatible? Yes!

Darwin's "dangerous idea" should have made atheists out of everyone. Yet the vast majority of students who learn about evolution in public schools still believe in God. Either they doubt what they are taught in biology class or are content keeping evolution and religion in separate parts of their brain, and never the two shall meet.

Many scientists say that science has nothing to do with belief in God, but let's be realistic. If God played no role in formation of the human species, then what else didn't He do? Attempts to reconcile facts with faith have led to fanciful conjectures filled with contradictions that paint believers into corners.

These attempts to reconcile religion with science include:

- *God put evolution into motion, knowing that its random path would produce humans someday.* Why use a wasteful, indirect process when He could just as easily have zapped everything into place at once? This scenario means apes are our kin, a point many people find distasteful; gone would be the special creation of Man, starting with Adam and Eve and their "original sin."

- *God made each species separately but in stages to prepare the earth for future epochs.* This is a poor attempt at explaining the indisputable evidence of the fossil record that shows simple life preceded more complex life. There is no getting around the fact that trilobites came before fish, fish before birds, birds before mammoths, and dinosaurs before humans. In this scenario, God's first shot at creating life would have to have been something like blue-green algae. But why would God have needed to make such primitive life first? Did He need eons of practice to reach the level of mammals? Is He not powerful enough to make snails, flowers, reptiles, and birds all at once? God's supposed work parallels what fossil dating shows, which is well explained by the theory of evolution. So "God" as an explanation is entirely unnecessary.

- *An Intelligent Designer is responsible.* This argument claims that an "Intelligence" of some sort made life, and that this "Intelligence" doesn't necessarily have to be God or even be supernatural. It opens up the farcical notion that there could be multiple Intelligent Designers, yet no one attempts to explain what made them. Presumably God stands by and merely watches the Designer(s) work animal creating magic.

- *God created the illusion of evolution to throw scientists off.* Then He is a manipulative, deceitful god who is not to be trusted.

- *Evolution explains the origin of all species except for man, who was specially created in God's image, complete with eternal spirit.* Then why did He use primates as a template? We look like chimps, our DNA is closer to chimps than chimp DNA is to orangutans, a chimp fetus is a spitting image of a human fetus, and we share many behaviors. In fact, chimps are so close to us that biologists have considered adding "homo" to their Latin scientific name.

- *Evolution is fact, but God exists too.* For starters, the Bible says God created the world and all its creatures in six days (and, strangely for an omnipotent being, rested on the seventh). It doesn't say a mindless process is involved. To believe in God and to accept the fact of evolution is to invalidate an important part of the Bible. To acknowledge that life got a foothold on earth all by itself is also to acknowledge that God is uninvolved, if not entirely absent. If God doesn't care enough to choose what life to seed a planet with, then He's surely not going to care about a hairless primate's cancer or hope for an afterlife. Such a God would be distant, not the personal savior so many people want to believe in. In all honesty, evolution voids the entire supernatural content of the Bible and its petty, intrusive God.

An alarming percentage of the general public remain ignorant of the theory of evolution. They find it hard to accept that such complex creatures as humans evolved from a chemical soup. Perhaps our ignoble beginnings foster a fear that we aren't so special after all.

Why do Christian fundamentalists focus on this field of science? They feel it is a threat to their faith. And they are right.

Got Proof?

Ironically, lack of evidence is a reason that some people believe in God, for it automatically designates God as being supernatural, and hence no physical evidence is necessary. The trouble is this logic leaves the door open for magical gnomes, invisible twelve-dimensional sentient trees, and other figments of the imagination.

Much more convincing than lack of evidence is the fact that humans believed in gods long before the Bible was written. It is our nature to want to believe in something higher than ourselves. But why should the biblical God be any more credible than Zeus, Ra, or a volcano god?

Not surprisingly, theists have an answer. They claim their god is purely spiritual and not limited by superstitious beliefs based on ignorance of physical phenomena like erupting volcanoes or the changing seasons. Show how a volcano works, and, poof, there go the volcano gods. Show how species arose on their own and every god's existence is in danger; so it's no surprise that Muslims and Christians oppose evolution, though the supernatural status of God allows even people who accept evolution to maintain their faith.

Once a culture has concluded that some ultimate "higher power" must be "out there," a fear and reverence of this power, this God, naturally follows. Such a God is a product of believers' faith alone, which puts it conveniently out of reach of the physical world. This mental construct effectively makes various cultures' Supreme Being a single deity. Muslims, Jews, and Christians believe in the same single God, despite variations in doctrine, and Muslims openly acknowledge this. Such a God becomes by default, the creator of the universe. Clearly, this points to God as being simply an end product of thinking about abstract "ultimates"; but is this a rational basis for believing that God actually exists.

Another flaw involves circular reasoning. God exists through blind faith, but why is blind faith needed to believe in God? The Bible is the inspired Word of God. How do we know? The Bible says so.

An episode of *The Simpsons* involves Homer becoming a genius. One of the feats he accomplishes with his enhanced brain is writing a proof showing that God does not exist. Alas, there can never be such a proof, because the supernatural is supposed to be beyond proof. God "exists" because He must be supernatural in order to be God. Such logic in effect says God must exist, because He cannot be disproven. This demonstrates that God is a thought experiment and nothing more.

Still, this doesn't stop us from believing. Lack of evidence has never been a hindrance to belief. When prayers aren't answered or when nothing happens, we think there must be a purpose to it. But what's the difference between "not intervening" and "there is no God to intervene"? God is a product of faith, faith is a product of the mind, the mind is a product of evolution, which in turn is a product of other non-divine physical processes.

Watering the Seeds of Doubt: Where Did God Come From?

If some people have a hard time accepting that simple life formed from non-life in a natural chemical process and diversified into species from there, imagine the giant leap one must make to suppose that a complex intelligence such as God arose ex nihilo, or that such an entity had no beginning at all! Some have shoved God back to the beginning of time and left Him there as a remote, non-personal Cosmic Cause, in an attempt to explain the origins of the universe. But this is not an explanation. Rather, it's the use of a convenient label ("God") as a means of *evading* explanation. While the circumstances "before" the universe existed are still unknown to science, ignorance is no excuse to invoke the supernatural.

Why Is Life Unfair? Why Is There Evil in the World?

This seems a tricky spot for God to wriggle out of. If He made everything, then He made evil too, so how can he be "all good"? If He allows evil to continue, He's negligent. If He can't fully control evil, He's not omnipotent.

There really is no such thing as "evil" per se, just the undesirable choices of a species with free will. But it's hard to explain why millions were murdered during the Holocaust, while God is credited with tiny "miracles" like putting a tumor into remission. Can the same God really allow children to starve to death in Third World countries and yet help someone in California find a missing wedding ring or win a golf tournament? Disturbingly, the "answer" is all too easy to fabricate: "We wouldn't understand." "God works in mysterious ways." "The meaning will be clear later." Yada, yada, yada.

Free Will or Sock Puppet?

Monotheistic religions posit that an all-knowing, all-seeing, omnipotent God is everywhere and everywhen. If so, is our free will an illusion? A sham? Are we living a predestined lie? It would seem so if God knows our every action in advance. He must laugh at the deep thought we put into our puny daily decisions and presumptuous prayers. He's always known the outcome; He knew it trillions of years ago. An eternity ago.

Anthropocentric Humans

We humans have always thought of ourselves as special. Since ancient times, we've assumed that the earth was the center of the universe. When the ancients discovered other planets, they assumed that the earth was at the center of the solar system, with the sun revolving around it. As recently as the early twentieth century, we believed ours was the only galaxy. Now we know there are billions of galaxies, and that our solar system is in the outskirts of an arm of an average spiral galaxy. The evidence has continually dashed our hopes of being center stage.

Today, many people wrongly assume that evolution had us in mind as its ultimate goal, and some charts depict humans occupying the top branch of life's tree. We continue to be pompous by anthropomorphizing animals. We project ourselves onto other creatures in order to make them less like animals and more like us, as if that somehow improves them.

And, of course, we think ourselves the special creation of a single perfect God, who thought so much of us that he granted us an eternal soul which lives on in a glorious afterlife. This last bit of self-flattery cannot be disproven by science but neither can believers prove it, and the burden of proof lies on those making assertions not those denying them.

Nails in the Coffin

God's coffin has more than enough nails in it. Notice how we have given it, God, a gender, a male gender: He, Him, the Heavenly Father, etc. This is still more evidence that God is a fabrication of self-centered humans.

To Err Is Divine

For a deity who is supposedly inerrant, Jehovah has a lot of explaining to do. Mistakes were made.

Extinction is a prime example. A large majority of earth's species have gone extinct. Estimates put it at 99 percent, with today's species representing a mere 1 percent of all life-forms in the planet's history. It seems that most of God's "perfect" creatures weren't quite perfect enough. They couldn't adapt quickly enough, compete well enough, or weather natural disasters successfully enough (disasters that God could have averted).

This is not to say that today's species are perfect. They are simply adapted to current conditions.

But God is said to have created each life-form "as is" using His infinite powers of wisdom and perfection. Why then do giraffes have a hard time bending down to drink? Female kiwi birds struggle to deliver an enormously large egg. Mammalian eyes have the optic nerve passing through the retina, and, consequently, a blind spot. Humans suffer from obsolete wisdom teeth and from lower back problems caused by relatively recent bipedalism.

Vestigial organs also point to less than perfect workmanship. They betray a creature formed by evolution not a perfectionistic Designer. The whale's shrunken pelvis. A python's residual back leg stumps. A human's pesky appendix. Vestigials can still be utilized by an animal's body for other purposes than they originally served, but they are the telltale signs of evolution not of a perfectionist Creator.

God's planning ability is as dubious as His designing. How do the dinosaurs fit in? Why create such a diversity of "terrible lizards" to dominate the planet for so long when He planned to make humans later on? Did He tire of them and allow an asteroid to wipe them out? Dinosaurs are not given the play in the Bible one would expect of such incredible creatures, undoubtedly because the authors were unaware of them. God must not have thought much of them if He left them out of his "dictations."

God's trouble with planning becomes obvious in the story of Adam and Eve. When God allegedly created humans, He initially made only Adam. It was after Adam expressed loneliness that the Lord created Eve. This shows an incredible lack of foresight. God gave each animal a mate but felt Adam could go it alone? Could He not foresee that Adam would need a partner too? Poor Adam had to bring this to God's attention, after which he awoke, minus a rib.

Are such oversights and imperfections the intent of God's "mysterious ways"? No. The answer is much more straightforward. There is no need to second-guess God, for the world behaves exactly as it would if there was no God at all.

Which there isn't.

Paradoxes

Can God create another God equal to Himself? This feat would be impossible, since the newly minted "God II" would be "younger" than the original and hence would not be equal in duration to the God that had no beginning. The very notion that this second God had a creator makes such a deity lesser. So, no, God could not make an equal God. If God did decide to produce multiple copies of Himself, how would we know? If we were to be oblivious to two, twenty, thirty, or sixty thousand Gods, why believe a single God exists?

Can God kill Himself? Let's suppose an eternity of being all-knowing and all-seeing wore thin on Yahweh. Could He commit suicide? Any method that worked would have to be more powerful than God Himself, an impossibility for the Almighty. As long as we're speculating, say He did manage to pull it off. Again, how would we know? Why then believe he exists right this moment? Perhaps the universe would vanish as soon as God ceased to exist. We'd be unaware of this as well. An impossible premise yields impossible questions. God is impossible.

But . . . the Universe Is Fine-Tuned for Life!

The universe seems like Goldilock's porridge: not too hot, not too cold, but just right for life. Some take this to mean the cosmos was designed. Earth is just the right distance from the sun to support life, and the sun is just the right type of star. Conclusion: a Creator was needed. This "anthropic universe" scenario is a case of using an unnecessarily complex answer when a simple one is better. Hindsight in this case is blinding, not 20/20. If the universe didn't turn out the way it did, we wouldn't be here to discuss it. We focus on how astonishing it is that we exist, the same way a lottery winner is astonished that he won, despite a 100 percent chance that somebody would win. If we weren't here or if no sentient life existed at all in the universe, something would be around, even if just a hodgepodge of atoms or empty space, just as "lucky" to exist as we are. We are a self-centered species that gasps, "Golly gee!" The universe doesn't know it's "suited" for life and that humans would come along and ask such questions.

Life Is Too Diverse and Complex to Have Formed on Its Own!

But it only had to happen once. Again, we're like the starstruck lottery winner mentioned above. A God isn't needed to explain any natural phenomenon. The only place He is needed is to give false hope to a death fearing primate species.

Then Is Human Life Purposeless?

Leave it to us prideful humans to think that we are so wonderful that there must be a reason we are here. We are inventors and designers who do things with intent, so we figure since we are here, something made us for a purpose. Some take this "purpose" as a personal destiny or "calling," while others think their purpose awaits them in heaven. There is no reason why we are here or why some people die sooner than others or were spared from harm. The "purpose" of living organisms is to pass along their DNA, but even then, there is no reason why it must happen. The universe and everything in it is an ongoing natural process, and we evolved brains to ponder what we consider "big questions." This need not be a bleak view. Our purpose is what we make it. Who needs a God for that?

Why Believe? Fear of Death/Hope for an Afterlife
"There are no atheists in foxholes," goes an old quip. We don't want to die. We don't want this life to be the only one. We yearn to be reunited with loved ones.

Justice
If a wrongdoer escapes punishment here on earth, it feels good to think the person will have a personal "judgment day" with God.

Experience
Many people swear that they feel God's/Jesus's presence, have witnessed miracles, experienced divine healing, dreams, or visions, and that their personal relationship with God is as real as any tangible event or object. The human mind has enormous aptitude for believing in the non-verifiable. Psychics, horoscopes, and alien abductions all have their true believers. The mind can convince itself of anything. It can invent significance out of thin air. Personal experience is subjective and in no way can be used as evidence that something is real.

The Bible
The Bible is the Word of God, so there must be a God. Sure. Just as the Koran is the Word of God, so there must be a God. Just as the Book of Mormon is the Word of God, so there must be a God. . .

Upbringing/Social Pressure
Many folks indoctrinated into believing in God from an early age never even conceive of questioning their faith. This is why conservative Catholics, fundamentalist Muslims and evangelicals, and other

religionists are so insistent upon giving their children a religious "education." The desire to please one's parents or to fit in with the traditions of society also plays a large role.

Belief Gives Comfort

The security of hoping one's life has meaning in some bigger picture is a huge inspiration to maintaining belief. It helps many to cope during a crisis to imagine God's "hands" holding them and the world. Who wants to believe that one's life is a purposeless, one-shot event? Apparently, not many! Insisting that a higher power is "out there" is a comforting crutch.

Loose Ends

Ask people if they believe in gods, and they'll likely answer, "No, that's for superstitious villagers or the ancient Greeks." Ask people if they believe in God, and they'll likely answer, "Of course, what kind of question is that?"

Announcing that you don't believe in gods is a moot point, but stating you don't believe in God will raise eyebrows. Why? Atheism is viewed as bleak, cold, cynical. To be "Godless" is to be on par with being immoral and uncaring. "What went wrong to make you an atheist?" they'll ask. Evolution, which is often equated with atheism, has been blamed for fostering an attitude of "we're just animals," which in turn leads to social decay. But social problems have always been around, long before the theory of evolution was formulated. In fact, some of the very worst problems, such as slavery, rampant infectious diseases, and the routine use of torture (all abundantly common in the Age of Faith), have markedly declined since the theory of evolution was propounded.

Often people will remark, "I'm not very religious," and then hasten to add, "but I believe in God," as if it's horrible not to believe. Yet a recent survey by Public Agenda reported that 58 percent of respondents said, "It's not necessary to believe in God in order to be moral and have good values."

The pious find it hard to swallow that atheists do not have some form of belief. "Surely you believe in something?" they'll inquire. Well, atheists believe that all religions have it wrong. Atheists believe there is no God, or, to be more precise, that it's silly to believe in something for which there is no evidence.

Agnostics like to declare that atheists and preachers share something in common: both are positive their respective beliefs are correct. Agnostics claim it's illogical to be strongly certain either way. How illogical of them! It's a black-and-white issue. There either is a God or there isn't. There are only two options, and one must be the correct one; and given the total absence of the desperately longed for evidence supporting the existence of God, not to mention all of the above listed paradoxes and absurdities, it's simply not reasonable to beg the question by saying, "No one has disproved the existence of God, so it's an open question."

By saying the subject is open, agnostics are actually giving believers the benefit of the doubt that God might exist. But note the absence of magical elf agnostics or supernatural gnome agnostics. No one has disproven their existence, either.

So, one strongly suspects that agnostics maintain their stance for social reasons—to be acceptable to their religious neighbors and, perhaps, to flatter themselves that they're more "open-minded" than atheists.

Believers ask, "What would it take for you to believe in God?" A giant hand parting the clouds and resurrecting the dead would help. As would spying a purple unicorn in one's neighbor's yard bolster the case for the existence of unicorns. But that evidence has never appeared and never will. Only in your mind can you imagine a day when trumpets blare and a legion of angels descends from the heavens, followed by a bearded man on a white horse.

Atheists can still be in awe of the cosmos and of a delicate flower and other wonders of nature. Atheists have more reverence for life and nature than most religious believers, because we know that we're here only by chance.

We don't consider the world a "vale of tears," the testing ground of a capricious God. Rather, we treasure our brief and only lives, and we treasure the beauties and wonders of the world in which we live.

CHAPTER X

Disbelief 101: A Young Person's Guide to Atheism (excerpt)

by S.C. Hitchcock

One of the more annoying aspects of talking to believers in god is that they always consider the god hypothesis to be the default position in any argument about the natural world. For example, a believer might ask you if you know how life could have "sprung up" in the first place. If you say science isn't sure yet but has some pretty good and testable hypotheses about how it might have happened, the religious person will seize on this. "But you're not sure, are you? Nobody was there!"

All of a sudden, people who will believe anything the Bible says on faith become the most careful skeptics when it comes to science. The implication of the above comment is that if there isn't any conclusive evidence on a topic involving the natural world, then "god must have done it." The religious seem to be saying, "If you can't prove it in front of my eyes, then my belief must be true." Or, if you can't absolutely show me how science explains this beyond a shadow of a doubt, then my religious ideas and your science must be on equal footing.

Nothing could be further from the truth. In fact, the claim that science is killing god is not true. God committed suicide a long time ago. The sharpest arguments put together to "prove" god's existence end up cutting god to pieces.

I'll go into the three most common arguments for the existence of a god, but before I get to them let me explain why they are so deadly to the very god idea they are designed to protect. Normally, when people argue endlessly about a topic it is because they are arguing from different beginnings or prepositions. (As you've probably heard, there has to be some original point of agreement before two people can argue about anything.) For example, the argument over whether abortion should be legal or not will likely never go away because people cannot agree on the proposition. For someone who thinks that human life begins at conception, abortion at any stage is "murder." However, for people who think that human life begins at birth, then abortion is not murder. (The abortion debate is more complex than this, but the purpose here is to explain how arguments work.)

We are fortunate, then, that we have no such problem when dealing with the three most common arguments for god's existence. I disagree with all of their premises, but that won't be an issue, because even when I pretend that I agree with them they obliterate the concept of a god. Here, then, are god's "suicide arguments."

God's Suicidal Arguments

1. The Prime Mover

It is a religious trick to dress absurdities up with solemn ceremonies in the hope that no one will notice their silliness. The taking of communion, for example, where Catholics eat a very sacred wafer that is supposed to change, at some point, into the flesh of Jesus is about as bizarre as you can get. Yet if everyone goes through the procedure with a solemn face, as if this is all very serious and important, then it appears to have some weight.

Sometimes atheists fall into the same trap and treat religious arguments with the same type of seriousness. So any discussion about the prime mover argument generally begins with a long preamble about the deep philosophical thought of Aristotle, St. Thomas Aquinas, and blah, blah, blah. It's like putting a mule in a tuxedo.

Essentially, the prime mover argument makes the case that something had to cause the universe. That something, according to the religious believer, must be god. No effects exist without a cause, so there must have been some "first cause."

The reason this argument is so suicidal to god is that it brings up an even bigger question. Where did god come from? How does adding an all-powerful invisible entity at the beginning help us at all? (In fact, this argument is flawed scientifically. The universe did not need a first cause, and this will be explained shortly.)

Let's all just accept the Big Bang theory for a moment. The Catholic Church does, saying that it was the finger of god that sparked the creation of the universe. Well, we might then ask the scientific question of what existed before the Big Bang? We can have a lot of fun just throwing out theories without evidence. I could say that before the Big Bang all that existed were two wart-covered aliens playing video games. And one of the aliens got angry and threw his controller through the television set, thus providing the spark for the Big Bang. So, what we see now as "reality" is simply the video game running on, broken and partially haywire. You would laugh at this. Where did the aliens come from? Where did the television set and video game console come from? Sure, it's possible that this happened. After all, no one can prove conclusively that it didn't, but the absurdity of it makes this hypothesis seem unlikely.

And yet, people who would laugh at the alien/video game theory will simply believe in the existence of a being who is infinitely more complex than they are, and who has created reasons for our existence which are equally bizarre. In fact, every "effect" we see in the universe has an easily explained cause. When I see a baseball flying through the air, I don't have to look very far to see what caused it—someone threw it or hit it. We could then ask a seemingly endless set of questions, such as, "Where did the thrower come from," etc., and we would have unremarkable answers all the way back until the Big Bang. Now, if we accepted god as the prime mover, he would be the only cause in this massive chain for which we have no explanation or hope of an explanation. This, somehow, makes him more likely to exist?

Science, as always, will simply say, "Well, we won't know until we can gather enough evidence to create a decent theory." Science does not insist upon anything that it can't prove. The idea of god being the first mover in the universe is silly and utterly without evidence. It should be of no more intellectual merit than the notion that a talking tractor, video game playing aliens, invisible flying clowns, or angry raccoons created the universe. None of the arguments for a god are any better than the arguments for any of these things.

When talking about the origins of life, that is, when life actually began, religious people will often bring up a concept related to the prime mover argument. This is the principle of Occam's Razor, which is maybe the most misunderstood concept in philosophical history. (Even many professional philosophers miss what Occam's Razor implies.) According to the medieval philosopher William of Occam, if you are presented with two explanations for a phenomenon, then the explanation with the fewest assumptions is generally the right one. This is usually paraphrased as, "All else being equal, the simplest explanation is best."

To put this another way, Occam's Razor simply means that we have to consider the evidence without any "extras." We'll see what this means in a moment and also why Occam's Razor is so dangerous to religion. (The medieval church, by the way, at least seemed to sense what Occam was up to and was not pleased—he died in exile. So, I'm not sure why religious people think his razor should be used on their behalf.)

When talking about the creation of the universe, religious folks will often invoke Occam's Razor and say: "What could be simpler than 'god did it'?"

Well, this is not such a simple explanation. First of all, we must make the mother of all assumptions—the existence of an all-powerful, invisible deity. Then we have to tack that notion on to any explanation we give for anything. So, god becomes a tumor that grows on the back of any explanation.

Let me show how Occam's Razor can be used to cut away the tumor from a more sophisticated argument made on god's behalf. The passage below is from a liberal and respected theologian who spoke up on behalf of evolutionary theory (and hence against the "intelligent design" proponents) at a trial in Dover, Pennsylvania. Catholic theologian John Haught was arguing that there was no conflict between science and religion, because, he believes, the two do not intersect:

> Suppose a teapot is boiling on your stove, and someone comes into the room and says, "Explain to me why that's boiling." Well, one explanation would be it's boiling because the water molecules are moving around excitedly and the liquid state is being transformed into gas.
>
> But at the same time you could just as easily have answered that question by saying, "It's boiling because my wife turned the gas on."
>
> Or you could also answer the question by saying, "It's boiling because I want tea."
>
> All three answers are right, but they don't conflict with each other because they're working on different levels. Science works

at one level of investigation, religion at another.... The problems occur when one assumes that there's only one level.
—quoted in Matthew Chapman [Charles Darwin's great grandson], *40 Days and 40 Nights* (New York: HarperCollins, 2007), 106

This line of reasoning made me think for a while, which is something that the god arguments have been inspiring people to do for years. However, it seems that Dr. Haught's argument cannot survive Occam's Razor. The idea that explanations can work on different levels is interesting. In fact, most actions do have several layers of explanation. The fallacy in this is in thinking that this includes a supernatural, rather than natural, explanation.

If I stated that the water was boiling because I wanted tea, then my want of tea could be easily explained through biological means. My body needs moisture and sends me signals to make sure that I get it. Ancestors that didn't have such signals would have died of thirst. Perhaps I was tired and my intellect, derived through evolution, would remind me that tea has caffeine.

If my wife turned on the stove for me, it may be because we have found that doing small favors for one another makes our marriage work better. Where, exactly, would I need god in any of these explanations? You see, if I was trying to observe and explain why water on a stove boils, the simplest explanation would be to say that heat causes the particles inside the water to move, that heat was caused by the electricity flowing through the heating element, and that the electricity came from a power plant, etc. If I believed in god, I would still have to explain the water particles, heat, etc., but I would have to tack on an extra layer of explanation at each point. Instead of saying, "The particles in the water are moving quickly because of the heat source," I would have to say, "The particles in the water are moving quickly because of the heat source and because an eternal, invisible deity of unlimited complexity designed this." Or, to use Occam's Razor to cut through Dr. Haught's several layers of explanation, I would have to say, "I want tea because I'm thirsty, and because an eternal invisible deity of unlimited complexity wanted me to be." Adding a god or an invisible flying clown or any other supernatural cause to an explanation makes it more complicated, not less. Occam's Razor cuts no tumor more deeply than the one called god.

So, we see that the "prime mover" argument holds the seeds of its own destruction, as does its companion, the misused Occam's Razor. If everything that exists must have a cause, and god exists, then where did he come from? (By the way, if he's all powerful, could he make a rock so big that he couldn't lift it?)

2. The Watchmaker, er, Cell Phone Maker

The second of god's suicidal arguments is roughly two hundred years old and was first put forth by the Anglican philosopher William Paley. The argument is rather simple. If something looks designed, then it must have a designer. A watch must have a watchmaker. In other words, if something is complex then it requires something more complex to create it. The universe, obviously, is very complex, therefore its creator must be, well, you get the picture.

Now, let's refer back to the believer's assertion that god as a prime mover, in keeping with Occam's principle, is a simple solution. As the great science writer/teacher/atheist Richard Dawkins has pointed out, any "creator" must be at least as complex as his creations. It makes no sense to explain how something became complex by invoking an invisible, undetectable something that is infinitely more complex. In other words, if the universe is too complex to not have had a creator, then what does that say about the creator? If a watch needs a designer, then how could an incredibly complex creator just have sprung into existence?

In fact, the watchmaker argument, often used in conjunction with the human body, is not just suicidal but deeply flawed. For one thing, it ignores that many people are born with harmful birth defects that almost immediately cause suffering and death. Was the watchmaker drunk? Secondly, the most complex things actually have teams of inventors, so it would seem that this argument actually is a better proof for the existence of many gods.

Thirdly, this argument is historically preposterous. Imagine a watch just popping into existence, fully formed. This is absurd. Everything that is complex in the universe has less complex origins. Modern cell phones include cameras, video games, telephones, radio transmitters and receivers, and computers. The cell phone was not created before any of these other inventions but was made up of them. And each of the cell phone's components had ancestors which were less complex.

Digital cameras did not come out, indeed could not have come out, before Polaroids. Flat screen televisions with DVR capabilities did not come out before black and white television. The Grand Theft Auto video games did not come out before Pong. Nothing that is complex just pops into existence. The very nature of complexity is that it is made up of things that are less complex.

Further, if you grasp this, you would understand that the phones from the 1950s, the kind that Andy Griffith spoke into when he was calling Aunt Bee and Opie from the sheriff's office, could be considered a different species from the modern cell phone. Andy's phone did not want to become another type of phone. It did not consider itself to be a "transitional species" of phone but merely survived for its time, and then eventually found itself outcompeted, and then extinct. Only its fossil record survives in thrift stores, attics, and museums.

You might say, yes, the phone has evolved, but it took humans (something more complex) to guide that evolution. Humans are a good metaphor in this case, but not for god, since no human being who grew up on an isolated island away from modern technology could ever hope to create a cell phone, or even conceive of what it is. (For that matter, imagine telling people fifty years ago that one day they would carry a phone in their pocket; I would bet that, almost universally, their first comment would be about how long the extension cord would have to be.) Human "inventors" aren't a good metaphor for god; but they are a good metaphor for natural selection. All that humans can do is look at all the phone designs that don't work (experiment) and then pick the ones that do. This is just a faster version of what nature does through environmental and sexual selection.

If I were ever brought into court to refute the watchmaker argument, I would find it an easy task. Every part of a watch had, at one time, uses that were entirely unrelated to its use in a watch in the same way that many of the features of a modern cell phone were once completely unrelated to being part of a cell phone. Numbers obviously had uses other than just being on a watch face. Gears were used for mills. The glass on the face of a watch was used for windows, and the strap is just a shrunken belt. When they all came together they turned out to have another use, at least partially unrelated to their original uses. Better yet, I could prove this. It would not be difficult to show the origins of numbers, of glass, of gears, of straps and to show that they had other uses prior to being part of a watch. I could even show "fossil" evidence of the antecedents of the modern watch. Egyptian sundials, Chinese water clocks, and the great designs which came from John Harrison's workshop (google his name; he's pretty cool) could all be used to prove the point that the watch evolved from smaller, less complex pieces. The evidence table would be full, and the court reporter would have to stop and massage the tendons of her wrist when I was through.

And I could be confident that god would never show up to testify on his own behalf.

3. Why Is There Something Rather Than Nothing?

The third of god's suicidal arguments is not really an argument. It actually involves an interesting question that theologians hope has an assumed answer. That is not to say the answer that believers give is interesting; it isn't. Religious people simply have to hope that believers will assume that the uninteresting answer is true.

We will now examine the biggest question of them all: Why is there something rather than nothing? Personally, I don't know why people assume there ever was nothing. What if the natural state of the universe is to be here? I don't know why people who live in a world of something should assume that there was at one point nothing.

Here's the problem with this question: Religious people don't believe there was ever really nothing, do they? According to them, god was hanging around, just waiting to create a universe so that he could make humans and play his little "faith or hell" game with us. This, then, is the problem. You cannot ask the question of why is there something rather than nothing if you don't assert that there actually was nothing. Instead, religious believers assert that rather than nothing, there was an Ultimate Something. This argument is the most persuasive when it is being used against the notion of a god. Why is there a god rather nothing? Again, this argument is suicidal for the god idea.

It is here that we can also address the point I raised earlier about the universe not needing a "first cause" or "prime mover." Stephen Hawking (the really smart guy in a wheelchair who is often depicted in *The Simpsons*) addressed the issue of the universe's creation from nothing to something and stated this in his best-selling *Brief History of Time*:

[T]he quantum theory of gravity has opened up a new possibility, in which there would be no boundary to space-time and so there would be no need to specify the behavior of the boundary.... The universe would be completely self-contained and not affected by anything outside itself. It would be neither created nor destroyed. It would just BE.

—Stephen Hawking, *A Brief History of Time* (New York: Bantam Books, 1988), 141

Dr. Hawking is careful to point out that this is just a proposal based on the mechanics of quantum gravity and will remain a proposal until all the evidence is in. That being said, doesn't it make much more sense to theorize about the universe's "beginnings" (if the word even applies) from the standpoint of science than it does to theorize about it from the standpoint of religion? What, exactly, makes anyone think that a religious proposal is likely to be helpful here?

I prefer to address the question in this way. The question "Why is there something rather than nothing?" answers itself, since it is not possible to ask its opposite.

And

In our culture, perhaps no single word conjures up such positive overtones as the word *faith*. Religious people often proudly proclaim themselves to be "people of faith." Children are taught that faith is an important aspect of their upbringing. "We're raising our child in faith" is a common parental boast.

Faith is a central aspect of Christianity and Islam. But even religions that claim not to put a high premium on faith (that is, those that don't claim it's the golden ticket to heaven) still need faith. Religious Jews need to have faith that there is worth in carrying out the same rituals as people who lived and died thousands of years ago in a desert. They need to have faith that there really is a savior on the way. Hindus must have faith in myriad (it doesn't hurt to look up a word now and then) gods and to have faith that good works will move them up the reincarnation chain to enlightenment. Buddhists have to have faith that the serene feeling that they get from meditation is somehow more spiritual than the feeling I get after going for a jog. In one way or another, faith, the ability to "believe," is an important aspect of all religions.

But why is "faith" held in such high regard. What does it mean anyway? The Oxford Dictionary defines faith like this: "1. complete trust or confidence. 2. firm belief, especially without logical proof. 3. a system of religious belief; b. belief in religious doctrines."

Isn't this a strange set of definitions? First of all, faith implies a firm belief. The person of faith is usually a person who strongly believes in something. People of faith have little or no doubt about what they believe in.

Okay, you would think that people would have this kind of faith in things that have been proven to work, that is, things that have been proven true. I have unswerving faith that dawn will come tomorrow. It's come every day for billions of years! And I have faith that the gravity which has kept the earth swirling around the sun will continue to work tomorrow and the next day and the next. Why? It's always worked. It's easy to have firm belief in something that is proven by evidence to be true.

And yet, the next part of the Oxford definition makes the first part seem bizarre. Faith is not just a firm belief; it's "a firm belief, especially *without* logical proof." (emphasis added)

Now wait a minute. How can anyone have a firm belief in something without proof for it? If I were to say that I had a firm belief in the existence of sound-carrying angels or an invisible flying clown, people would think I was weird. If I said I had firm belief that the invisible flying clown would rescue me if I jumped off a building, I'd be considered insane. After all, gravity is known to exist. One can have real faith in gravity. If something goes up, it comes down (unless it leaves the earth's gravitational pull), but to put so much faith in something for which I have no evidence, to the point where I'd wager my life on it, would be nuts.

Let's revisit a slightly different version of an example I used earlier but go into greater detail. Let's say there's a very religious farm family living out in the middle of nowhere, and the youngest boy has his leg mangled in a farming accident. The boy's mother and father, having been raised to have faith in the power of god, simply cover the boy's leg with a sheet and pray for him.

After one day of this, the boy is in extreme shock and delirium from pain and loss of blood. The mother calls her pastor who contacts the other members of the church, and they gather to pray for the boy's healing. The boy gets worse and worse despite the prayers. One of the members of the congregation finally suggests that the mother and father take the boy to the hospital. They don't, thinking that if they show a lack of faith in god he will take the boy's life. The boy is only appearing to get sicker and sicker to test his and their faith.

The boy dies.

Any rational person, even a deeply religious one, would consider the actions of everyone involved, except for the injured boy, to be criminal. Why? Isn't faith a good thing, and the more faith the better? Why should having so much faith in god be a criminal and negligent act? Why should it be considered child endangerment?

Many religious people would answer that, while they believe in a god, they also believe that he wants them to visit a doctor. Most people see no contradiction in taking a loved one to the hospital and then praying to god for his or her recovery while that loved one gets all the help of modern medical science.

But if you really have faith, why go to the hospital?

In his wonderful book, *The God Delusion*, Richard Dawkins, wrote about a study called "The Great Prayer Experiment." It involved 1802 patients in six hospitals. All were recovering from the same type of heart surgery. The patients were divided into thirds. One group was prayed for and knew it; the second group was prayed for and didn't know it; and the last group was not prayed for and didn't know it.

It turns out that those in the two groups that were unaware of their prayer status had no difference in their health or recovery. The only ones to show a difference were the people who were prayed for and knew it. They "suffered significantly more complications than those who did not [know they were being prayed for]" (Richard Dawkins, *The God Delusion* [Boston: Houghton Mifflin Company, 2006], 63). Dawkins attributes this to the added stress the knowledge brought.

This should have been an unnecessary study. A simple look at history shows that prayer does nothing. The infant mortality rate used to be much higher than it is now. Plagues used to ravage medieval Christian Europe and the Islamic nations of the Middle East. I presume that many people in these deeply religious societies prayed often and fervently and died horrible deaths regardless. Nobody in America dies of plague or smallpox anymore. Is it because we pray harder than our medieval predecessors? Or is it because science has given us better medicines?

Do we no longer have epidemics in this country because god likes us better than people in the past, or is it because we discovered that sanitation and hand washing are effective in preventing outbreaks?

Ask yourself why it is that you're supposed to have just the right amount of faith. You're not supposed to have so much faith that you actually expect god to do anything useful, like heal the sick or rescue the helpless, but just enough so that you believe in very old texts and in wild stories. Believe just enough, the church seems to be saying, to get your behind in the seats every Saturday or Sunday.

Why do all religions put such a high premium on faith? Why do they ask their followers to "grow in faith," when clearly growing too much in faith can become a problem and can even land you in jail? What do the religions want? They want your faith to grow but only in certain untestable areas. Religious Jews want you to have faith that a messiah is coming to save the world and that the books of the Old Testament are literally or figuratively true. They want you to have faith that Jesus was not a messiah or savior. The Christians want you to have faith that Jesus was the son of god and that he was born of a virgin, walked on water, healed the sick, talked to Satan, was crucified for the sins of humanity, and that he died and came back three days later. The Muslims want you to have faith that Jesus was a prophet, but not the son of god, that god is named Allah, and that his true prophet was Mohammed, who was visited by an angel in a cave and spent his life conquering territory to spread Islam, taking many underage "wives" along the way.

How can these linked religions all exist? Simple: none of them have any evidence for their claims, so there's no way to test their validity. Each claim, without any real evidence to back it, is just as valid as the next. It is the absence of evidence, of logic, of reason, that forces all religions to put a high premium on faith. Because they have no evidence for their claims, they have to make it a virtue to believe in things that are illogical—even though in any other area to have faith in something without evidence is crazy.

Every single religion in the world teaches that you exist for only one reason: to find and believe in that religion, whatever it may be. They all teach that god went through all the trouble of creation just so you can have free will and discover his one true religion.

And most people believe that the one true religion is whichever one they grew up with.

How do the many churches of the world sell something as blatantly stupid, as sadistic, as faith? Well, they promise a lot, don't they? These religions claim that faith is the one thing that god requires. Many believers of various sects of Christianity and Islam think that god requires that we believe in him despite all evidence against his existence and the truth of the scriptures. It is a virtue, for example, to believe in creationism and not evolution because of all the evidence stacked against the idea of creationism; and the fact that there is not a single shred of real evidence in favor of creationism is only a test of faith. God wants to see if you will trust your own mind over the ancient holy texts he had written on his behalf. If you trust your own mind, if you lose faith that these comically flawed documents are the actual truth, then you will be punished. If you keep your faith, then you will be rewarded.

We might ask, "What are the rewards of having such faith?"

Heaven. A place of eternal bliss.

When do you go to heaven?

After you die!!

Of course, our next question is obvious: If you don't go to heaven until after you die, how does anyone know it exists? I think you know the answer: you have to have *faith*!!!

And if you don't believe in all of this nonsense, what do the many religions of the world say awaits you?

Hell. A place of eternal torment.

Take a wild guess when you go. That's right: after you're dead. (You're getting good at this.) And how do we know that hell exists if people only go there after they're dead.

Drum roll, please. . .

You have to have *faith*!!!

Oddly enough, these extremes of reward and punishment, heaven, on one hand, and hell, on the other, are enough to scare many people into being religious. Many people go to church and give money to it like they put money into a retirement account, hoping to do just enough to get into the nice gated community that is heaven and, perhaps more importantly, avoid that nasty slum called hell.

Isn't this insane? Isn't this a crazy wager? What if you picked the wrong religion? What if you're Catholic and god is a Southern Baptist? What if you're a Hindu and god is an African Animist?

What if god wants you to conclude he's not there, and the only people who get into heaven are those wicked atheists? Why not? If you believe in a god who enjoys playing little games, how hard is it to believe in a god who tells everybody he wants them to believe in his holy books, but who really wants them to buck the system and not believe?

Of course, I don't believe any of this for a second. Many Christian and Muslim religious people are put off by the notion that people of other faiths, billions of people, are going to go to hell. And yet, if religious people want to believe that god lets people of all faiths into heaven, then what's the point of believing in any particular religion?

You see the problem? If you can get into heaven being a Buddhist, Muslim, Jain, or whatever, then why should you come to—and give money to—some Christian church? From the point of view of members of any particular religion, it makes no sense to say that everyone gets into heaven; and yet it seems cruel to condemn most of humanity to hellfire for believing, with total faith, in whatever holy book and religion happened to be fashionable in the area in which they were born.

This is a real problem for those seeking to sell religion, so they mostly ignore it. In America, it is a social convention not to argue about religion. We seem to have a policy of "if you don't mess with my nonsense, I won't mess with yours." It's downright impolite to bring up the topic of logic to a religious person.

If you ever ask people who attend a "megachurch" why they give money to it, when it's plain for anyone to see that the tax-free cash is being used to build media empires and to line the pockets of already wealthy preachers, they'll probably look at you funny. The truth is they don't care where the money goes. They give the money because they have faith that god is pleased with them for giving it and is building them a nice retirement condo in the clouds. Because religion is a business built on faith, it has to make faith into a virtue. Religions have to get to you when you are young and plow into your impressionable mind the idea that faith is a good thing, that it's the only thing that matters, that it's important. Not total faith, no, just enough faith to believe what god's spokesmen (and it is almost always men) are telling you, even when what they're telling you is complete rubbish.

Religions have to do this. After all, faith is their only product. Faith may consume your whole life and a good deal of your money and your intellect, but it costs religions next to nothing to produce it. And the best part: Every indoctrinated child grows up to sell the product to the next generation.

CHAPTER XI

Dogspell

by Earl Lee

A new book recently came across my desk, called *Dogspell: The Gospel According to Dog*. At first I thought maybe *Dogspell* was a new version of the musical *Godspell*, but using barking dogs—kind of like the Christmas music CDs put out by "Jingle Dogs," or the even more annoying "Jingle Cats" music CDs, where a group of cats meow out Christmas classics like "Here Comes Santa Claws" or "Meowy Christmas."

As it turns out *Dogspell* is a book that wants to guide Christians to a better understanding of their relationship with God. According to the publisher, the author "uses [the] metaphor of [a] dog's unconditional devotion to its human and the joy it finds in [this] relationship."

This idea is disturbing in so many ways.

Can this be the spiritual goal of most Christians—to view the universe on all fours while sniffing the crotch of God? And think of all the theological questions it raises. Is it appropriate to hump God's leg only on Sundays? Or Saturdays? Or should this be a daily ritual?

And then there is the question of evil. How can we address the fact that I have fleas? Why doesn't God do something about this? Get me a flea collar! Buy some flea powder! Please, God, do something to clean up all these horrible problems in the world.

I love my neighbor. So can I ask God to send the city's Mobile Spaying Unit to my neighbor's house and "fix" them all? (Just my idea for cleaning up the local gene pool.)

What if it turns out that my God is violent and brutal, and he beats the hell out of me with a two-by-four and sells me out to dogfights, like Michael Vick? Am I still expected to lick his hand?

Why is it that people look up to the sky, searching for some invisible master and abase themselves like dumb animals?

What is it about this idea that makes me want to lie down and lick my own ass, just to get the taste of this out of my mouth? Oops, I can't reach. A little help here!

The religious never cease to amaze. Sometimes their weird ideas are pretty funny. Other times their violence and senseless bigotry are downright shocking. From female circumcision to abortion clinic bombings, these people are seriously disturbed. Maybe they're trying to work out overwhelming feelings of worthlessness? At least that would explain the self-identification with dogs.

And their ideas and practices are truly crazy. Ritual cannibalism on Sundays. Confessing one's "sins" to a pedophile in a dress. Not using birth control. Praying in front of candles and statues. Wishing for miracles. Denying dying children medical care. Then they accept whatever crazy shit the preacher tells them and reject the evidence of their own eyes.

I know of a Baptist preacher in our town (pop. eighteen thousand) who has a congregation of only twenty-five people. Every Sunday (and Wednesday and Friday) he subjects them to two hours of yelling and personal abuse (I am *not* exaggerating). Why do they put up with this jerk? And worse yet, a few months ago he emptied the church bank account and left town. And some church members still want him to come back! How sick is that?

I guess it does all comes back to the self-identification with dogs: *Here boy! Good boy! Kill that unbeliever! Roll over for your heavenly daddy!*

Afterword
by Chaz Bufe

Pamphlet

A booklet that consists of up to several dozen pages printed on both sides, folded in half, and bound with a staple in the center. (Pamphlets are distinguished from fliers and handbills in that pamphlets are bound and contain at least a few pages printed on both sides, whereas handbills and fliers consist of single pages and often are printed only on one side.)

Historical Background

Pamphlets have been around nearly as long as the printing press. They've been, and still are to some extent, a handy and cheap means of spreading information and oftentimes controversial opinions. In sixteenth- and seventeenth-century Europe, early pamphlets often dealt with political and religious matters, a famous example being by John Knox, the Calvinist father of Presbyterianism: *The First Blast of the Trumpet Against the Monstrous Regiment of Women*, which appeared in 1558. (It's not *quite* as bad as it sounds: Knox was railing against rule ["regiment"] by female monarchs.)

At about the same time, what could well be considered the first anarchist pamphlet appeared: *Discourse on Voluntary Servitude* (*Discours de la servitude volontaire*), by Étienne de la Boétie. While he apparently wrote the essay during his university years, it was only published in 1578, fifteen years after his tragically early death in 1563. De Boétie's *Discourse* was very much an outlier, and nothing remotely similar in political tone appeared until well into the eighteenth century.

In Britain's American colonies, a similar situation prevailed from the seventeenth century on, with pamphlets published on religious and political matters, often mixing the two topics, as with Knox's *First Blast*. The most famous and by far the most influential of these pamphlets was Tom Paine's *Common Sense*, an impassioned plea for American independence, which can rightly be considered the spark that ignited the Revolutionary War. In all likelihood, it remains the biggest selling pamphlet of all time. During its first year, at least one hundred thousand copies were sold in the U.S. (with a [white] population of three million), and several hundred thousand more were sold in Great Britain and (in translation) France.

Paine followed this up with another famous pamphlet, *Rights of Man*, in 1790, which argued that human beings have inherent ("natural") rights, and that the sole purpose of government should be to safeguard those rights. After that, in 1794, his influential book *The Age of Reason* appeared. In it, Paine attacked organized religion, especially Christianity, and advocated deism. Because of his attack on Christianity, he was forced to flee to the United States, where he was again ostracized for his views and died in poverty in 1809.

In both the U.S. and Europe, atheism had long been proscribed, and its few open advocates often cruelly tortured and murdered for "blasphemy." Jean Meslier, a French priest, was the author of the first openly atheist book, in part titled *Clear and Evident Demonstrations of the Vanity and Falsity of All the Religions of the World*; like Copernicus, he had the good sense to delay publication of the book until after his death, in 1729.

In the late eighteenth century, especially in the wake of the French Revolution, openly atheist and deist works began to appear, including, in 1782, what was likely the first atheist pamphlet in England, *Answer to Dr. Priestley's Letters to a Philosophical Unbeliever*, of which the authorship remains a matter of dispute.

Still, it remained dangerous to openly express atheist opinions while blasphemy laws remained on the books in Britain, the United States, and much of continental Europe. Atheist publishers continued to be persecuted for blasphemy throughout the nineteenth century, with the final British atheist jailed for the "crime" of publishing atheist materials being George Jacob Holyoake, in 1842. Nonetheless, suppression of "blasphemous" materials and their authors continued, though not systematically, in the British Isles, with blasphemy laws wiped off the books only in 2008 in the UK and 2018 in the Republic of Ireland.

In the U.S., blasphemy and "obscenity" laws were used throughout the nineteenth century, in contravention of the First Amendment, to suppress atheist materials and their authors and publishers. The last person convicted for blasphemy in the United States was Charles Lee Smith in Little Rock, Arkansas, in 1928, for giving away atheist pamphlets he had written. He was sentenced to twenty-six days in jail after the blasphemy charge was thrown out, and he was convicted instead of publishing "scurrilous" or "seditious" materials. It wasn't until 1952, in Joseph Burstyn, Inc. v. Wilson, that the U.S. Supreme Court declared blasphemy laws unconstitutional. Despite the Supreme Court ruling, blasphemy laws remain on the books, unenforced, in a number of American states.

Despite the danger of blasphemy laws, atheist and political—especially socialist and anarchist—pamphleteering greatly increased in the latter part of the nineteenth century in both the U.S. and Britain. In Britain, atheist publishing picked up steam with the founding of the Rationalist Press Association (now the Rationalist Association; in the early days, it underwent several name changes) in the 1890s, which published both books and pamphlets, including, in 1898, the pamphlet *God Eating: A Study in Christianity and Cannibalism*, by John T. Lloyd.

In the United States, where pamphleteering—especially anarchist and socialist pamphleteering—was quite common by the late nineteenth century, there was no corresponding organization; and there still isn't. Instead, small independent publishers took up the slack. One notable early atheist pamphlet was Johann Most's *The God Pestilence* (included in this volume), which appeared in print in Most's newspaper in 1883 and was a blistering attack on both religious belief and capitalism, as can be seen in the following passage:

> The more man clings to religion, the more he believes—the more he believes, the less he knows—the less he knows, the more stupid he is—the more stupid, the easier he is governed—the easier to govern, the better he may be exploited—the more exploited, the poorer he gets.

Twentieth-Century American Pamphlet Publishing:
The Haldeman-Julius Company

In 1895, the pamphlet publishing situation in the United States began to change. In that year, Julius Wayland founded the socialist *Appeal to Reason*, a weekly newspaper, in the small town of Girard, Kansas. (The reason for this apparently odd choice of location was that Girard had a station on the Atchison, Topeka, and Santa Fe Railway, had a socialist local government, and was near the geographical center of the United States.) By 1910, the *Appeal* had a circulation of over five hundred thousand and occasionally printed special editions with print runs in the millions. It was the largest-circulation political publication in the world and, according to at least one estimate, was the largest-circulation periodical in the world, period.

The *Appeal* also published pamphlets, and within a decade of its founding had published hundreds of them, a good majority bearing on various aspects of socialism; authors included such luminaries as Marx, Engels, Eugene V. Debs, and Clarence Darrow.

By 1915, the *Appeal* was in decline, though it and its publishing operation would shortly undergo a metamorphosis. In 1916, one of the *Appeal*'s editors, Emanuel Julius, married Marcet Haldeman, a banker's daughter and reputedly the richest woman in Kansas. In 1919, they purchased a majority interest in the *Appeal* and changed the emphasis of the publishing operation from the severely weakened newspaper (now titled the *New Appeal*) to pamphlet publishing.

Along with this change in direction, they also drastically increased the number of pamphlets published and drastically decreased the price of most to only five cents. These very cheaply produced 3.25" × 4.75" pamphlets set in 8-point type (this is 8-pt. type) became the famous *Little Blue Books* issued by the Haldeman-Julius Company. The company also issued a smaller number of 5.5" × 8.5" pamphlets, so-called *Big Blue Books* (though most didn't have blue covers), priced at between twenty-five cents and a dollar. In all, during its active pamphlet publishing period of 1919 to 1951, the company issued roughly 2,500 titles with a press run, according to one historian, of 500,000,000 copies. That seems optimistic, but it's almost certain that the Haldeman-Julius Company sold at least 100,000,000 copies. (They sold the pamphlets by mail and took out large ads in major newspapers across the country listing hundreds of pamphlets in a single ad and selling them twenty for a dollar.)

One notable aspect of this pamphlet publishing empire was that once they assumed control of it in 1919, Emanuel Julius (name changed to E. Haldeman-Julius [EHJ] at the time of marriage) drastically diversified the topics of the pamphlets, with the issues addressed now including philosophy, self-improvement, classic works of fiction, poetry, and any other subject EHJ thought would sell.

Importantly, the published topics now included atheism. For the first time in U.S. history, a major (though highly unorthodox) publisher was issuing atheist pamphlets as both *Little* and *Big Blue Books*. EHJ published a lot of such pamphlets—almost certainly well over one hundred—and even wrote one *Little Blue Book* on the issue himself, *The Meaning of Atheism*. In it, he outlines the primary reason he considered religion a menace:

> Perhaps religion might be dismissed as unimportant if it were merely theoretical . . . but there is and has always been sternly and largely a disposition of religion to enforce its theory in the conduct of life; religion has meant not simply dogmatism in abstract thinking but intolerance in legal and social action. Religion interferes with life.

Atheist titles EHJ published included *The Anti-Christ*, by Friedrich Nietzsche; *Religion: A Dialogue* and *A Few Words on Pantheism*, by materialist philosopher Arthur Schopenhauer; and *Christianity, a Continuing Calamity*, by Clay Fulks, in which Fulks states, in an unfortunately still relevant passage:

> Having fundamentalists in a nation is like having congenital imbeciles in the family—it's a calamity. Allow their mountebank, swindling leaders enough control over society and though religious faith would flourish fantastically, society would revert to the sheep-and-goat stage of culture.

But by far EHJ's most prolific atheist author was former Catholic priest and theologian Joseph McCabe. McCabe wrote dozens upon dozens of both *Big* and *Little Blue Books* attacking religion on many, many fronts. His topics included Christian misogyny (*Degradation of*

Woman), sexual prudery and authoritarianism (*The Catholic Church and the Sex Problem*), Christianity's syncretic nature (*Pagan Christs* and *How Christianity Grew Out of Paganism*), and Christianity's woeful record as regards slavery (*Christianity and Slavery*).

The Haldeman-Julius Company's glory days were in the 1920s and 1930s, when it undoubtedly sold a majority of its hundreds of millions of copies. But sales began to go downhill with the approach of World War II and the appearance of the still familiar 4.25" × 7" mass-market paperback book—importantly, a cheap book with a *spine*.

Sales were already in decline by the beginning of World War II, and following the war they plummeted. With the postwar economic boom and the arrival en masse of cheap paperbacks often priced at twenty-five cents, the day of the cheap-looking *Little Blue Book* had passed. Following the war, EHJ all but ceased publishing new titles, and with his death in 1951 (while being hounded by the IRS during the post–World War II anti-communist hysteria), his company entirely stopped publishing new works. It continued to slowly sell off its remaining stock until 1978, when its printing plant/warehouse was destroyed by fire. Today, the funky-looking *Little Blue Books* have become cheap collectibles, oddball reminders of early twentieth-century America.

The Post–World War II Period

Following the downfall of the Haldeman-Julius Company, pamphlet publishing fell to a low ebb in the United States. Undoubtedly fewer were being published than even in the latter part of the nineteenth century prior to the rise of *Appeal to Reason*'s publishing program. One of the primary reasons for this is that in the post–World War II period leftist political activity in the U.S. all but ceased, but for the heavily persecuted and deeply deluded (Stalin worshiping) Communist Party USA (CP). Politically, the CP had sucked all the air out of the room—aided and abetted by reactionaries who ceaselessly promoted the false dichotomy of Soviet-style "communism" vs. American-style "free enterprise"; and in seemingly endless economic boom times, with a rising standard of living, the appeal of both socialism and anarchism had waned.

This began to change in the 1960s with the Vietnam debacle and the rise of the largely inchoate leftist opposition to it. With that opposition, weekly newspapers sprang up in every major American city and in many medium-sized ones, and books and pamphlets by "alternative" publishers began to appear. One amusing example from the 1970s was produced by the Fifth Estate group in Detroit. Its title was a play on the classic *Twilight Zone* episode, "To Serve Man." The title of the pamphlet was *To Serve the Rich*, and it featured recipes for such delicacies as "Rocky Mountain Oysters Rockefeller."

The pamphlet's authors comment:

> A note on brains: "You are what you eat" should not be taken too literally; unlike some primitive tribesmen, you needn't fear that the brains of the wealthy will endow you with their personality traits and transform you overnight into an avaricious, exploitative parasite.

As for atheist pamphlet publishing, very little was going on in postwar America prior to the founding of American Atheists (AA) in 1963 by the Elmer Gantry–like figure, Madalyn Murray O'Hair (MMO'H). She was a confirmed and charismatic atheist, but she used the organization and its membership to enrich herself, squirreling away millions in offshore bank accounts before her murder in 1995 by a disgruntled ex-employee during a kidnapping gone wrong.

By the 1970s, American Atheists had begun publishing books, pamphlets, and a monthly magazine, *American Atheist*. Under MMO'H, American Atheists published reprints by historical atheist figures such as Joseph McCabe and Robert Ingersoll, as well as original books and pamphlets, some by MMO'H herself.

American Atheist's pamphlets tended to be pricey and poorly produced; one reason for this was that MMO'H ran the organization with an iron hand, and, among other things, decreed that all American Atheist publications be typeset in the Souvenir typeface, a display face very common in the 1970s that veritably reeks of hot tubs and granola, and is difficult to read in extended passages. (This is Souvenir.)

Sales for American Atheists books and pamphlets have never extended much beyond its membership, largely because they've apparently made little effort to expand sales beyond that base, but also because very few bookstores (and no chains) would accept pamphlets, and because their books (especially the covers) are usually so poorly designed that they'd be unsalable in bookstores. As for the pamphlets, since sales have always been almost exclusively to members, at most we're looking at total sales in the low six figures and quite possibly below that.

Following MMO'H's death in 1995, American Atheists has continued under much more ethical leadership, and the group continues to occasionally publish books and pamphlets. Their prices are now much more moderate than in the time prior to 1995, but the design problems continue.

Other smaller atheist groups and publishers also began to issue pamphlets in that period, including See Sharp Press. (Disclosure: I'm the publisher.) From the mid-1980s through the first decade of the twenty-first century, See Sharp issued fifty pamphlets with a total press run of well over one hundred thousand. The predominant publishing areas were anarchism and atheism, with atheist titles comprising probably 60 percent of the total.

During the 1980s and 1990s, See Sharp's pamphlet sales boomed, largely because of the presence of well-organized anarchist distributors (who also carried the atheist pamphlets), such as A Distribution, Left Bank Distribution, and AK Press in the United States, and Freedom Distribution, Active Distribution, and AK Press in the UK.

Sales began to dip in the late 1990s, and by the end of this century's first decade, See Sharp's pamphlet sales had all but ceased. There were three reasons for this: first and most importantly, the internet spelled doom for short-form publications, because it offers easy and often free access to such short-form materials; the abovementioned distributors went under or drastically curtailed their activities; and the Republicans in Congress kneecapped the U.S. Postal Service in 2006, with the fallout from that including astronomically higher overseas shipping rates, which made sales to the UK all but impossible.

Today, See Sharp is selling off its remaining pamphlet inventory but continues to publish atheist books.

As for other post-millennium atheist pamphlet publishers, as mentioned above, American Atheists continues to put out the occasional pamphlet, and PM Press publishes a couple of pamphlets per year, including an atheist pamphlet every now and then (next up, reportedly, Sébastien Faure's *Twelve Reasons for the Nonexistence of God*, which is included in this volume). Beyond that, atheist pamphlet publishing is all but dead.

The Materials in This Collection

The original intention with this collection was to feature only materials that originally appeared as pamphlets. However, upon reflection I decided to also include several pieces that appeared in other forms, in order to provide a more well-rounded compilation. (Restricting this to a pamphlets-only anthology would, among other things, have precluded including Emma Goldman's "The Failure of Christianity," and it would have precluded including almost anything from the current century.)

So, while many of the following essays first appeared as pamphlets, there are also excerpts from books by small publishers, essays that originally appeared in newspapers, and two short pieces that originally appeared as blog posts.

As for the materials and their authors:

"The God Pestilence," by Johann Most, first appeared in 1883 in German in Most's anarchist paper, *Die Freiheit* (Freedom). A fiery anarcho-communist and proponent of armed insurrection, Most was viciously persecuted in both his native Germany and in the U.S. following his exile from Deutschland.

"Woman, Church, and State," by prominent early feminist Matilda Gage, was published in 1893 by The Truth Seeker Company, which also published the very long-running (over a century) freethought magazine *Truth Seeker*. The excerpt included here was the final chapter of the book.

"The Devil's Dictionary", by muckraking journalist and author Ambrose Bierce, appeared originally in newspapers and magazines in San Francisco over a period of more than thirty years in the late nineteenth and early twentieth century. "Bitter Bierce's" collection first appeared in book form in 1906 and in more complete form in 1911. The accompanying "American Heretic's Dictionary" was written by the editor of this collection, Chaz Bufe, and published by See Sharp Press in 1992.

"The Failure of Christianity," by America's most famous and most admired anarchist, Emma Goldman, was first published in her magazine *Mother Earth*, in April 1913. Although Goldman's anarchist and feminist views are well-known, many are still unaware that she was also a militant atheist.

"Twelve Proofs of the Nonexistence of God," by Sébastien Faure, was published in Paris as a pamphlet in 1914. Faure was a leading member of the French anarchist movement for over five decades, from the late nineteenth century to his death in 1942. The first English version that we're aware of appeared in the 1930s, and was translated by two Italian anarchist refugees from fascism, Aurora Alleva and D.S. Menico. The version in this compilation is a new translation specifically for this volume.

"The Meaning of Atheism," by publisher and socialist E. Haldeman-Julius, appeared as a pamphlet (*Little Blue Book*) issued in 1942 by the Haldeman-Julius Company, the most important American pamphlet publisher of the twentieth century. (See above for more information on Haldeman-Julius.)

"How Christianity Grew Out of Paganism" (1926), "Christianity and Slavery" (1926), and "Judeo-Christian Degradation of Woman" (1943) all appeared as Haldeman-Julius *Little Blue Books* and are all by ex-Catholic priest and theologian Joseph McCabe, Haldeman-Julius's most prolific author. For this compilation, I've edited down all three pamphlets to some extent in order to eliminate tangential passages entirely unrelated to the topic (of which there were many). The most extreme elision occurred in "How Christianity Grew Out of Paganism," where I eliminated the entire first half of the pamphlet, because, as McCabe himself states in his introductory remarks, the first half is completely unrelated to the title topic.

"May the Farce Be with You: A Lighthearted Look at Why God Does Not Exist," by contemporary graphic artist and feminist Pamela Sutter, was published as a pamphlet by See Sharp Press in 2001. While the pamphlet is no longer available, "Farce" is now "in print" as an e-book.

"Twenty Reasons to Abandon Christianity," by Chaz Bufe, was published as a pamphlet in 2001 by See Sharp Press, and is currently available in both pamphlet and e-book form. Chaz is currently expanding it to book length, with the tentative title, "Twenty-Four Reasons to Abandon Christianity." Chaz's other piece, "Why Science Leaves Religion in the Dust," appeared in 2014 on the See Sharp Press blog: https://seesharppress.wordpresss.com.

"Disbelief 101: A Young Person's Guide to Atheism (excerpt)," by contemporary American educator and labor activist Christ Edwards (as S.C. Hitchcock), was published as a short book in 2009 by See Sharp

Press. (I insisted on his using a pseudonym, as at the time he had a young family, lived in the Bible Belt, and had received anonymous death threats for writing letters to the editor opposing the Iraq War.)

"Dogspell," by recently deceased American author and humorist Earl Lee, appeared as a post on the See Sharp Press blog in 2013. It's an excellent example of Lee's acidic, earthy humor.

About the Authors

Chaz Bufe is the author, editor, or translator of over a dozen books, including: *Alcoholics Anonymous: Cult or Cure?*; *An Understandable Guide to Music Theory*; *The Heretic's Handbook of Quotations*; *The American Heretic's Dictionary*; and the science fiction novel *Free Radicals: A Novel of Utopia and Dystopia* (under the pseudonym Zeke Teflon). Chaz has also been the publisher and primary editor at See Sharp Press since 1984.

Dan Arel is a journalist, activist, and author of the critically acclaimed book *Parenting without God*.

ABOUT PM PRESS

PM Press was founded at the end of 2007 by a small collection of folks with decades of publishing, media, and organizing experience. PM Press co-conspirators have published and distributed hundreds of books, pamphlets, CDs, and DVDs. Members of PM have founded enduring book fairs, spearheaded victorious tenant organizing campaigns, and worked closely with bookstores, academic conferences, and even rock bands to deliver political and challenging ideas to all walks of life. We're old enough to know what we're doing and young enough to know what's at stake.

We seek to create radical and stimulating fiction and nonfiction books, pamphlets, T-shirts, visual and audio materials to entertain, educate, and inspire you. We aim to distribute these through every available channel with every available technology—whether that means you are seeing anarchist classics at our bookfair stalls, reading our latest vegan cookbook at the café, downloading geeky fiction e-books, or digging new music and timely videos from our website.

PM Press is always on the lookout for talented and skilled volunteers, artists, activists, and writers to work with. If you have a great idea for a project or can contribute in some way, please get in touch.

PM Press
PO Box 23912
Oakland, CA 94623
www.pmpress.org

PM Press in Europe
europe@pmpress.org
www.pmpress.org.uk

FRIENDS OF PM PRESS

These are indisputably momentous times—the financial system is melting down globally and the Empire is stumbling. Now more than ever there is a vital need for radical ideas.

In the years since its founding—and on a mere shoestring—PM Press has risen to the formidable challenge of publishing and distributing knowledge and entertainment for the struggles ahead. With over 300 releases to date, we have published an impressive and stimulating array of literature, art, music, politics, and culture. Using every available medium, we've succeeded in connecting those hungry for ideas and information to those putting them into practice.

Friends of PM allows you to directly help impact, amplify, and revitalize the discourse and actions of radical writers, filmmakers, and artists. It provides us with a stable foundation from which we can build upon our early successes and provides a much-needed subsidy for the materials that can't necessarily pay their own way. You can help make that happen—and receive every new title automatically delivered to your door once a month—by joining as a Friend of PM Press. And, we'll throw in a free T-shirt when you sign up.

Here are your options:

- **$30 a month** Get all books and pamphlets plus 50% discount on all webstore purchases

- **$40 a month** Get all PM Press releases (including CDs and DVDs) plus 50% discount on all webstore purchases

- **$100 a month** Superstar—Everything plus PM merchandise, free downloads, and 50% discount on all webstore purchases

For those who can't afford $30 or more a month, we have **Sustainer Rates** at $15, $10 and $5. Sustainers get a free PM Press T-shirt and a 50% discount on all purchases from our website.

Your Visa or Mastercard will be billed once a month, until you tell us to stop. Or until our efforts succeed in bringing the revolution around. Or the financial meltdown of Capital makes plastic redundant. Whichever comes first.

Parenting without God: How to Raise Moral, Ethical, and Intelligent Children, Free from Religious Dogma, Second Edition

Dan Arel
with a Foreword by Jessica Mills

ISBN: 978-1-62963-708-2
$15.95   176 pages

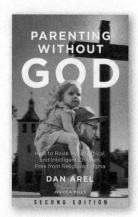

Children inevitably turn to their parents for more
than just food and security; equally important are assurance, recognition, and
interpretation of life. A child develops best in an environment where creativity and
discovery are unimpeded by the artificial restrictions of blind faith and dogmatic
belief. *Parenting without God* is for parents, and future parents, who lack belief in a
god and who are seeking guidance on raising freethinkers and social-justice-aware
children in a nation where public dialogue has been controlled by the Christian
Right.

Dan Arel, activist and critically acclaimed author, has penned a magnificently
practical guide to help parents provide their children with the intellectual tools for
standing up to attempts at religious proselytization, whether by teachers, coaches,
friends, or even other family members. *Parenting without God* is also for the parent
activist who is trying to make the world a better place for all children by first
educating their own children about racism, sexism, and all forms of discrimination
that continue to serve as a barrier to the fundamentals of human dignity and
democracy. It's for parents who wish for their children to question everything and
to learn how to reach their own conclusions based on verifiable evidence and
reason. Above all, Arel makes the penetrating argument that parents should lead
by example—both by speaking candidly about the importance of secularism and
by living an openly and unabashedly secular life.

Parenting without God is written with humility, compassion, and understanding. Dan
Arel's writing style is refreshingly lucid and conveys the unmistakable impression
of a loving father dedicated to redefining the role of parenthood so that it also
includes the vitally important task of nurturing every child's latent human impulse
for freedom and autonomy. This second edition has been expanded with new
material from the author.

"*Parenting without God is not just about the absence of religion—it's about the
glorious space that opens up for secular parents and their lucky kids once the clutter
and smoke of religion is gone. Dan Arel's voice is clear, smart, and a welcome addition
to the growing chorus of parents taking the hands of their children and running at full
speed into the real world.*"
—Dale McGowan, author/editor of *Parenting Beyond Belief* and *Raising Freethinkers*

Anarchy and the Sex Question: Essays on Women and Emancipation, 1896–1926

Emma Goldman
Edited by Shawn P. Wilbur

ISBN: 978-1-62963-144-8
$14.95   160 pages

For Emma Goldman, the "High Priestess of Anarchy," anarchism was "a living force in the affairs of our life, constantly creating new conditions," but "the most elemental force in human life" was something still more basic and vital: sex.

"The Sex Question" emerged for Goldman in multiple contexts, and we find her addressing it in writing on subjects as varied as women's suffrage, "free love," birth control, the "New Woman," homosexuality, marriage, love, and literature. It was at once a political question, an economic question, a question of morality, and a question of social relations.

But her analysis of that most elemental force remained fragmentary, scattered across numerous published (and unpublished) works and conditioned by numerous contexts. *Anarchy and the Sex Question* draws together the most important of those scattered sources, uniting both familiar essays and archival material, in an attempt to recreate the great work on sex that Emma Goldman might have given us. In the process, it sheds light on Goldman's place in the history of feminism.

"Emma Goldman left a profound legacy of wisdom, insight, and passionate commitment to life. Shawn Wilbur has carefully selected her best writings on that most profound, pleasurable, and challenging of topics: sex. This collection is a great service to anarchist, feminist, and queer communities around the world."
—Jamie Heckert, coeditor of *Anarchism & Sexuality: Ethics, Relationships and Power*

"Shawn Wilbur has done a great job assembling and introducing Emma Goldman's writings on women, feminism, and sexuality. As he notes, Goldman's essays continue to provoke and inspire. The collection artfully documents the evolution of Goldman's views on freedom, sex, and human liberation."
—Robert Graham, editor of *Anarchism: A Documentary History of Libertarian Ideas*

No Gods, No Masters, No Peripheries: Global Anarchisms

Edited by Raymond Craib and
Barry Maxwell

ISBN: 978-1-62963-098-4
$27.95   408 pages

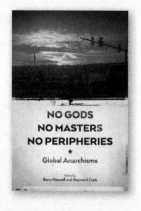

Was anarchism in areas outside of Europe an import
and a script to be mimicked? Was it perpetually at
odds with other currents of the Left? The authors in
this collection take up these questions of geographical
and political peripheries. Building on recent research that has emphasized the
plural origins of anarchist thought and practice, they reflect on the histories and
cultures of the antistatist mutual aid movements of the last century beyond the
boundaries of an artificially coherent Europe. At the same time, they reexamine
the historical relationships between anarchism and communism without starting
from the position of sectarian difference (Marxism versus anarchism). Rather, they
look at how anarchism and communism intersected; how the insurgent Left could
appear—and in fact was—much more ecumenical, capacious, and eclectic than
frequently portrayed; and reveal that such capaciousness is a hallmark of anarchist
practice, which is prefigurative in its politics and antihierarchical and antidogmatic
in its ethics.

Copublished the with Institute for Comparative Modernities, this collection
includes contributions by Gavin Arnall, Mohammed Bamyeh, Bruno Bosteels,
Raymond Craib, Silvia Rivera Cusicanqui, Geoffroy de Laforcade, Silvia Federici,
Steven J. Hirsch, Adrienne Carey Hurley, Hilary Klein, Peter Linebaugh, Barry
Maxwell, David Porter, Maia Ramnath, Penelope Rosemont, and Bahia Shehab.

*"Broad in scope, generously ecumenical in outlook, bold in its attempt to tease apart the
many threads and tensions of anarchism, this collection defies borders and category.
These illuminating explorations in pan-anarchism provide a much-needed antidote to
the myopic characterizations that bedevil the red and black."*
—Sasha Lilley, author of *Capital and Its Discontents*

*"This wonderful collection challenges the privileging of Europe as the original and
natural laboratory in which anti-statist ideas developed as well as the belief that
anarchism and Communism could not intersect in fruitful ways. Drawing on non-
Western locations (from Latin America, the Middle East, North Africa, and South Asia)
its authors demonstrate how antiauthoritarian movements engaged with both local
and global currents to construct a new emancipatory politics—proving that anarchy
and anarchism have always been global."*
—Barry Carr, La Trobe University

Shout Your Abortion

Edited by Amelia Bonow and
Emily Nokes with a Foreword by
Lindy West

ISBN: 978-1-62963-573-6
$24.95   256 pages

Following the U.S. Congress's attempts to
defund Planned Parenthood, the hashtag
#ShoutYourAbortion became a viral conduit for
abortion storytelling, receiving extensive media coverage and positioning real
human experiences at the center of America's abortion debate for the very
first time. The online momentum sparked a grassroots movement that has
subsequently inspired countless individuals to share their abortion stories in art,
media, and community events all over the country, and to begin building platforms
for others to do the same.

Shout Your Abortion is a collection of photos, essays, and creative work inspired
by the movement of the same name, a template for building new communities
of healing, and a call to action. Since SYA's inception, people all over the country
have shared stories and begun organizing in a range of ways: making art, hosting
comedy shows, creating abortion-positive clothing, altering billboards, starting
conversations that had never happened before. This book documents some of
these projects and illuminates the individuals who have breathed life into this
movement, illustrating the profound liberatory and political power of defying
shame and claiming sole authorship of our experiences. With *Roe vs. Wade* on the
brink of reversal, the act of shouting one's abortion has become explicitly radical,
and *Shout Your Abortion* is needed more urgently than ever before.

"**Shout Your Abortion** *reflects what makes me most hopeful for this next century, that
there's a whole new generation of young people who refuse to be judged and shamed
about who they are, whether it's their gender identity, their sexual orientation, or what
they do with their body.*"
—Cecile Richards, president of Planned Parenthood Federation of America

"*By presenting a collection of nuanced narratives,* **Shout Your Abortion** *aims to
advance a message of broader acceptance: If your abortion experience was hard and
sad, that's okay. If your abortion experience wasn't hard or sad, that's also okay. This
marks a significant tonal shift in the cultural conversation about abortion.*"
—Caitlin Gibson, *Washington Post*

"**Shout Your Abortion** *has altered the landscape. We all knew that abortion stigma
was a central tool in keeping women silent and isolated. Amelia Bonow busted down
that door and women poured through it like a dam had burst.*"
—Martha Plimpton, actor and cofounder of A is For

Witches, Witch-Hunting, and Women

Silvia Federici

ISBN: 978-1-62963-568-2
$14.00   120 pages

We are witnessing a new surge of interpersonal and institutional violence against women, including new witch hunts. This surge of violence has occurred alongside an expansion of capitalist social relations. In this new work that revisits some of the main themes of *Caliban and the Witch*, Silvia Federici examines the root causes of these developments and outlines the consequences for the women affected and their communities. She argues that, no less than the witch hunts in sixteenth- and seventeenth-century Europe and the "New World," this new war on women is a structural element of the new forms of capitalist accumulation. These processes are founded on the destruction of people's most basic means of reproduction. Like at the dawn of capitalism, what we discover behind today's violence against women are processes of enclosure, land dispossession, and the remolding of women's reproductive activities and subjectivity.

As well as an investigation into the causes of this new violence, the book is also a feminist call to arms. Federici's work provides new ways of understanding the methods in which women are resisting victimization and offers a powerful reminder that reconstructing the memory of the past is crucial for the struggles of the present.

"It is good to think with Silvia Federici, whose clarity of analysis and passionate vision come through in essays that chronicle enclosure and dispossession, witch-hunting and other assaults against women, in the present, no less than the past. It is even better to act armed with her insights."
—Eileen Boris, Hull Professor of Feminist Studies, University of California, Santa Barbara

"Silvia Federici's new book offers a brilliant analysis and forceful denunciation of the violence directed towards women and their communities. Her focus moves between women criminalized as witches both at the dawn of capitalism and in contemporary globalization. Federici has updated the material from her well-known book Caliban and the Witch *and brings a spotlight to the current resistance and alternatives being pursued by women and their communities through struggle."*
—Massimo De Angelis, professor of political economy, University of East London

Re-enchanting the World: Feminism and the Politics of the Commons

Silvia Federici
with a Foreword by Peter Linebaugh

ISBN: 978-1-62963-569-9
$19.95   240 pages

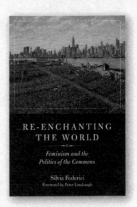

Silvia Federici is one of the most important contemporary theorists of capitalism and feminist movements. In this collection of her work spanning over twenty years, she provides a detailed history and critique of the politics of the commons from a feminist perspective. In her clear and combative voice, Federici provides readers with an analysis of some of the key issues and debates in contemporary thinking on this subject.

Drawing on rich historical research, she maps the connections between the previous forms of enclosure that occurred with the birth of capitalism and the destruction of the commons and the "new enclosures" at the heart of the present phase of global capitalist accumulation. Considering the commons from a feminist perspective, this collection centers on women and reproductive work as crucial to both our economic survival and the construction of a world free from the hierarchies and divisions capital has planted in the body of the world proletariat. Federici is clear that the commons should not be understood as happy islands in a sea of exploitative relations but rather autonomous spaces from which to challenge the existing capitalist organization of life and labor.

"Silvia Federici's theoretical capacity to articulate the plurality that fuels the contemporary movement of women in struggle provides a true toolbox for building bridges between different features and different people."
—Massimo De Angelis, professor of political economy, University of East London

"Silvia Federici's work embodies an energy that urges us to rejuvenate struggles against all types of exploitation and, precisely for that reason, her work produces a common: a common sense of the dissidence that creates a community in struggle."
—Maria Mies, coauthor of *Ecofeminism*

Romantic Rationalist: A William Godwin Reader

Edited by Peter Marshall
with a Foreword by John P. Clark

ISBN: 978-1-62963-228-5
$17.95   192 pages

William Godwin (1756–1836) was one of the first exponents of utilitarianism and the first modern proponent of anarchism. He was not only a radical philosopher but a pioneer in libertarian education, a founder of communist economics, and an acute and powerful novelist whose literary family included his partner, pioneering feminist writer Mary Wollstonecraft, and his daughter Mary Godwin (later Mary Shelley), who would go on to write *Frankenstein* and marry the poet Percy Bysshe Shelley.

His long life straddled two centuries. Not only did he live at the center of radical and intellectual London during the French Revolution, he also commented on some of the most significant changes in modern history. Shaped by the Enlightenment, he became a key figure in English Romanticism.

This work offers for the first time a handy collection of Godwin's key writings in a clear and concise form, together with an assessment of his influence, a biographical sketch, and an analysis of his contribution to anarchist theory and practice. The selections are taken from all of Godwin's writings including his groundbreaking work during the French Revolution, *An Enquiry Concerning Political Justice*, and arranged by editor Peter Marshall to give a coherent account of his thought for the general reader.

Godwin's work will be of interest to all those who believe that rationality, truth, happiness, individuality, equality, and freedom are central concerns of human enquiry and endeavor.

"Peter Marshall has produced the most useful modern account of Godwin's life and now the most useful modern anthology of his writings. Marshall's selection is sensible and valuable, bringing out the important points. . . . His introduction is a good summary of Godwin's life and work. . . . Marshall is right to see him as 'the most profound exponent of philosophical anarchism.'"
—Nicolas Walter, *New Statesman*

"A handsome and handy little book, excavating nuggets of Godwinian wisdom from the whole range of his writings."
—Colin Ward, *Times Educational Supplement*

Kropotkin: The Politics of Community

Brian Morris

ISBN: 978-1-62963-505-7
$24.95   320 pages

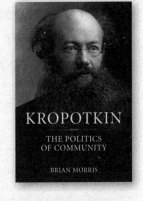

The nineteenth century witnessed the growth of anarchist literature, which advocated a society based on voluntary cooperation without government authority. Although his classical writings on mutual aid and the philosophy of anarchism are still published today, Peter Kropotkin remains a neglected figure. A talented geographer and a revolutionary socialist, Kropotkin was one of the most important theoreticians of the anarchist movement.

In *Kropotkin: The Politics of Community*, Brian Morris reaffirms with an attitude of critical sympathy the contemporary relevance of Kropotkin as a political and moral philosopher and as a pioneering social ecologist. Well-researched and wide-ranging, this volume not only presents an important contribution to the history of anarchism, both as a political tradition and as a social movement, but also offers insightful reflections on contemporary debates in political theory and ecological thought. After a short biographical note, the book analyzes in four parts Kropotkin's writings on anarchist communism, agrarian socialism, and integral education; modern science and evolutionary theory; the French Revolution and the modern state; and possessive individualism, terror, and war.

Standing as a comprehensive and engaging introduction to anarchism, social ecology, and the philosophy of evolutionary holism, *Kropotkin* is written in a straightforward manner that will appeal to those interested in social anarchism and in alternatives to neoliberal doctrines.

"Peter Kropotkin has been largely ignored as a utopian crackpot, but Brian Morris demonstrates in this wide-ranging and detailed analysis that Kropotkin addressed significantly and perceptively the major issues of the present day."
—Harold B. Barclay, author of *People without Government: An Anthropology of Anarchy*